THE VIETNAM STORY

THE VIETNAM STORY

First published in the United States by
Chartwell Books, Inc.
A Division of Book Sales, Inc.
110 Enterprise Avenue
Secaucus, New Jersey 07094

Produced by Winchmore Publishing Services Limited
40 Triton Square, London NW1 3HG

Edited by Sue Butterworth
Designed by Roy Williams and Laurence Bradbury
Picture Research by Jonathan Moore
Maps by Pierre Tilley

ISBN 0 89009 681 3

Printed and bound by Mladinska knjiga, Ljubljana, Jugoslavija

CONTENTS

I.THE END OF FRENCH RULE

IN 1945 THE FRENCH started to re-establish their colonial rule in Vietnam. The Japanese had moved into Indo-China during the power vacuum created by the fall of France in 1940 and the subsequent establishment of the Vichy government. At that time Vietnam was part of the Indo-China Union established in 1887 by France and incorporating Laos and Cambodia. The French had colonised an area where they already exercised control. Improved sea communications and the value of rubber and rice made Vietnam an attractive colony.

The country stretches from the northern mountains bordering China down to the Red River delta with Hanoi and its port Haiphong. The Annamite chain runs from Laos down the length of the land until it ends to the north-east of Saigon. The Mekong delta is the southern rice bowl for the country, which has prompted some writers to describe Vietnam as a peasant's balancing pole with the two major cities and agricultural areas at either end, like the baskets at the end of a pole. The terrain varies from jungle, through paddy fields to plantations and coastal sand dunes. While some areas are heavily populated, others are covered by dense jungle that offers a haven for simple aboriginal people who are known as Montagnards by the French or Moi (savages) by the Vietnamese.

Before the war the French interest in their colony had been the traditional extractive process of exporting raw materials to France. The standard of their governorship can be judged by the fact that in 1939 80 per cent of the population was illiterate, French and Vietnamese Catholic priests being the only ones to provide education to the Vietnamese. French was the language of the 7,000 Vietnamese landowners who were the only real indigenous supporters of colonial rule.

Opposition to the French had begun before 1939 and, like many of the revolutionary movements which seized power after 1945, it benefited from the assistance and support of the Western Allies who used it as a resistance movement against the Japanese.

However, the vestiges of French government, with its Vietnamese civil servants, continued to function. It was a time of great humiliation for the French who had not only lost prestige following their defeat in Europe but were also aware that real power in Vietnam was in the hands of the Japanese. On 9 March 1945 a military putsch in which the Japanese slaughtered or imprisoned Europeans, soldiers and civil servants, put the Emperor Bao Dai in power.

This prompted the US to increase OSS support for the only obvious leader of the underground resistance. This leader had united the mixed political and religious groups into a resistance movement despite French and Japanese attempts to neutralise him. He was Ho Chi Minh, who had used a variety of names though he had been born Nguyen That Thanh in 1890. He had learned his brand of revolutionary communism from the French while he had been living and working in France. The Indo-Chinese Communist Party had been founded in the 1930s, and drew much of its support from men and women who had a simple nationalistic desire to see the French colonial rule ended in Indo-China.

On 14 August 1945 the war with Japan ended with the dropping of the atomic bombs on Hiroshima and Nagasaki – creating another power vacuum in Vietnam. The Vietnamese Communists seized the opportunity and Ho Chi Minh declared a Democratic Republic of Vietnam in Hanoi on 2 September 1945. In Saigon, Tran Van Giau, heading the Communist-dominated Provisional Executive Committee of South Vietnam, recognised Ho Chi Minh's authority.

Meanwhile, at the Potsdam Conference in July and August the Allies had decided that the control of Vietnam would be divided between the Nationalist Chinese and the British. The former would take control of the north, while the latter would land and control the south. Major-General Douglas D. Gracey, commanding 26,000 troops of the 20th Indian Division with two RAF squadrons and a Royal Navy port party, landed in Saigon and declared martial law in September 1945. They were withdrawn when French troops landed.

By 5 October 1945 General Leclerc, who had also landed in Saigon, had an expeditionary force of 21,500 French troops ready to re-establish French rule. But he had been pre-empted by a mixed group of Gaullists and armed colons (white residents in the colony). On 23 September they had attempted to arrest the Saigon committee but most of its members escaped.

As the French drifted towards the first Indo-Chinese war they identified their enemy as the

Overleaf: A French paratrooper takes cover from Viet Minh shell fire during the battle of Dien Bien Phu.

Right: Major-General Douglas D. Gracey, who commanded the 26,000 men of the 20th Indian Division who took control of Saigon in 1945 and later handed it over to General Leclerc in October 1945.

Left: A young Ho Chi Minh toasts the Vietnamese liberation with General Leclerc in 1945. The good relations between the Viet Minh and the French were to deteriorate rapidly and the two sides were soon in armed conflict.

Viet Minh. This name was the contraction of Doc Lap Dong Minh or League for the Independence of Vietnam – the umbrella political/military organisation that had been set up by Ho Chi Minh in 1941. At first it looked as if the French and Viet Minh might work together and in the north, as the Japanese withdrew, 25,000 French and French-officered Vietnamese troops landed at Haiphong.

Any negotiations between French soldiers and officials and the Viet Minh were undermined by the fact that the government in Paris was lurching through a series of political crises and many leaders were anxious for their own careers. Their only concern was that Indo-China should remain French in some form. Negotiations dragged on with both sides becoming increasingly entrenched. The French were willing to recognise the Vietnamese republic if it remained in union with France. Negotiations that might have led to a painless independence, rather in the style of the British Commonwealth, collapsed when Admiral d'Argenlieu, the French High Commissioner for Indo-China, proclaimed Chochin China an autonomous republic. 'The Indo-Chinese Federation' of 1 June 1946 was in fact a French puppet state.

Fighting was not yet widespread and after joint French and Viet Minh patrols in Haiphong, the French moved in to take over the customs sheds in the port on 15 October 1946. This was not merely a political gesture, but was also a way of cutting off supplies to the Viet Minh. In reply to Viet Minh provocation the French escalated their pressure violently when on 23 November they subjected the Vietnamese quarter of Haiphong to a naval bombardment which killed 6,000 civilians. The Viet Minh rose in revolt in the port but were crushed by the weight of French fire-power. However, it took the French a week to root out the ill-equipped guerrilla forces from the port. Ho Chi Minh's military leader Vo Nguyen Giap was learning the hard way how to fight a guerrilla war. Previously his military experience had been limited to the anti-Japanese resistance, when OSS officers had trained the Viet Minh.

Early in the new year, as the French established their control in Indo-China, there was fighting for several weeks in January and February around Hue. The ancient capital had been under siege by Viet Minh forces, but the garrison was relieved by French troops.

Though France was not economically strong, after four years of occupation in World War II, she did have manpower that could be employed in her Asian colony. Peter Scholl-Latour, the veteran West German television and radio journalist, recalled the returning British troop convoys passing the outgoing French ships in the winter of 1945. The French convoy with their mixture of European nationalities from the recently defeated Axis powers and the now unemployed victors looked at the bronzed British veterans of Burma and Malaya. They failed to find any humour in a Royal Navy officer's shout, 'You are going the wrong way!'

Later, the men who would make up the French forces in Indo-China were drawn from other colonial forces in Africa and from indigenous Vietnamese, with regular career soldiers from Europe (France never used her conscripts in the Far East). Observing this build up, the Viet Minh realised that the best tactics to adopt were the currently successful guerrilla methods employed by the Chinese Communists in their war with the Nationalists.

The French attempted an offensive on the political front by trying to bring back the Emperor Bao Dai to head a Vietnamese government – a government that was linked closely to France. By mid-1949 there were 150,000 French troops in Indo-China. The French employed tactics which had been successful in their operations before World War II in North Africa: hold the cities and defend roads and communications, then use these bases to spread out and secure the countryside.

The Chinese Communists had supported the Viet Minh during World War II and in 1946 Chinese Communist forces rolled southwards to the border with Indo-China. A modest garrison watched as the troops paused at the border – and stopped. For the Viet Minh this was the guarantee of final victory. They had a border sanctuary and now Giap could deploy his two infantry divisions that had been in training in the mountains of the north-west.

Arms from China (many supplied by the USA to the Nationalists) were beginning to reach the Viet Minh and in January 1950 as China and the USSR recognised the Viet Minh, the USA began

Right: An M36B2 Tank Destroyer crosses a dried-up paddyfield during the French operations in Indo-China. The French forces were supplied with large quantities of World War II military equipment by the US Government and without it would have been unable prosecute their war against the Viet Minh.

to supply more arms and equipment to the French. French troops had returned to Indo-China with a mixture of British, French and German arms and equipment; they were also supplied with the tested tracked vehicles used in the Pacific in World War II and the transport and fighter bomber aircraft used by the Allies. Many thought France would easily defeat the Viet Minh.

However, on 16 September 1950, Giap attacked on ground of his own choosing and after an accurate and heavy mortar barrage launched waves of troops against a French Foreign Legion outpost in the border village of Dong Khe. The 260 Legionnaires fought fiercely against an estimated 2,000 assailants and after hand-to-hand fighting and a second barrage of mortar fire managed to withdraw.

Below: French infantry and armoured officers confer during a break in operations. Their equipment is a mixture of French, American and British, weapons and radios are American.

The first major victory for the Viet Minh was the fighting for Cao Bang. As the French garrison withdrew after the assault on their outpost in the north-east corner of Vietnam, the Viet Minh ambushed the relief column of the 1st Foreign Legion Parachute Battalion.

By the end of October Ho and Giap had secured much of the north and driven the French out with a loss of 6,000 casualties or prisoners out of a garrison of 10,000. In addition the French had lost 900 machine-guns, 125 mortars, 13 field guns, 1,220 automatic weapons, 8,000 rifles and 450 trucks.

French fortunes began to improve with the arrival of a new Commander-in-Chief in Indo-China in December 1950. General Jean de Lattre de Tassigny was not only a gifted soldier, but an aristocrat who could inspire his forces down to the lowliest private or Foreign Legionnaire. Freed from the requirement to get clearance from Paris, he set about organising his troops for defence and made good use of the US aircraft that had been supplied. The Bearcat, Corsair and Invader gave him air power that could be directed at the front line and the enemy communications.

On 22 December 1950, French aircraft armed with napalm hit a Viet Minh troop concentration near Tien Yen. It was the first time this devastating weapon had been used and as the years passed it proved consistently effective. On the night of 14-15 January 1951, two Viet Minh Divisions were sent against a defended post at Hinh Yen near Hanoi. The French garrison of 8,000 held firm and de Lattre, taking personal command, deployed air power to its maximum. Thousands of Viet Minh died in the flames and black smoke. By the afternoon of the 17th it was all over and the

Left: The charismatic French leader in Indo-China, General de Lattre, talks to his son at a French position on one of the rivers in Vietnam. His son, on the left of the picture, was to die during operations in Indo-China soon after his father had returned to France.

Viet Minh were in retreat. Their estimated losses were 6,000-9,000 killed, 7,000-8,000 wounded and 600 prisoners.

De Lattre had seen the victory of the defensive battle and established the 'de Lattre Line' a complex of concrete bunkers and wire that protected Hanoi and Haiphong. Like the Maginot Line, it was well built and sited, but tied up troops who should have been used for mobile operations against the Viet Minh.

Giap again made the error of attacking well-established French positions. In two savage battles at Mao Khe US-supplied 155-mm guns pounded the attackers. At the Day River, operations against the over-extended Viet Minh lines of communications, which used local friendly guerrilla forces, forced a withdrawal. Following Maoist principles the Viet Minh political and military commands examined their mistakes and decided to return to guerrilla operations while they regrouped.

De Lattre, capitalising on his successes, ordered an air assault with road follow-up against Hoa Binh, a Viet Minh staging post about 50 miles west of Hanoi. On 14 November three French parachute battalions successfully captured the town. The road relief column however took casualties as it moved forward and, as a diversionary attack, Giap assaulted the outpost at Lang Tu Vu. His pressure on the garrison at Hoa Binh was well chosen since the French regarded this as a prestige position which they refused to evacuate.

The French suffered a heavy reverse when de Lattre resigned as Commander-in-Chief because of ill health. He died in January 1952 from cancer – though he was already a shattered man following the death of his son in Indo-China. His successor was General Raoul Salan, known as *Le Chinois*, who later became notorious as an OAS leader in Algeria. Salan accepted that Hoa Binh could not be defended and attempts to open the road were halted. He ordered the abandonment of positions along the Black River between Hoa Binh and Viet Tri. Giap took advantage of this opportunity and

Left: Jacking up a 1000lb bomb on to a Bearcat fighter bomber at Dien Bien Phu. This battle, planned by the French to draw in Viet Minh forces and destroy them, was in fact to lead to the destruction of French military power in Indo-China.

Top: General Gilles (*left*) and General Raoul Salan inspect a detachment of the Foreign Legion Regiment in Indo-China. The French did not use conscript forces during this war but relied on their colonial and volunteer armed forces to fight the campaigns.

Above: An M24 Chaffee light tank on patrol. The tanks are escorted by an infantry patrol who can be seen either side of the road. This combination of tank and infantry was essential to protect the armour from close-range Viet Minh anti-tank weapons.

as the French withdrew from their fortifications they were easy meat for ambushes. As well as suffering casualties, there was a bad fall in morale.

The campaign season drew to a close and as the French re-armed with trucks, tanks and APCs provided by the US, the Viet Minh brought their units up to strength. The smallest unit in their forces was a three-man cell; three men, it was established, were better than two or four, since one or two could keep an eye on the politically weaker member of the group.

The offensives in 1952 took the Viet Minh into the watershed of the Black and Red Rivers, clearing positions from the high ground covering Nghia Lo. Salan committed his forces to operation Lorraine on 29 October 1952, a thrust deep into Viet Minh territory. The operation involved 30,000 troops and used the now well-tried tactics of an air assault with ground follow-up. Athough the supply base at Doan Hung was captured, logistic strains forced a withdrawal before the Viet Minh could be brought to battle by the French. Once again the ground forces had to fight their way through a series of ambushes.

In March 1953 General Henri Navarre succeeded Salan. The new Commander-in-Chief had some successes and pressed on with attempts to increase the numbers of Vietnamese in the French forces. Known as *le jaunissement* (or 'yellowing') it was more effective with Legion units than other

Right: A French Dinnasaut Riverine Naval Unit. These forces, composed of small warships and armoured landing craft, fought pitched battles with the Viet Minh as they endeavoured to patrol the main rivers of Vietnam and keep the static garrisons supplied with ammunition and rations.

corps or units. Navarre was able to use the tracked amphibious APCs from the US which were employed on the coastal swamps and rivers. The advantage was that APCs could cross the paddy fields which in the past had been the sole domain of the foot soldier.

However, it was Navarre who committed the French to their major setpiece battle. Lacking the manpower to wage war on his own terms, Navarre opted for the 'Honey Pot' tactic. In simple terms this presents the enemy with a threat he cannot afford to ignore. It had worked well in Burma in World War II where the British had put troops in by air behind the Japanese lines and had thus created a threat to Japanese communications, as well as a battle-ground away from the front line. Air power had been the critical factor; it had allowed the British to evacuate casualties and keep their troops supplied.

Navarre looked at the likely Viet Minh moves and identified a position on their main axis. Giap would probably send his forces south-westward into Laos and a likely position astride this route was the small village of Dien Bien Phu. It had the

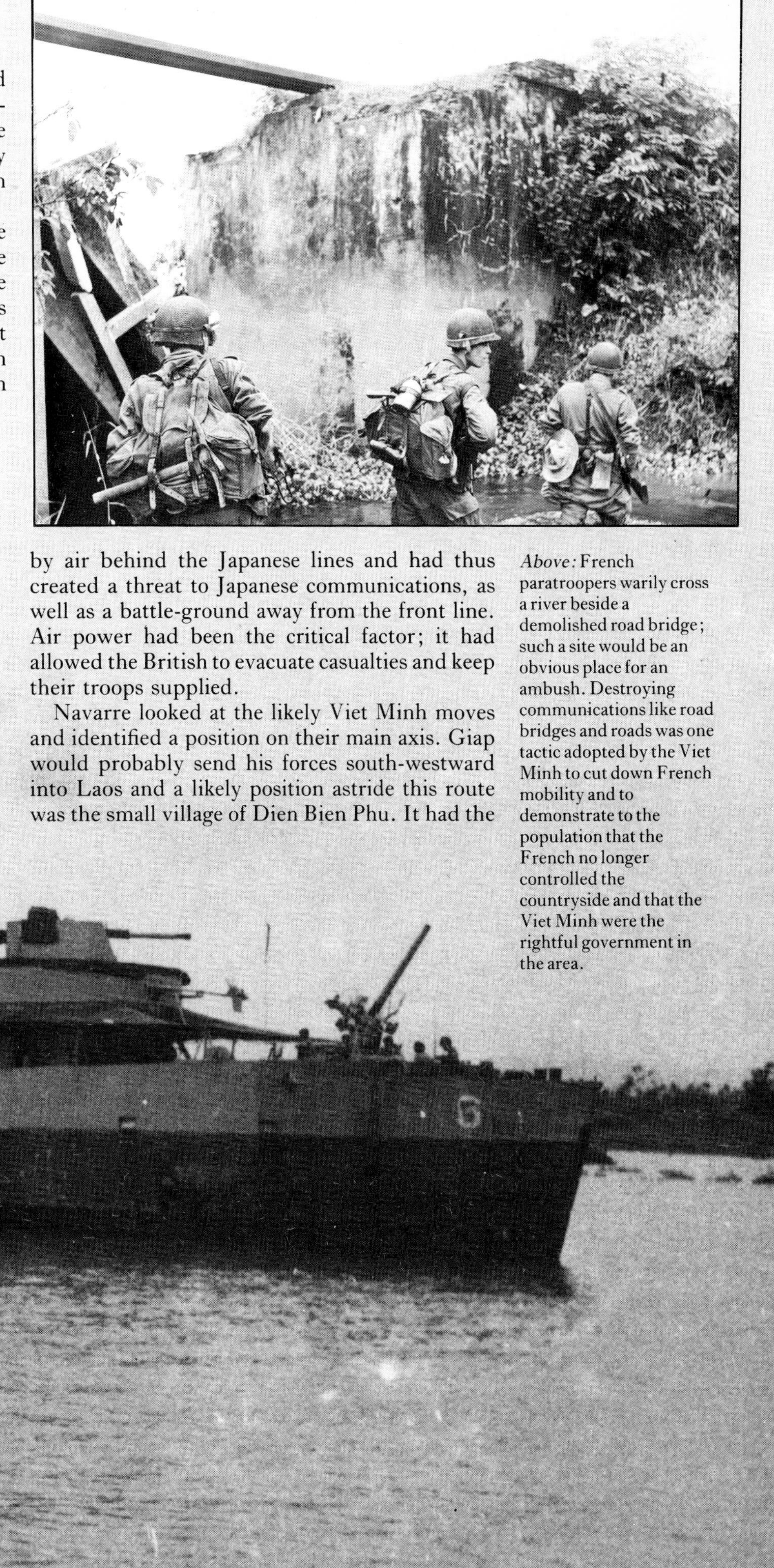

Above: French paratroopers warily cross a river beside a demolished road bridge; such a site would be an obvious place for an ambush. Destroying communications like road bridges and roads was one tactic adopted by the Viet Minh to cut down French mobility and to demonstrate to the population that the French no longer controlled the countryside and that the Viet Minh were the rightful government in the area.

Above: French-armed and equipped Vietnamese soldiers plod through the harsh sunlight in both the first and second Indo-Chinese War. It was the population of Vietnam that was to bear the heaviest load of the fighting, as soldiers fighting for the Viet Minh or the Viet Cong or as civilians caught between the fire of the communists and Vietnamese Government Forces.

Right: General de Castries (*left*) and General Navarre in conference at Dien Bien Phu. De Castries was to command the garrison there and is seen wearing his red Spahis side hat.

Far right: The Bearcat fighter bombers at Dien Bien Phu. In the background can be seen the high ground which dominated the French fortress and from which the Vietnamese gunners and observers were able to direct accurate shell fire on the French garrison, eventually forcing the French to rely on parachute drops of ammunition and supplies and preventing effective use of the airfield that had been built there.

added advantage that an airstrip already existed.

It was here that on 20 November 1953 three paratroop battalions were dropped to set up the position, committing the French to a battle which was to become a military legend – and a defeat. Dien Bien Phu is situated in a valley about 2½ miles wide and 10 miles long. It is 200 miles from Hanoi by air and the only road communications are by Route 41, now Route 6, which is a twisting road through mountains over 300 miles long. Navarre was eventually to commit about 16,000 men with 28 105-mm guns and four 1550mm howitzers, 10 M24 Chaffee light tanks, and heavy mortars. One addition, suggested by a US officer, was the inclusion of two quadruple ·50-in AA guns in the ground defences – they were to do grim service in breaking up Viet Minh ground assaults. Having thus established themselves the French were able to invite VIP visitors to see the position.

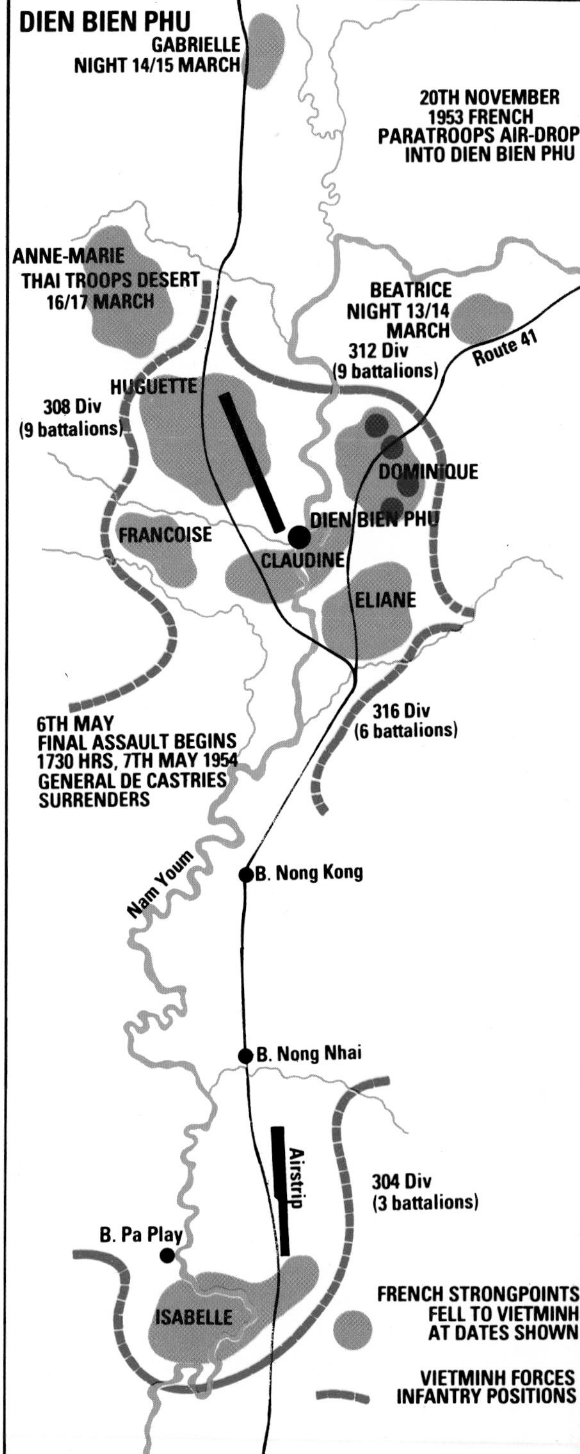

It was indeed a logistic triumph – the light tanks had been flown in stripped-down and rebuilt at Dien Bien Phu.

The confident feeling was that a mix of air power and artillery would do what it had in the past – break up and defeat Viet Minh ground attacks. There was also the belief that Giap would not be able to sustain a siege or move sufficient emn and equipment to make effective attacks against the garrison.

In fact Giap was able to move both men and artillery over some of the grimmest terrain imaginable and get them into position around Dien Bien Phu. Redoubtable bicycle porters. with their load-carrying machines used like two-wheeled carts, each carried 150 lb of equipment. The 105-mm guns were dug-in in the jungle and, instead of having an open gun pit, were placed in bunkers and caves with a narrow embrasure. AA guns were moved in to cover the likely re-supply routes and pilots who had flown over the Ruhr in World War II reported later that the flak concentrations were greater.

By Christmas Day 1953 the fortress was surrounded and the Viet Minh had bypassed it to attack targets in Laos. A month later the Viet Minh had amassed forced in the hills overlooking Dien Bien Phu which outnumbered the French by five to one.

On 19 February 1954 the Geneva conference on Korea opened with delegates from France, Britain, the USSR and USA. Indo-China had been added to the agenda and its inclusion gave the Viet Minh a new deadline for victory.

Up to 13 March, the day that Giap committed troops to the first major ground action, he had employed his men on probes and patrols and had driven back any French attempts to make reconnaissance patrols into the hills adjoining Dien Bien Phu.

With a style typical of the French, the strongpoints had been named after women. At the north was Gabrielle, north-east was Beatrice, with the central core of the defences composed of Anne-Marie, Huguette, Françoise, Dominique, Claudine, Eliane and to the south the isolated position of Isabelle,

At 17.10 hours on 13 March, massed artillery fire hit the fortifications and assault troops stormed Beatrice. It fell with heavy casualties on both sides. The Viet Minh then captured Gabrielle, but with their casualties running at 2,500 killed after the fall of Anne-Marie they were forced to pause and employ tactics. However, their flak cover, which was moving closer to the garrison, prevented aircraft from landing and the parachuted supplies delivered by French Air Force pilots and US-contracted civilians could not be guaranteed to fall on to the intended dropping zone.

On 30 March the siege temporarily halted when further assaults shrunk the French perimeter. Now the defenders had only Huguette, Eliane, Claudine and Isabelle. Sinking morale among the Viet Minh forced another pause and Giap rebuilt his forces until they stood at 50,000 to the French 16,000, while some of the French colonial troops had become 'internal deserters' hiding in dugouts along the banks of the river Nam Yum which flowed through the camp.

On International Labour Day the Viet Minh were once more back on the offensive; seven days later the Viet Minh 308th Division broke through to the command post bunker and the fighting was over. During the siege the French with their Viet-

The legendary Major Marcel Bigeard who commanded the 6th Colonial Parachute Battalion at Dien Bien Phu. A forceful and effective leader, he was to fight from World War II through Indo-China into the Algerian War to become a cult figure with the French paratroop forces. Below: French paratroops double to cover as smoke rises from the stores and ammunition dump hit by Viet Minh shell fire at Dien Bien Phu.

namese paratroopers had fought with extraordinary courage. Men had volunteered from all over Indo-China and had been flown in at night to join the garrison.

Before the fighting ended there was serious discussion whether the US could be persuaded by the French government to give direct military assistance. Though this could have been massed conventional air attacks against the Viet Minh rear areas, the French were reported to have wanted an atomic weapon to be employed. The US was at that point spending over a billion dollars a year on Vietnam, almost 78 per cent of French war costs.

The French had lost 2,293 killed, 5,134 wounded with 11,000 prisoners (including wounded). Some 62 aircraft were destroyed with 167 damaged. Estimated Viet Minh losses were 8,000 killed and 15,000 wounded. However, it was not the number of losses that was significant, but the quality of the troops and the timing of the defeat. France had lost her best men at Dien Bien Phu. A day after the surrender, the Geneva Conference addressed itself to the subject of Indo-China on 8 May 1954.

However, on 17 June 1954 a new French National Assembly headed by Premier Pierre Mendes-France was mandated to arrange a ceasefire in Indo-China by 20 July. In the grim bargaining at Geneva the Communists agreed to withdraw from Laos and Cambodia, and that the dividing line between the Communist and Non-Communist parts of Vietnam would be at the 17th, rather than the 13th, parallel. Elections were set for 1956 to see if the two halves of Vietnam would be prepared to be united. The original date had been 1954, but the two years breathing space were seen as time to allow the southern politicians more time to organise themselves.

When the Conference ended on 21 July 1954 it was agreed that within 300 days forces would be redeployed with refugees free to move into or out of different political zones. During this time all French forces would leave the country. Elections were set for July 1956 and delegates gave a spoken agreement to these terms. No one was completely happy with them, but they were felt to be the best solution and a way out of the war for France.

Below: French medical attendants race between a Sikorsky helicopter and the underground hospital, loading some of the last casualties to be evacuated from the fortress. Subsequently Viet Minh shellfire closed the airstrip and prevented many of the wounded being evacuated. Many were to die in captivity, unable to stand the rigours of the Viet Minh prison camp.

Far left: Doctor Grauwin on an inspection of his underground hospital. It was to become grossly overcrowded during the battle of Dien Bien Phu but his tireless efforts saved many lives although he operated under the crudest conditions imaginable.

Left: The end of French Indo-China: a French soldier places his US-supplied helmet on top of a jungle headstone, the last resting place of a soldier who had died trying to win a war that was later reckoned to be unwinnable.

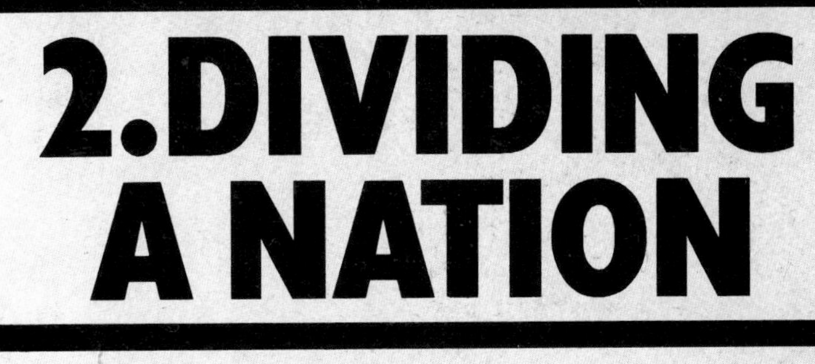

2. DIVIDING A NATION

THE UNITED STATES ENTERED THE WAR in Indo-China in a series of almost unnoticed steps. In 1950 the Truman administration had taken the decision to give military and financial assistance to the French during their war. The Korean war had reinforced the view that the Far East was an area the Communists had designs on – and therefore merited assistance. It was thus that civilian American pilots flew re-supply missions to the garrison at Dien Bien Phu; indeed the troops on the ground were to comment bitterly that many of these US pilots flew lower and slower to deliver their cargoes more accurately, while the French military pilots made greater efforts to avoid the Viet Minh flak, and so dropped less accurately.

Following the division of Vietnam between the Communist north and the newly independent south, the French began to withdraw their military presence, though for a time they retained men to train the new Army of the Republic of Vietnam. Years after the second Indo-Chinese war was over, an American officer on a visit to the French airborne forces remarked that his stay with the French had at last helped to explain many of the attitudes that he could not understand when he commanded Vietnamese troops – the uniforms had changed, but the manners and attitudes had remained.

Following the Geneva Conferance that divided the nation, there was a dramatic exodus by men and women from the north. The tough Catholic communites who had no intention of living under a Communist state, and ethnic groups that had sided with the French and knew that they would face extermination by the Viet Minh, trooped south. At the same time the Viet Minh cadres who had prosecuted their guerrilla war in the delta and highlands, moved north. They were later to be invaluable as the advance guard of the new insurgency in the south.

In the south the new nation was headed by Ngo Dinh Diem. The Americans were keen to promote him as an important democratic leader in South East Asia. One publication coined the description 'the Mandarin democrat in the sharkskin suit'. However, despite the public support there were private reservations.

By July 1955 the migration between the two nations was over. Over one million people had come south, while between 80,000 and 100,000 had moved north. By the autumn of that year Diem had stabilised his country, absorbed the refugees and disarmed the private armies that terrorised the population in their territories.

A year later Senator John F. Kennedy was to say:

> Vietnam represents a proving ground for democracy in Asia ... If this democratic experiment fails, if some one million refugees have fled the totalitarianism of the North only to find neither freedom nor security in the South, then weakness not strength will characterise the meaning of democracy in the minds of still more Asians. The United States is directly responsible for this experiment – it is playing an important role in the laboratory where it is being conducted. We cannot afford to permit that experiment to fail.

Kennedy pressed that the US and South Vietnam should have no part in the elections that were intended to unite north and south. Speaking of the Viet Minh agreement with the French he said:

> Neither the United States nor Free Vietnam was a party to that agreement – and neither the United States nor Free Vietnam is ever going to be a party to an election obviously stacked and subverted in advance, urged on us by those who have already broken their own pledges under the agreement they now seek to enforce.

Certainly the north presented an unattractive place to live in. One visitor who returned to Hanoi said that the city he remembered under the French had colour and style, and so did the people, he now found it unrecognisable even without seeing the purges that had been conducted after the partition of the north from the south. In fact the elections did not take place.

In the south there were problems with the spirit role, that Diem contributed to the rise of the Vie

Overleaf: Capt Robert W Butler and 1st Lt Dale W Shipley, US advisors to the 42nd Ranger BN, discuss defence measures with South Vietnamese troops following the action near Ca Mau when government troops killed 59 Viet Cong and captured 58 in October 1964.

Below: ARVN soldiers are transported by an H-21 helicopter of the 57th Transco in the vicinity of Ap Trach, south-west of Saigon, during operations against the Viet Cong in February 1963.

Right: The administrative divisions of South Vietnam.

Cong. In parallel to the failure of the carrot of land reform, he applied the stick of military operations against the remaining Viet Minh/Cong enclaves. However, in the north the decision had been taken to prosecute a guerrilla war against Diem. It was begun by those former members of the Viet Minh who had moved north, and whose return would go unnoticed when they settled back into the country. Many had families who would accept and protect them. Moreover, the Viet Minh were the national heroes who had driven the French out of Vietnam.

The Viet Nam People's Workers Party (VWP) or Lao Dong met in Hanoi in 1959. The Central Committee decided on the war in the south and was subsequently pleased by the way in which the West assumed that the insurgency was home grown.

To foster this image the southern Communists were given the front organisation called the People's Revolutionary Party (PRP). The peasants in the country had lived with the Communists long enough to know that the names were not relevant – the party drew its instructions from Hanoi. However, the intellectuals in the cities like Hue and Saigon saw the PRP as an independent force that they might join or try to arrange a truce or agreement with.

Though the US was committed to supporting Diem – 'Sink or Swim with Ngo Dinh Diem' – he rejected their attempts to direct the policies of the country. Diem also had the advantage of a record of resistance to the French that gave him a stature in the people's eyes. However, after an attempted military coup he began to turn to his family circle and to men who could be trusted but lacked the ability to go with their loyalty.

In 1961, with Kennedy as the new President of the United States, General Maxwell D. Taylor was sent on a fact-finding tour of Vietnam. His report was worrying reading. In order to raise morale within the Vietnamese Army and guarantee greater efficiency, a task force of about 6,000 to 8,000 men should be sent. They would be engineers and support troops sent as assistance for flood relief, but with them would go a headquarters that could co-ordinate operations.

US advisors had been in the country since 1960 when their strength stood at 875 – hardly a breach of the vague Geneva Accords. A year later they had more than trebled to 3,164 and the first serviceman had died in action. By 1962 the war was hotting up: some 11,326 men were in Vietnam and 2,334 USAF sorties had been flown; four helicopters had been downed and seven fixed wing aircraft lost. Thirty-one men had died in action.

The US Rules of Engagement (ROE) under the code name FARMGATE required that a Vietnamese had to be aboard a USAF aircraft when it went into action. In theory the Vietnamese was a of democracy. Diem had held the nation together, but in doing so had suppressed opposition including the newspapers, and thus had alienated influential members of the middle classes.

In the country the Americans urged that land reform should be pushed through as rice exports were an important foundation for the country. However, the reforms that were begun in 1956 had hardly advanced in three years. Only 10 per cent of the farmers had received their land, and so the majority found themselves paying rent. Some of these tough canny farmers had been working their land free – having been given it by the Viet Minh who had expropriated it from absentee landlords. Now the only benefit they received from democracy was to be obliged to pay rent.

It was in the mid-1950s, before any US forces were involved in anything other than an advisor's

Top: A US Special Forces advisor, Lt William Stymiest, briefs a Vietnamese Special Forces Unit on a proposed night ambush during operations southwest of Tay Ninh City in November 1966.

Above: Maintenance crews of the US Army Support Group Vietnam prepare H-21 helicopters of the 33rd and 81st Transport Company for flight to Tan Son Nhut Airport just outside Saigon.

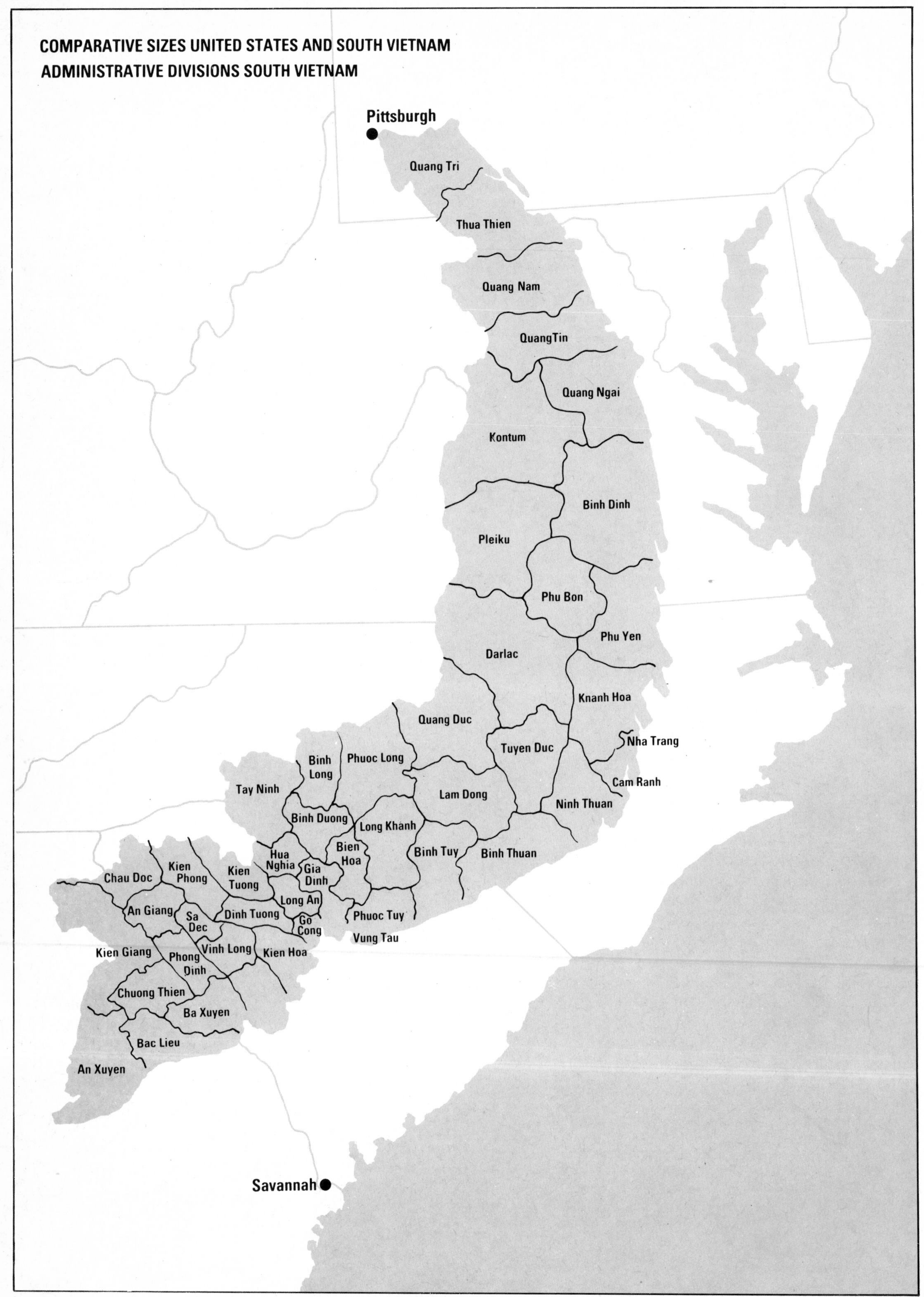
COMPARATIVE SIZES UNITED STATES AND SOUTH VIETNAM
ADMINISTRATIVE DIVISIONS SOUTH VIETNAM
Pittsburgh
Quang Tri
Thua Thien
Quang Nam
QuangTin
Quang Ngai
Kontum
Binh Dinh
Pleiku
Phu Bon
Phu Yen
Darlac
Knanh Hoa
Quang Duc
Tuyen Duc
Nha Trang
Cam Ranh
Binh Long
Phuoc Long
Tay Ninh
Lam Dong
Ninh Thuan
Binh Duong
Long Khanh
Bien Hoa
Binh Tuy
Binh Thuan
Hua Nghia
Gia Dinh
Kien Phong
Kien Tuong
Chau Doc
Long An
An Giang
Sa Dec
Dinh Tuong
Go Cong
Phuoc Tuy
Vung Tau
Kien Giang
Vinh Long
Kien Hoa
Phong Dinh
Chuong Thien
Ba Xuyen
Bac Lieu
An Xuyen
Savannah

rainee pilot – thus the fixed wing aircraft were argely twin seat T-28 trainers and later the Dougas Skyraider. Both types flew with the red and ellow markings of the South Vietnamese Air Force and could carry an under-wing load of ombs, rockets and napalm.

In 1963 the advisors had risen to 16,263 and vith the increase in the commitment and level of ction, so too had the casualties. Some 77 men had lied, 14 fixed wing aircraft had been lost and nine elicopters. The USAF had flown over 6,000 orties.

By 1964, when the number of advisors stood at 3,310, the casualties had reached three figures. ome 137 men died and, while 30 fixed wing ircraft had been lost, the helicopter losses had umped to 22 – the Viet Cong had mastered this hreat. The USAF had flown over 5,000 sorties.

All the sorties listed above were on attack, scort or combat patrol activities and do not inlude the logistic support which was now becoming important for the Army of the Republic of Vietnam (ARVN). The French watched these moves with jealousy. They felt that had they enjoyed these resources in their war, it would have had a different outcome.

A contemporary issue of *Paris Match* magazine ran a picture feature on the US involvement. It showed the crew-cut advisors arriving in Vietnam. They wore garlands of flowers around their necks. The French caption remarked ruefully that this was not a Vietnamese tradition, the Americans had imported it with them from Hawaii. Later in the same magazine there was a picture of an officer in smart olive-green shirt and trousers stepping out of the clinging mud of a paddy field – the Americans, the French commented, were enmired in the '*guerre subversive*'.

For the advisors who were paired off with Vietnamese counterparts, each with the same rank, there were moments of agonising frustration. The US officers and senior NCOs who had volunteered to serve in Vietnam represented the best in both the armed forces and the ideals that Kennedy had offered the nation. It was a time when the USA believed in its role as an international police-

Below: Crew men of a unit of the Vietnamese Junk Force searching a fishing boat for contraband and arms in May 1962. The man standing on the junk resembles his Viet Cong enemy with the black cotton two-piece overalls known as pyjamas by the Americans and his Thompson sub-machine gun – there is little to distinguish him from the Viet Cong.

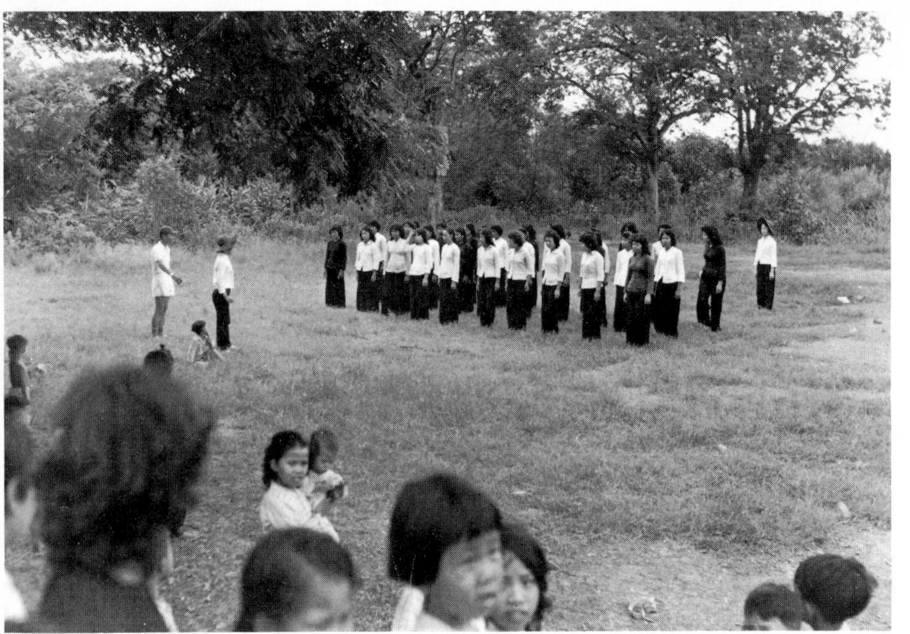

man. The Peace Corps and agricultural advisors as well as doctors and nurses, were going out t many parts of the Free World to assist rural com munities. The American military presence i Vietnam was an armed equivalent of this commit ment to assist the third world.

However, just as the agronomists and doctor had to combat local prejudice and practice, so to the advisors found that the ARVN had its way o fighting the war. Central government under Dien tried to prevent generals developing a power base so men with ability and ambition found them selves moved around, while at lower levels ther was a reluctance to become involved in action Advisors were maddened to discover that opera tions had been mounted in areas that held no Vie Cong, while when an ARVN unit had becom caught up in a fire fight it would be prepared to let the enemy withdraw after dark. Sometimes for the benefit of the advisor the Vietnamese would produce their VC prisoners. Some were genuine members of the Viet Cong, but all too often they were hapless farmers brought in because they were of an age that could make them VC. These actions and operations did little to assist the government's cause in the country.

Another operation that started as a good idea, but which went very wrong was the strategic hamlet. This scheme had been drawn from the Malaysian Emergency, but one war's success did not necessarily work for another. The strategic hamlets consisted of peasant farmers grouped behind barricades of panji stakes (bamboo trimmed to razor-sharpness and planted in the ground at an angle to catch a running man). The hamlets had their own armed defence group, a watch tower and bunkers. The theory was that the village popula-

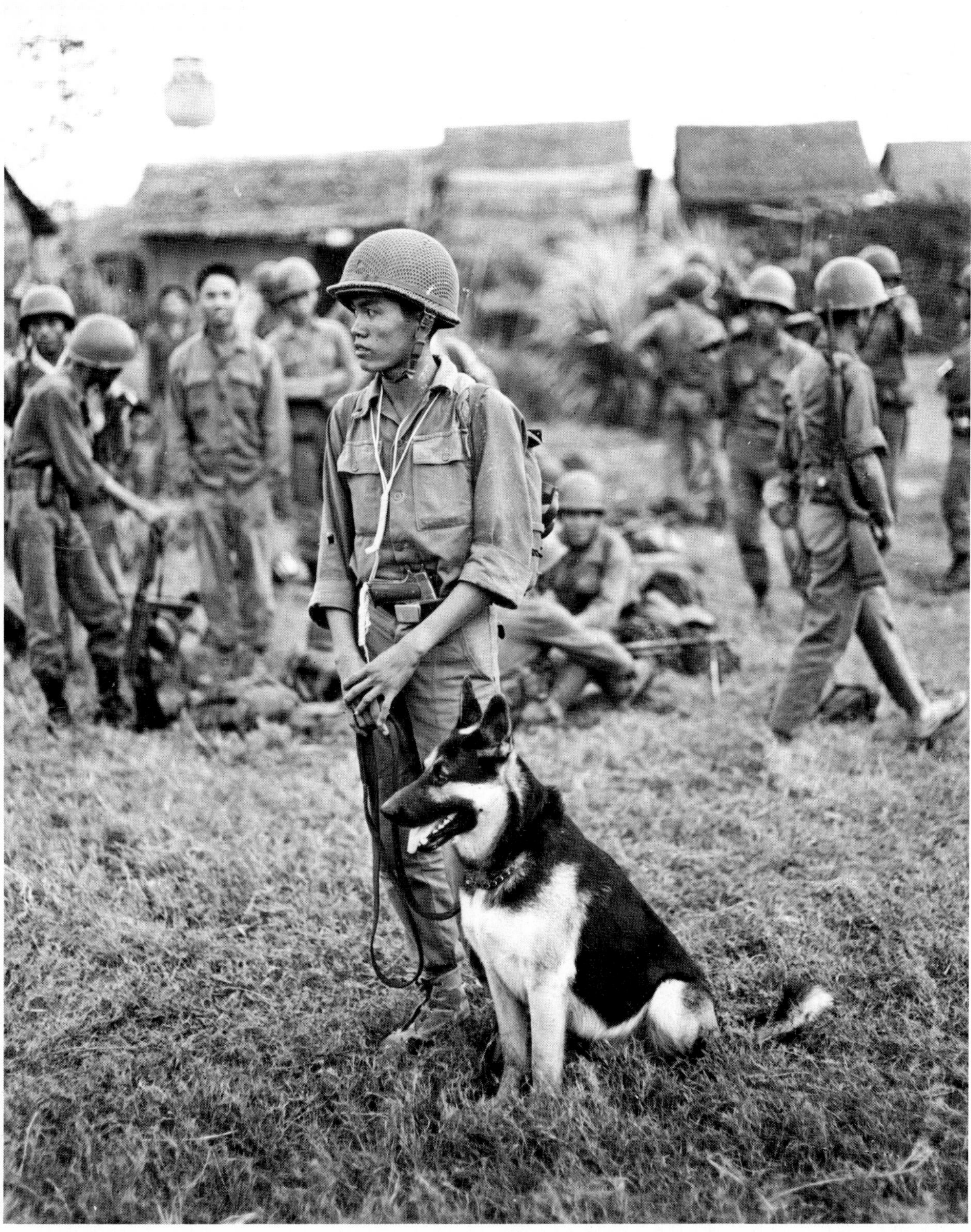

Left: A group of ARVN troops prepare for an operation. They are waiting at Ca Mau prior to being lifted into the vicinity of Ap Trach, south-west of Saigon, for a sweeping operation against the Viet Cong in February 1963.

Far left above: Members of the Women's Self-Defence Corps drill in the village of Vinh Phuok in October 1962. The Self-Defence Corps was part of a concept of strategic hamlets that had been suggested to the Vietnamese by the Americans.

Far left: Vietnamese troops with a German Shepherd war dog guard a group of women and children during a search for Viet Cong suspects. The dogs were used to locate men hiding underground in the villages during the search.

Right: President Lyndon B. Johnson with Vietnamese civilians and government officials. Johnson had hoped to be the President who would lead the United States into the 'Great Society', but he is sadly remembered as the President who led the country into the Vietnam War.

Below: The USS *Maddox* arriving at Pearl Harbor, Hawaii in 1964. The *Maddox* was one of the two US warships that were attacked by North Vietnamese torpedo boats and so precipitated the Gulf of Tonkin Incident which led to American involvement in Vietnam.

tion would deny the VC food and shelter and defend themselves if they were attacked. The practice was different.

One hamlet was bitterly nicknamed the VC PX – a Viet Cong Post Exchange – because the VC could attack it and simply re-stock with captured arms and ammunition. Moreover, after Diem had been deposed and killed, it emerged that he had exaggerated the number of hamlets. In 1962 he said that 3,225 had been established and so about one third of the population was enclosed. In reality the number was far less.

A policy that made 'open zones' of areas that had not been penetrated by the government forces produced more refugees. Diem claimed that these were men and women fleeing from the Viet Cong. In reality they were fleeing the random artillery and air attacks that were directed against them.

Both the 'open zones' and the hamlets served only one group, the Viet Cong. They emphasised that the Saigon government was out of sympathy with the rural population.

The US political and military experts in Saigon were aware of some of the deficiencies of the Diem government. The most dramatic was the repression of the Buddhist opposition which was to lead to the public suicide by fire of Buddhist monks. As the monks were a highly political group, the pressures were beginning to build up against Diem. He was not helped by his family circle who now assisted in the running of the country. His brother Nhu acted as confidant and advisor and Madame Nhu horrified the West with her comment about 'Buddhist barbecues' when talking of self-immolation by the monks. Diem's brother Can was proconsul in central Vietnam, while brother Thuc as Archbishop was the spiritual leader of the two million Roman Catholics.

On 1 November 1963, the event that Diem had feared took place. The army moved into the capital of Saigon and in a fire fight with the palace guards they closed in on the presidential palace. Diem and Nhu were captured. The tacit support of the army plotters by the US did not extend to the murder of Diem and Nhu, but this happened in the back of an APC. The hope had been that the

leaders would be flown out of the country.

Sadly the hopes that a new government led by Vice-President Nguyen Ngoc Tho (but dominated by General Duong Van Minh) would remove the corruption, patronage and crime did not materialise and moreover a succession of generals felt that as leaders of the nation they deserved to have their cut of the action.

1963 saw the final moves that would commit the United States deeply to the war in Vietnam. On 22 November 1963, Kennedy was killed and Vice-President Lyndon B. Johnson became President. Johnson, who would be remembered as the man who took the United States into Vietnam, would rather have been remembered as the man who introduced 'the great society'. Some commentators think that Kennedy might have been able to ease the US out of the quagmire that was to absorb them, but Johnson lacked the vision and ability to see what was coming and once in, how to get out of it.

In 1964 there was considerable pressure to increase the US military presence in Vietnam. Advisors muttered that what was needed was a US combat unit – they would show how the war should be fought. It was also a time when the Viet Cong began to receive their first supplies of new Soviet weapons. The AK 47 and related light machine-guns and heavier weapons gave them a fire-power that was deadly in ambushes and made up for the M113 APCs that the ARVN forces had received.

However, just as the south under US guidance was striking back at the north, an operation designated OPLAN 34A, or Operations Plan 34A, was putting raiding parties ashore in North Vietnam to attack facilities and increase the pressure on Hanoi. At the same time the US Pacific Fleet was sending destroyers along the coast to test the radar and coastal artillery (this operation was known as De Soto). The belief of the North Vietnamese that these two operations were inter-related produced the Gulf of Tonkin incident and all that followed.

Attacks by North Vietnamese patrol boats on the destroyers USS *Maddox* on 2 August 1964 and the USS *Turner Joy* on the 4th prompted US retaliatory air attacks against North Vietnam, and at a meeting at 6.45 pm on the 4th President Lyndon Johnson explained to 18 congressional leaders why he had ordered the strikes. The attacks launched from US carriers hit North Vietnamese patrol boat bases and oil storage areas in

Below: The USS *Turner Joy*, the second destroyer with the *Maddox* to be attacked by North Vietnamese patrol boats during operations along the coast of North Vietnam to locate enemy radar and coastal artillery.

the early hours of 5 August. In all 64 sorties were flown. The war had moved up a notch.

Johnson requested and received a congressional vote of support for his South-East Asian policy on 7 August, the Gulf of Tonkin Resolution being passed by a vote of 88 to 2. It included the words 'Congress approves and supports the determination of the President, as Commander in Chief, to take all necessary measures to repel any armed attack against the forces of the United States and to prevent further aggression'.

However, while there was resolution and commitment in Washington, Saigon was riven by political instability. At the same time in the US there was still a reluctance to become involved in ground fighting – 'American boys were not going to do the fighting for Asian boys'. In fact a French commentator speaking on British radio said that he feared the United States did not know what they were becoming involved with, and that they might not have the grim patience of the oriental who had fought for centuries in the area. The north was by now fully committed to waging a clandestine war in the south, and it would be false to assume that the arrival of US ground forces was a provocation that caused the beginning of the 'regular' war in the south.

Dave Richard Palmer in *Summons of the Trumpet* says that the north made four primary assumptions before committing their regular forces:

1) The United States would not commit ground forces to a land war in Asia.
2) ARVN, stretched taut by its counter-insurgency campaign against the Viet Cong, would be unable to cope also with regular formations of NVA troops.
3) A major North Vietnamese victory would precipitate a collapse of resistance throughout South Vietnam (the Dien Bien Phu syndrome).
4) The United States, fearing involvement with Red China, would continue to restrict its air operations to areas south of the Demilitarized Zone at the 17th Parallel.

By the end of 1964 the US had 23,000 advisors in Vietnam and it was these men and the air force personnel who became the target for Viet Cong attacks. Men had already died as advisors in the field, and in a mortar attack on Bien Hoa airbase casualties were caused to US men who were part of the ground crews, while on Christmas Eve in Saigon a bomb attack caused more casualties. In 1964 a soldier of the 5th Special Forces Group manning an isolated camp along the Cambodian border won the first Medal of Honor of the south-east Asian campaign as he directed the defence by the irregular forces against North Vietnamese assaults. America was being sucked deeper and deeper into the conflict, which she would then find difficult to pull out of.

3.THE U.S. GOES TO WAR

THE VIET CONG ATTACK which changed the war came just after midnight on 7 February 1965. It was a Sunday and the men at Camp Holloway and the neighbouring airfield of Pleiku were stood down. First it was incoming mortar rounds and then Viet Cong sappers were through the wire and on to the airfield. In a typically ruthless and well co-ordinated attack they left eight Americans dead and 109 wounded, and destroyed or damaged 20 aircraft.

The first reaction from the United States after the shock had passed was the implementation of air attacks under the awesome name of Rolling Thunder. It had been chosen from the Civil War epic *The Red Badge of Courage*. However, before Rolling Thunder began its series of attacks against military and economic targets in North Vietnam the US and South Vietnamese Air Force made raids across the border in operations named Flaming Dart and Flaming Dart II. Rolling Thunder began on 2 March; Hanoi called it 'The War of Destruction'.

The attacks aimed to reduce the southward flow of arms and men and also to demonstrate to the north that continued agression would not pay. It was, however, a campaign restricted by self-imposed rules that the USAF and US Navy strove to observe in action. Sadly they found that the north was quick to exploit these attempts to retain

Top right: Fuel tanks at Haiphong burn after attacks by carrier-based aircraft from the USS *Oriskany* in August 1966. These attacks were in retaliation for North Vietnamese naval operations in the Gulf of Tonkin.

Above left: South Vietnamese firemen damp down a building after the Viet Cong terrorist bomb attack on a building in Saigon used by Americans and Vietnamese on Christmas Eve in 1964.

Overleaf: US Marine Corps M60s machine gun crew from L Company 3rd Battalion, 3rd Marine Regiment watch as artillery fire falls on targets during Operation Harvest Moon, south of Da Nang in December 1965.

some humanity in operations that are in essence dangerously random. The river dikes and built-up areas that pilots were instructed to respect became sites for anti-aircraft guns, while trucks and stores were parked among buildings.

The north, however, was not only quick to develop and improve its passive anti-aircraft measures, but also to build up a SAM and flak system from the USSR that was the most efficient in the world. As operations progressed there was an increasing effort to either suppress the flak sites with separate attacks, or to use electronic measures to confuse the missiles that were being fired at incoming aircraft.

At the bottom end of the scale the North Vietnamese taught their militia to engage aircraft with massed small arms fire. In a time when men were soon to walk on the moon and space was opening up, a simple peasant soldier could bring down a multi-million dollar aircraft with small arms rounds that cost a few cents.

On 8 March 1965 a further step was taken into the war. Two battalions of US Marines came ashore to protect the facilities at Danang which had suffered from Viet Cong raids. Only 3,500 men landed, but by the end of the year the numbers had grown to 180,000.

With summer in Vietnam the Viet Cong moved their offensive operations into top gear. In Saigon Premier Quat attempted to govern a country that looked as if it would disappear as more and more areas came under Viet Cong control and were marked pink on the civil and military wall maps. General Westmoreland, who had taken command of the United States Military Assistance Command (COMUSMACV) in June the year before, pressed for more men, and the freedom to use them in operations away from static guard roles.

On 12 June, Nguyen Cao Ky, the South Vietnamese Air Force Commander-in-Chief seized control of the government from Premier Quat. It was the high (or low) point of political unrest in South Vietnam. By the end of the month Westmoreland had been granted freedom to 'commit US troops to combat independent of or in conjunction with GVN forces in any situation in which the use of such troops is required by an appropriate GVN commander and when, in COMUSMACV's judgement their use is necessary to strengthen the relative position of GVN forces'. A day after receipt of these orders the US, in conjunction with Australian forces, whose first

Below: US Marines wade ashore from landing craft at Da Nang as part of American reinforcements for the base on 30 April 1965.

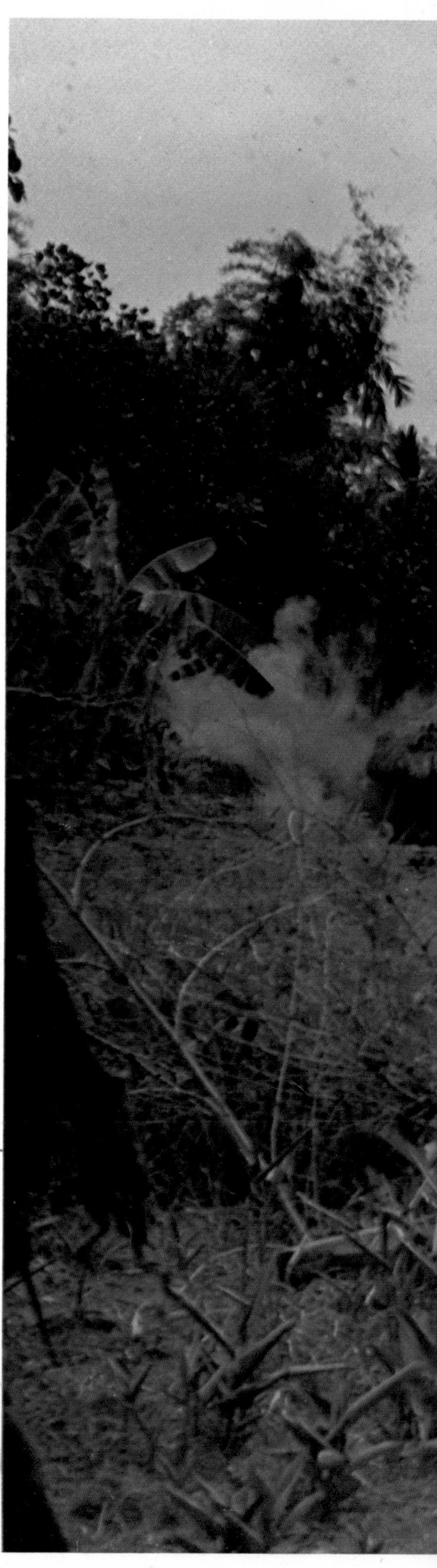

Top: An A-4E Skyhawk from the USS *Oriskany* returns to its carrier after a raid over North Vietnam in February 1967.

Above: Vietnamese children look on as a patrol of US Marines passes their home in the village of Ha Chou in South Vietnam.

Right: Marines of the 3rd Marine Division demolishing Viet Cong bunkers and tunnels in a village near An Hoa in May 1966.

contingents had arrived in August 1962, and ARVN troops, began search-and-destroy operations in the area known as War Zone D to the north-east of Saigon.

The operations were undertaken by men of the US 173rd Airborne Brigade. Before the men had flown from the USA their train had been delayed by anti-war protestors who had blocked the line. The soldiers' attitude when interviewed by a TV journalist was one of disbelief that anyone should wish to prevent them moving to their departure point.

The tactics that dominated the years up to the Tet offensive of 1968 included patrolling and ambushes as well as larger search-and-destroy operations. The object of these operations was to enter those areas of jungle and mountain terrain that had been denied to the ARVN forces and which had been used as sanctuaries by the Viet Cong. It was in these areas that the Viet Cong were able to train and recuperate after their sorties and plan the detailed attacks that they launched

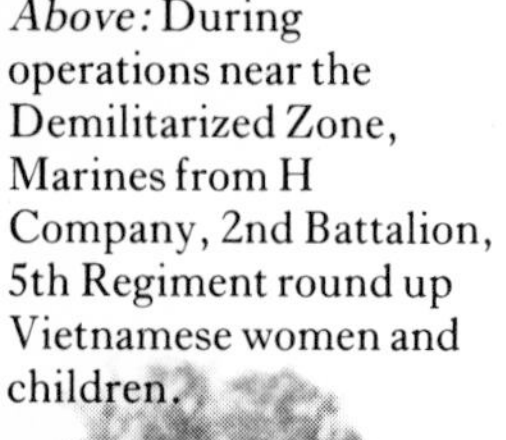

Above: During operations near the Demilitarized Zone, Marines from H Company, 2nd Battalion, 5th Regiment round up Vietnamese women and children.

Above right: Wearing the typical Vietnamese coolie hat, a group of villagers waits under guard prior to screening for Viet Cong suspects.

against government and allied forces. The sanctuaries had a complex system of tunnels and bunkers that allowed the men and women in them to survive the massive air attacks made by tactical and strategic bombers.

Parallel with the jungle and mountain sanctuaries there were villages defended by the Viet Cong militia. In effect these were a Viet Cong version of the strategic hamlets – turned against the government. The outward appearance of a village would conceal a system of tunnels and bunkers, but also there would be booby traps made from sharpened bamboo and long nails. These panji stakes would be concealed in the water of the rice paddy fields and hidden in shallow pits with a thin covering of leaves and branches. An unwary soldier would tread on them and have his foot or leg pierced. An uglier version included stakes smeared with animal or human excrement which would infect the wound. However, these traps were later replaced by bouncing anti-personnel mines or trip-wire traps which could include shells or aerial bombs as their main charge.

The operations that were intended to wear

Above: The gunnery sergeant and his officer, Gunnery Sgt Laurence A. Martin and 1st Lt Wes N. Firth on a patrol north of Phu Bai Marine airbase.

Below: US Marines with the typical range of equipment from the early days of Vietnam. This includes the flak jackets and the big 7.62 mm M14 rifle, later to be replaced by the more modern M16. Here an officer with his RTO advances on a patrol

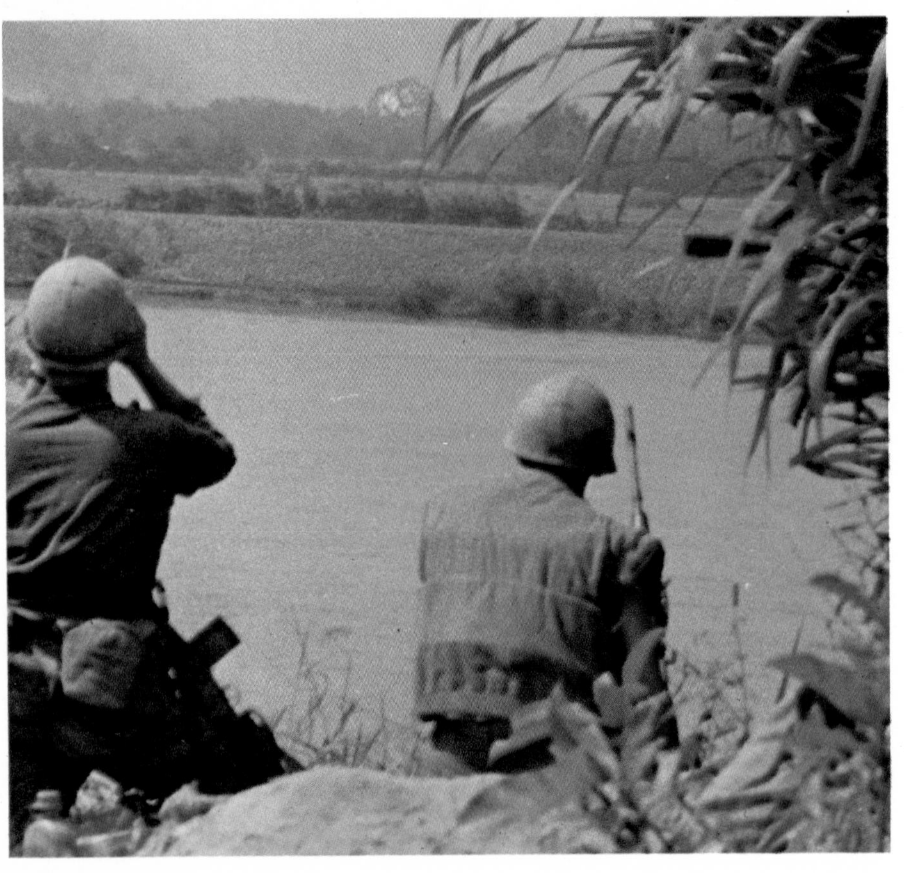

down the Viet Cong often seemed to be having the same effect on the Marines and soldiers who were plodding through the rice fields and highlands. The occasional sniper, the booby trap that killed and maimed, and the realisation that a man had a one year tour – 365 days – in Vietnam, made some short-timers (men with a few days to go before they returned to the USA) wary about their movements in the field.

However, at the close of 1965 the US forces with the ARVN scored a significant victory over the North Vietnamese regulars who had been sent south by General Vo Nguyen Giap. Giap hoped to slice South Vietnam in two by pushing three NVA divisions from Pleiku, through An Khe to Qui Nhon.

The increasing US commitment in Vietnam included the 1st Cavalry and airmobile force that had 450 helicopters – nearly five times the number in a normal infantry division. It not only had its own troop lift but could bring in artillery and place it on high ground, and also make preparatory rocket and machine-gun attacks against positions that might conceal enemy forces. Around Pleiku, Giap's front commander General Chu Huy Man had three regiments. The 32nd NVA had been in South Vietnam since February, the 33rd had arrived at about the same time as the 1st Cavalry and still on its way down the Ho Chi Minh trail was the 66th.

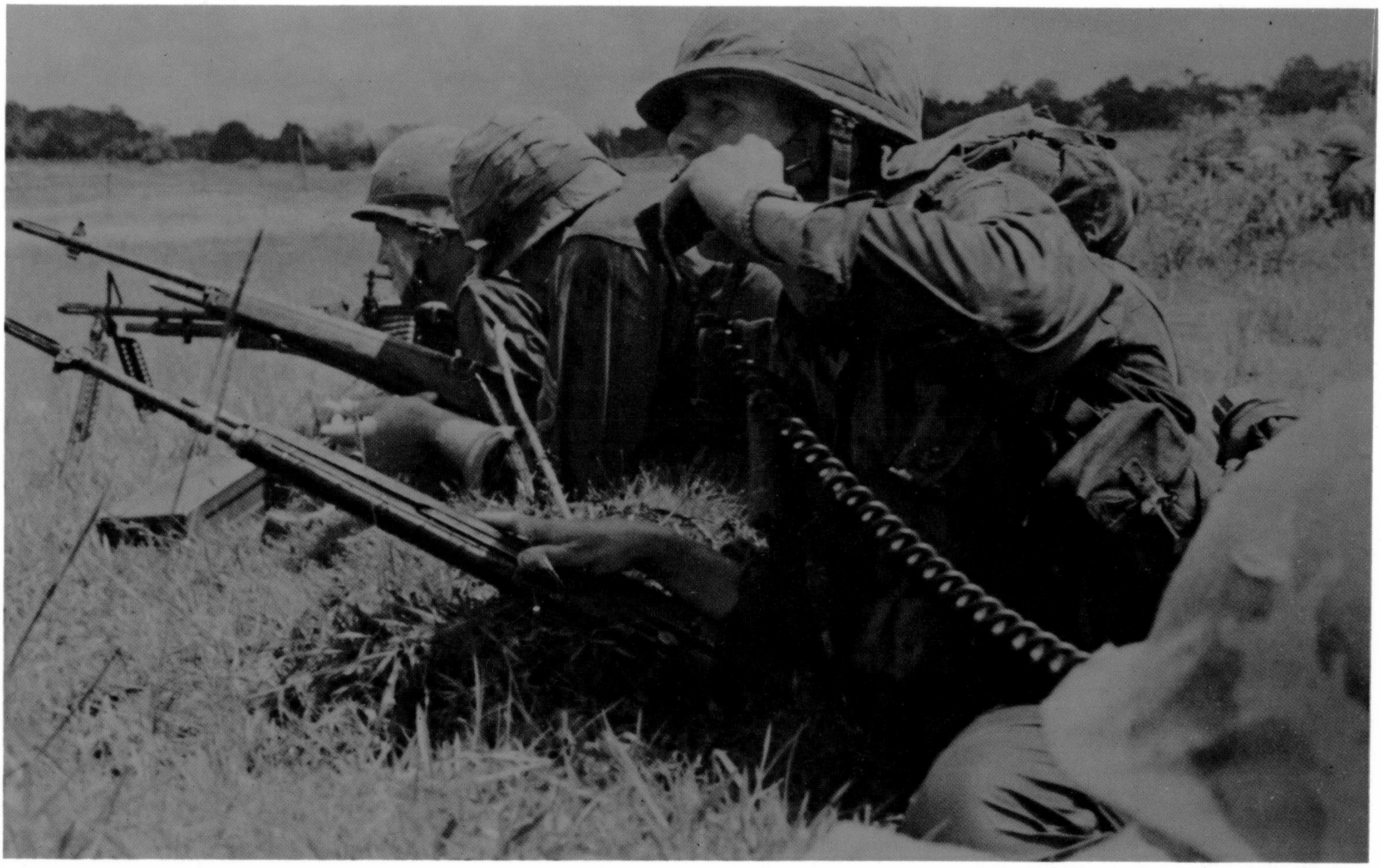

The first move was an attack on the US Special Forces camp at Plei Mei. The 33rd Regiment began a siege on the evening of 19 October, while the 32nd moved to ambush the relief column which was sure to be sent out. These were tactics well-tried during the war with the French.

The first problem was that, though the camp took a heavy pounding, the relief column did not set off pell-mell and fall into the ambush. It waited, and the camp held out. On the 23 October the ARVN column, with a strong armour element, set out. They fell into the ambush that they had nerved themselves to expect, but fought hard and the 32nd broke off the action. The 1st Cavalry lifted artillery batteries to cover the relief column on its march route and ARVN armour was able to break the week-long siege.

The first NVA move had been checked. They were keen to pull back and now General Westmoreland sensed that he should push for a counter-attack. The men were to be lifted into an area which combined elephant grass and jungle; though the man on the ground might not be able to see far, the air-mobility and radio communications compensated for this. Initially the search-and-destroy operation yielded nothing, then on 1 November helicopter reconnaissance saw movement along the Tae River. In a brief fire fight, cavalrymen captured a field hospital concealed at the edge of the jungle, but more importantly they killed an NVA officer and found on him a map marked with routes and details of the two regiments.

Major-General Harry O. Kinnard, commanding the 1st Cavalry, switched its operations and patrols immediately began to make contacts. Between the 3rd and 6th November NVA units attempting to reach the Chu Pong massif, to regroup for another attack, found their axes blocked by the 1st Cavalry. In a series of assaults on these positions the 33rd Regiment suffered heavily before it broke off to find other routes.

Above: Platoon leader 2nd Lt John L. Libs of C Company 16th Infantry, 1st Infantry Division, on a patrol near Bin Hoa.

Far left above: Marines man a machine-gun bunker as napalm explodes on the skyline during fighter ground attack operations in support of their patrol.

Far left below: A company headquarters watches smoke rise after an air attack. In front of them is the typical mix of agricultural land with tree lines and the mountains beyond.

Left: Marines sit out the rain during Operation Prairie near the Demilitarized Zone. Vietnam is a country of contrasts, hot dry weather and also downpours of tropical monsoon.

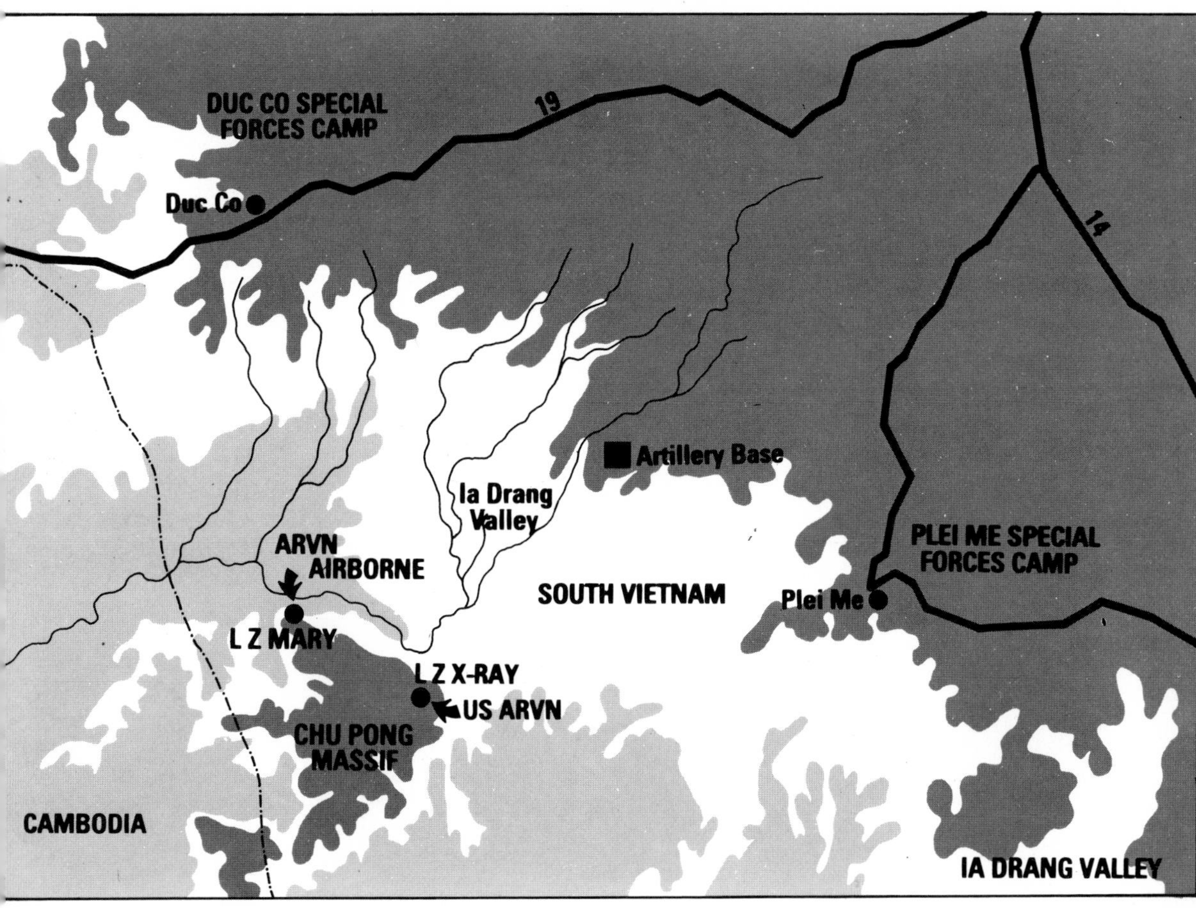

Kinnard switched his 1st and 3rd Brigades after ighting that had reduced the 33rd Regiment from 2,000 men to a weary 700. The NVA, thinking hat the rotation of US units was a withdrawal, lecided to return to the attack on Plei Mei, this ime using the fresher 66th Regiment with the two battered regiments in support.

Search-and-destroy operations by the 1st Cavalry brought them westwards towards the Chu Pong. This time General Chu Huy Man appeared o be about to get the concentration of men and ire-power that had evaded him. On 14 November ielicopters began to drop men in a landing zone (LZ) near the Ia Drang.

LZ X-Ray had been chosen by Lieutenant-Colonel Harold G. Moore, commanding 1st Battalion 7th Cavalry. He had the luck to capture in NVA straggler and, based on the interrogation, ie sent a company forward. B Company ran into NVA soldiers who were moving up for an assault and a violent fire fight ensued. A second company was inserted into the battle that had engaged all he companies of the 1st Battalion. It became a reserve and the battle continued with Lieutenant-Colonel Moore switching men and fire-power as he NVA attacks swarmed in. Fighting continued hrough the night but with the dawn there was no espite. A savage dawn attack reached a hand-to-iand struggle. However, the massive US fire-power was finding targets in the jungle – B-52 strikes, tactical air strikes and artillery pounded the enemy. By noon the battalion was no longer cut off as reinforcements had been inserted by land and air. Weak attacks were made in the night, but the LZ held and dawn on the 16th revealed that the enemy had left over 600 corpses on the battlefield. Many others were carried away, and it was estimated that about half of the 2,000 men in the 66th Regiment were killed or disabled at Ia Drang.

The ARVN added to the sufferings of the NVA when five battalions of paratroopers were air and heli-lifted to a stop line along the Cambodian border. US artillery fire and ARVN paratroopers finished the work of the Cavalry. The NVA could not give Giap a South Vietnam split open from west to east.

The victory was a triumph for US mobility and fire-power, though there were those who observed that US forces employed static tactics where the enemy would be blocked, but did not follow up on foot. These tactics kept casualties down, but even so the Cavalry lost nearly 300 dead. The helicopter had proved a war-winning and life-saving arm. Moving casualties to secure base hospitals and placing artillery on commanding heights, it had displaced batteries 67 times in the battle and re-supplied them so that they could fire 33,108 rounds of 105-mm ammunition during the action.

While this violent clash between the armed élites of two nations was being fought out in the jungle and mountains of central Vietnam, dissent

Left: Over the top: US Marines scale a rugged slope as they attack North Vietnamese regulars during Operation Hastings, two miles from the Demilitarized Zone.

Inset: Man of the 2nd Battalion, 503rd Infantry, 173D Army Airborne Brigade, struggle through the swollen streams around the base at Bien Hoa in 1965. This was the first operation by the 173D following their arrival in Vietnam.

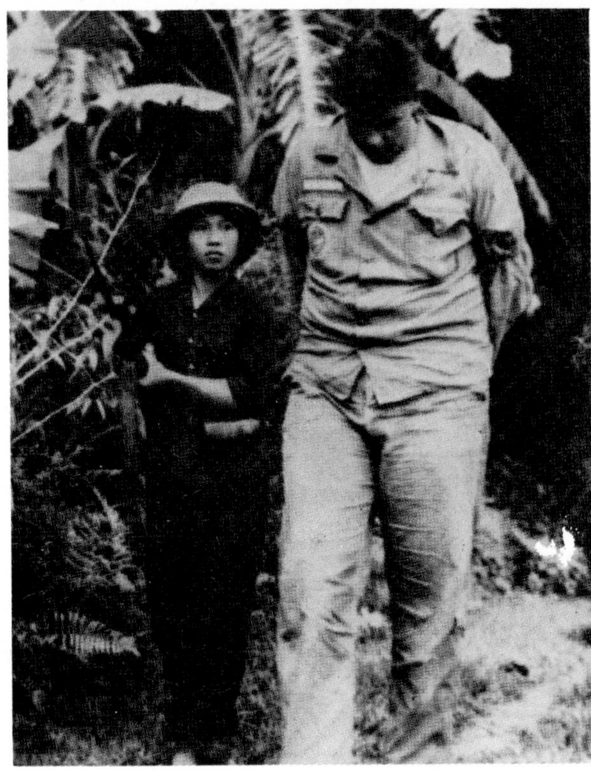

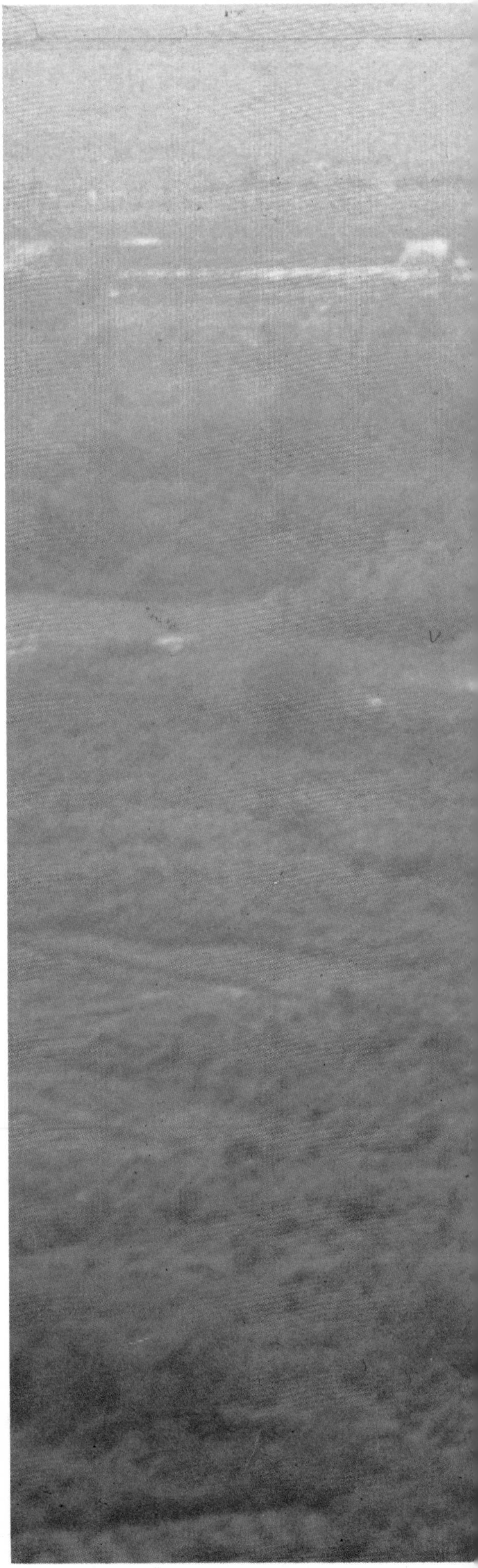

Top: A USAF SkyRaider fires rockets at Viet Cong positions in the mountain highlands during Operation Thayer.

Right: An image the Viet Cong were keen to exploit: an American serviceman is marched into captivity by a small female Vietnamese, part of the People's Militia in the North. Captured American servicemen were in some cases held for up to six years before their final repatriation.

Far right: An F-100 Super Sabre of the 416 Tac Fighter Squadron drops a Mk-82 Snake Eye bomb during operations against the Viet Cong in South Vietnam. Part of the problem of high technology weapons like Jet fighter bombers was their inaccuracy when pinpoint targets needed to be hit.

and discussion flared in the US. The morality and effectiveness of the Rolling Thunder bombing campaign was producing protests from the liberals in Washington and the east coast. There was the frightening figure of 28 battalions – 112,000 men – which MACV (Military Assistance Command Vietnam) had stated would be needed on top of the 181,000 men who were already in Vietnam.

A pause in bombing operations against North Vietnam which embraced Christmas and New Year produced no response from Hanoi. The air-power exponents pressed for a more ruthless attack – pin-point attacks on bridges and communications would not intimidate the hard men who made up the politburo in Hanoi. The North Vietnamese were also gaining propaganda from the air operations; film of captured pilots in their striped uniforms towering over their small but aggressive captors, and film of houses destroyed in air attacks, were being distributed around the western and eastern world. Vietnam was becoming a fashionable cause with the left of Europe.

4.1966 – ENTERING THE QUAGMIRE

Overleaf: A 175 mm self-propelled gun moves to a new location during Operation Seaward.

Below: A B-52 unloads bombs on the coast of South Vietnam.

BY 1966 THE UNITED STATES knew that it could not pull out of South Vietnam. To do so would not only plunge the country into communism, but be a breach of faith that would reflect on her dealings with other Asian countries. However, she could not go for the land actions that could win the war. The Viet Cong and North Vietnamese enclaves in Cambodia, the supply routes that twisted through the jungles of Laos and debouched into South Vietnam in a thousand anonymous tracks and paths were not open to major land attacks. Certainly the US Air Force waged a protracted air war against the Ho Chi Minh trail, and it was later to produce some of the, then, futuristic ideas of UGS – unattended ground sensors which could monitor the passage of men, animals and vehicles

›wn the trail.

The Ho Chi Minh trail, and the less well known hanouk trail (the sea route into Cambodia and ence overland to Vietnam) were to pose a con- ant problem for the planners of MACV. On the orth Vietnamese side the operation of the trail as a complex, well-organised operation in which nvoys would be switched as bombing blocked

one route and men and women were brought in to repair cratered stretches of the road.

The use of air power to interdict the route and the employment of B-52 bombers brought the war to the still neutral land of Cambodia. Prince Sihanouk attempted to strike a balance in his dealings with the North and the United States and for a time it seemed that he would manage to placate both sides. Tragically Cambodia was to suffer more than any country in Indo-China.

MACV now had the interest of the press to consider. Though much of the US press might rely on agency material there were a number of photographers and journalists who made Vietnam their major interest. They produced photographs, film and stories which, though they might pick on small groups and incidents, had a dramatic human interest.

Top: South Vietnamese paratroops jump from a C-123 Provider of the USAF in South Vietnam in 1966.

Above: South Vietnamese paratroops in training near Tan Son Nhut Airbase. These photographs, though not representative of operations in South Vietnam, were popular with news editors and journalists in the United States and the Western World.

Right: A US Marine prepares to throw a hand grenade into a Vietnamese bunker during village clearing operations in 1967. Part of the problem with hand grenades under these conditions was that the thin walls of a structure like this would provide no protection for the men throwing the hand grenades.

Below: The ubiquitous Huey: South Vietnamese Rangers of the 43rd Battalion wait for the helicopters to lift them on an operation in 1965. At the close of the operation they had killed four Viet Cong and captured eight. It was an indication of the, at times frustrating, ratio of effort to results that was a feature of the War in Vietnam.

Above: PFC David Reeve of the 7th Rgt, 1st CAV Div (Air Mobile) during Operation Masher near Bong Son in 1966.

For Westmoreland there was the realisation that he would only be able to make war by attacking the branches and not the roots of the guerilla and regular war that was being fought in the south. The war of attrition produced the grim and at times artificial system of 'body counts', which had once been a reliable way of gauging the outcome of an action. If you held the field at the end and the enemy had fled you would collect the corpses and weapons and report the total. It was a technique that had been used in the small unit actions in other counter-insurgency wars.

The body count was a way of recording success in the way that miles captured or cities liberated had been accepted in World War II. It was morbidly attractive to the press who would compare the list of men killed in the US forces with that of the ARVN and the reported NVA casualties. One comedian had a reported list that had awesome NVA and US deaths, and two for the ARVN – 'they died in a trolley car accident in downtown Saigon', he added.

While in 1966 US and allied troops fought with the NVA, the ARVN seemed happy to build up its strength and not prosecute the war. It was the beginning of a confusion and bitterness that marred US and ARVN relations. Sadly many of the US troops who arived saw little of the real Vietnam. Young men drafted into the US Army found themselves in a country they were asked to possibly die for, and yet seemed populated by corrupt politicians, bar girls, pimps and drug pushers.

Yet Vietnam was grateful for the assistance and

Below: F-105s of the 34th Tactical Fighter Squadron, 388th Tactical Fighter Wing, drop a 750-lb bomb on Viet Cong positions.

care that was being lavished on it. In Saigon a monument was erected bearing the words 'List of Nations having provided aid to the Republic of Vietnam' and in alphabetical order from Argentina to Venezuela were 45 countries. Some had given assistance in agriculture, others trained administrators or police, and others still sent soldiers and air crew.

For Westmoreland 1966 was a year when he aimed to keep the pressure up on the NVA and Viet Cong. Many of these operations took place

Inset: An H-46 Sea Knight helicopter disembarks Marines from the USS *Princeton* in April 1966. Heavy-lift helicopters like this were invaluable in Vietnam for both troop carrying and cargo lift.

along the coastal plain, and it was here that the heaviest concentrations of population made the operations slow and often costly.

Operations 'Masher' (re-named White Wing after Presidential pressure), 'Thayer' and 'Irving' were successful insofar as they penetrated the villages that had been Viet Cong for years, but the deployment of massive fire-power, the movement of the population for screening as Viet Cong suspects and the escape or evasion of the young male population produced a massive new refugee problem as the peasant farmers and fishermen moved towards the bigger cities where they thought they would be free of interference.

Masher, a series of actions fought by the 1st Cavalry between 25 January and 6 March, rooted out NVA and Viet Cong troops from a sanctuary area in the northern half of Binh Dinh province. After six weeks of almost continuous action in which 141,712 rounds of artillery had been expended, the 1st Cavalry could report 1,342 enemy killed in action (KIA), 633 captured and 1,087 Viet Cong suspects detained.

Thayer and Irving saw even greater use of fire-power. By 24 October 1966, Korean, ARVN and US troops had called in air strikes which had dropped 1·5 million pounds of high explosives an 292,500 pounds of napalm. Irving yielded 91 enemy killed, 550 possible kills, large quantities o captured foodstuffs and medical supplies, an 1,172 suspects.

Sadly, with this volume of violence the refuge problem grew and by December 1966 Binh Din province had 85 refugee camps housing 129,20 refugees.

The US forces may have kept the regular an hard core enemy forces on the move, but this ver movement by US forces prevented them achiev ing real successes in the pacification programm (see Chapter 5) that would have yielded real re sults. Some units attempted to put down roots i an area, but they would then be called on to par ticipate in a major search-and-destroy operation The Viet Cong infrastructure still remained – an with it the intelligence system.

The French had suffered from the problem o leaks of information during their operations an the US suffered too. One cause was that they use local labour inside their establishments and eve the delivery of ammunition as well as increase activity would give the local Viet Cong units a indication that something was in the offing Women would wash clothes and clean accom modation and this gave an insight into gossip an rumours in camps and barracks. The Australian and New Zealanders with experience of counter insurgency wars in Malaya took a professiona pride in the fact that there were no Vietnamese i their establishments, thus making their securit better.

For the US forces, in contrast, it seemed tha the more elaborate the operation the greater th chance it would be leaked to the Viet Cong. Earl in 1966 Operation Double Eagle against the 325 NVA Division, which had been operating on th border of Binh Dinh and Quang Ngai provinces drew an almost complete blank. It involved tw battalions of Marines who were landed 20 mile south of Quang Ngai and a third battalion that wa heli-lifted to a cut-off point 5 miles west of th beaches. The operation lasted from 28 January t 16 February, but its entire catch were snipe teams that harried the troops as they swept th area. In the after-action report the Marines wer to admit that PoW interrogation revealed that th NVA Division knew most of the details of th operation beforehand.

Westmoreland was keen to take the war to th enemy and this resulted in the disruption of an pacification programmes that units might b attempting. While these operations were unde way the US and Congress began to wonde whether they were on a course that would lead t an acceptable solution to the war in Vietnam and a chance to withdraw honourably. The phrase 'ligh at the end of the tunnel' was starting to be used i

Below: A helping hand during Operation Double Eagle in Trung Phan as Marines of F Co, 2nd BN, 3rd Marines cross a high rice paddy dyke in 1966.

informal conversations. The rising cost and the demands for manpower made it essential that the war should be seen to be winnable and being won. Statistics have always been a two-sided weapon in arguments, but they were mobilised to show that areas were under pacification and that men and women were rallying to the government. In some cases the Vietnamese who were 'voting with their feet' were in fact taking the chance to get out of areas that had become too dangerous to support life. In the daytime, ARVN and US forces would sweep through the countryside, while at night the NVA or Viet Cong would emerge to recuperate and propagandise. Stocks of rice and other possessions would be seen as VC or NVA stores and liable for confiscation or destruction.

The United States were also faced with the problem that they had vast resources which were seen as a means to save life. In contact with the enemy, drills emerged that involved 'calling in the world' – in other words, either on a patrol or in a defensive position, troops would call for artillery or air strikes against positions or locations that appeared to be concealing enemy groups. Men with experience of other wars remarked that there was less manoeuvre and a reluctance to sustain a contact. However, before the Tet offensive of 1968 there was still a high degree of commitment and a feeling that the offensive spirit and superior equipment and technology of the US forces would win the day. It was this message that was passed back to Congress and the people.

Above: During Operation Baker a US infantryman wades up a small stream during search and destroy operations 7 kilometres north of Duc Pho in Quang Ngai. Constant patrolling in flooded paddy fields and irrigation canals was a problem for soldiers who suffered from immersion foot, a fungal disorder contracted from constant soaking in polluted water. The soldier is carrying linked 7.62 ammunition for the M60 machine gun.

5. HEARTS AND MINDS

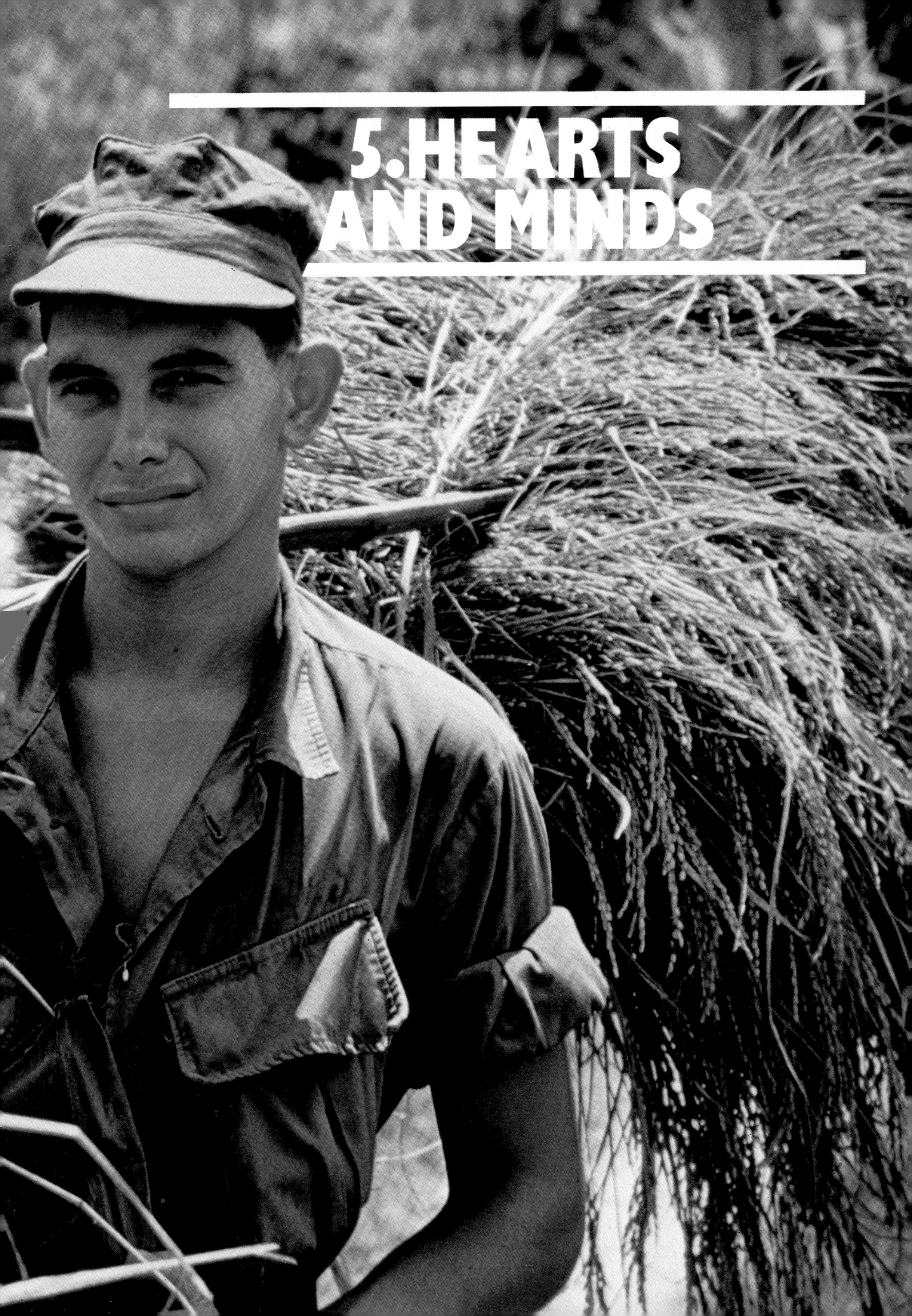

'PACIFICATION' WAS A WORD that the United States officials in Vietnam unwittingly took over from the French. In so doing they implanted in the minds of the Vietnamese the associations of the former French colonialists' programme.

In essence pacification is a well-tried tactic of counter-guerilla war. The government and armed forces give the people the very improvements that the insurgents have promised: land reform, so that farmers can own and work their own land; medical aid which brings clinics out to the people in the country; just and efficient taxation with benefits that can be seen by the people; the honest working of the law; advice and guidance on farming, health, small business and industry, and finally a respect for the honest religious and political aspirations of the people.

If these programmes are correctly implemented then the people will see that, instead of a 'pie in the sky' promise from the insurgents, they are getting genuine reforms and public works from the very people they are meant to hate. The insurgents will see these reforms and the men and women who make them work as a threat to their campaign, so the agricultural advisors, medical care teams and administrators become targets for assassination and intimidation. They too are in the front line.

For the United States the pacification war seemed to be a campaign that could be undertaken with considerable success. 'Throwing money at a problem' was a useful way of solving it. However the Pacification and later Civil Operations and Revolutionary Development Support c CORDS, were to face problems that had not dog ged the British in Malaya where pacification ha been used to good effect throughout the 1950 One of the problems was the neglect of populatio security. The theory was that the US forces we up in the hills or the river strongholds fighting th battle with the NVA and VC forces while th Government of Vietnam (GVN) was working restoring its power credibility 'behind the lines In fact the people were not protected, even thoug the war might not be on their doorstep.

US experts were to decide that at times th ARVN were operating a 'search and avoid' polic when it came to rooting out the VC infrastructu that existed in the villages. When on operatio they were often arrogant and abusive to the rur population. Secretary of Defence McNamara wa to remark bitterly:

> in almost no contested area designated fc pacification in recent years have ARVN force actually cleared and stayed to a point where cadr teams, if available, could have stayed overnight i hamlets and survived, let alone remain to accon plish their mission. VC units of company and eve battalion size remain in operation and they ar more than large enough to overrun anything th local security forces can put up.

The truth of this was borne out by the estimate figures of over 6,000 government officials assassin

Overleaf: A Marine attached to Combined Action Platoon 2-5-3 helps a Vietnamese lay out his rice to dry so that it can be threshed.

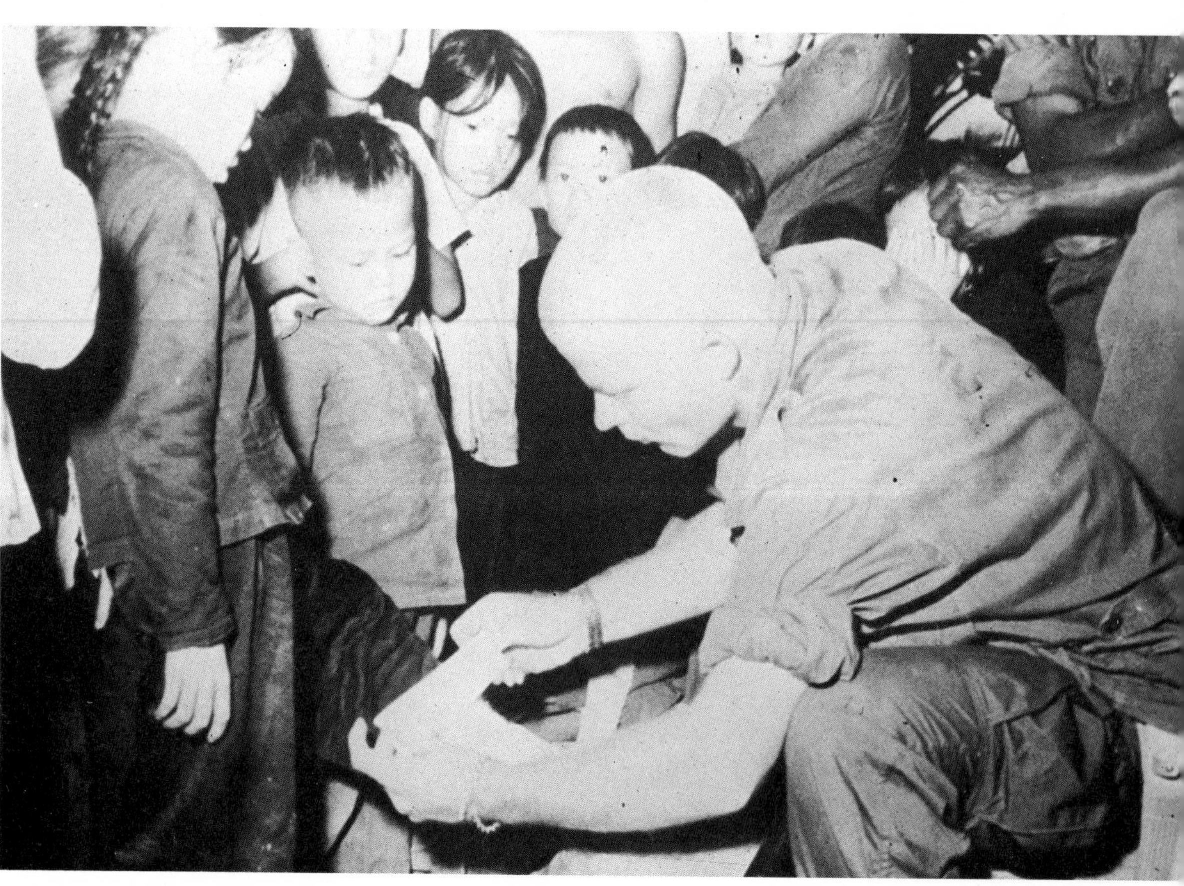

Right: An infantryman stops to treat and bandage the wounds of a small Vietnamese girl during a sweep against the Viet Cong in 1966.

Left: A US advisor with ARVN troops confers with his counterpart at their command post. A poncho liner and poncho have been erected to keep off the harsh sunlight.

ated between 1964 and 1967, not to mention those that were kidnapped and whose fate remains unknown.

However, the attraction for the military of funding these static and less dramatic operations was very small. The armed forces were doing what they had trained for and were best at, killing the enemy. This was evident from the figure of almost $14 billion spent on bombing and offensive operations, while only $850 million was spent on pacification.

For the men and women who were trying to assist the Vietnamese in the pacification programmes there was a feeling that they were in a backwater. This was not helped by the constantly changing names given to the operations. They included Reconstruction, Civic Action, Land Development Centres, Agglomeration Camps, Agrovilles (echoes of the French), Strategic Hamlets, New Life Hamlets, *Hoc Tap* (Co-operation), *Chien Thang* (Victory), Rural Construction, Rural Reconstruction and Revolutionary Development. Little wonder that the military could give scant time to a programme that changed its name, and the people in the scheme suffered problems of confidence and morale.

In the late 1960s the British defence commentator Richard Clutterbuck remarked that the big unit operations that netted VC and NVA stores complexes and a few prisoners were irrelevant. He cited an example of a US Marine Corps unit which had moved its men into the neighbouring villages to live with the families and look after their interests. In some cases the men of the village had departed and the suspicion was that they were with the VC. However, the big marines took to their families and made great efforts to see that they received the assistance and stores that were available through the government. A bond developed between the Vietnamese and the Marines, and these US servicemen grew to know the rural population better.

Nonetheless, despite the good intentions of the US advisors and some of the servicemen there were deep-seated problems in the community that could not be eradicated. The corruption in the Government of Vietnam was a mixture of national practice from previous years and the low pay of government servants.

Perhaps the most irritating aspect of corruption was that it gave the VC the clear opportunity to point the finger at government and show that it was not working for the people. A popular calculation was that the amount of cement that had been sent to Vietnam could have covered the country up to six feet deep. Some of the American aid made its way direct to the VC, and the capture of rice stocks with bags marked as 'a gift from the people of the United States' was an enraging experience.

However, more significantly, it made the assessment of the progress of the war less clear. The Third Party Inducement Program, a scheme that was related to the *Chieu Hoi* (Open Arms) surrender operation, was an attempt to get men of the VC and NVA to surrender and bring in a friend. In the end it was turned into a profitable scheme where the 'friend' was a civilian who split the reward money. The men who had rallied to the government appeared to have increased until the

Right: Private 1st Class James N. Jones, rocket man with H Company, 2nd Battalion, 5th Marines, assists a Vietnamese mother during the Tet Offensive in 1968.

corruption was exposed.

'Throwing money at a problem' might seem a cynical phrase, but between 1961 and 1968 the US government gave the GVN economic aid that was almost $3 billion. On top of this were the civic action programmes by local troops and engineers and doctors.

However, as Guenter Lewy says, in his valuable book *America in Vietnam*:

> While the VC offered to redistribute status, wealth and income, the GVN's efforts were perceived as the preservation of the social status quo, albeit at a higher level.

He quotes an article by Edward G. Lansdale which was writen in 1964 and says:

> there must be a heartfelt *cause* to which the legitimate government is pledged, a cause which makes a stronger appeal to the people than the Communist cause ...

No war can be fought without destruction, and the massive fire-power on call to US and ARVN forces was another problem for pacification. The South Koreans too used fire-power as a way of saving the lives of their men. In one instance a hamlet in Binh Dinh province had been hit by 2,000 artillery shells before troops moved in to clear it. Little remained.

Ironically the hardware itself was a tempting incentive for its use. High performance jets were employed to attack targets which could have been hit more accurately and for less cost by the prop-driven Spads with their substantial underwing loads. However, over 90 per cent of sorties were flown by jets.

For veterans of World War II and Korea, it was

Below: A Combined Action Platoon and villagers. The men of the village are grouped around their Marine advisor who stands in the centre back row. The Combined Action Platoon was an attempt to integrate Marines and villagers together, advising and assisting them with their self-defence and civilian activities.

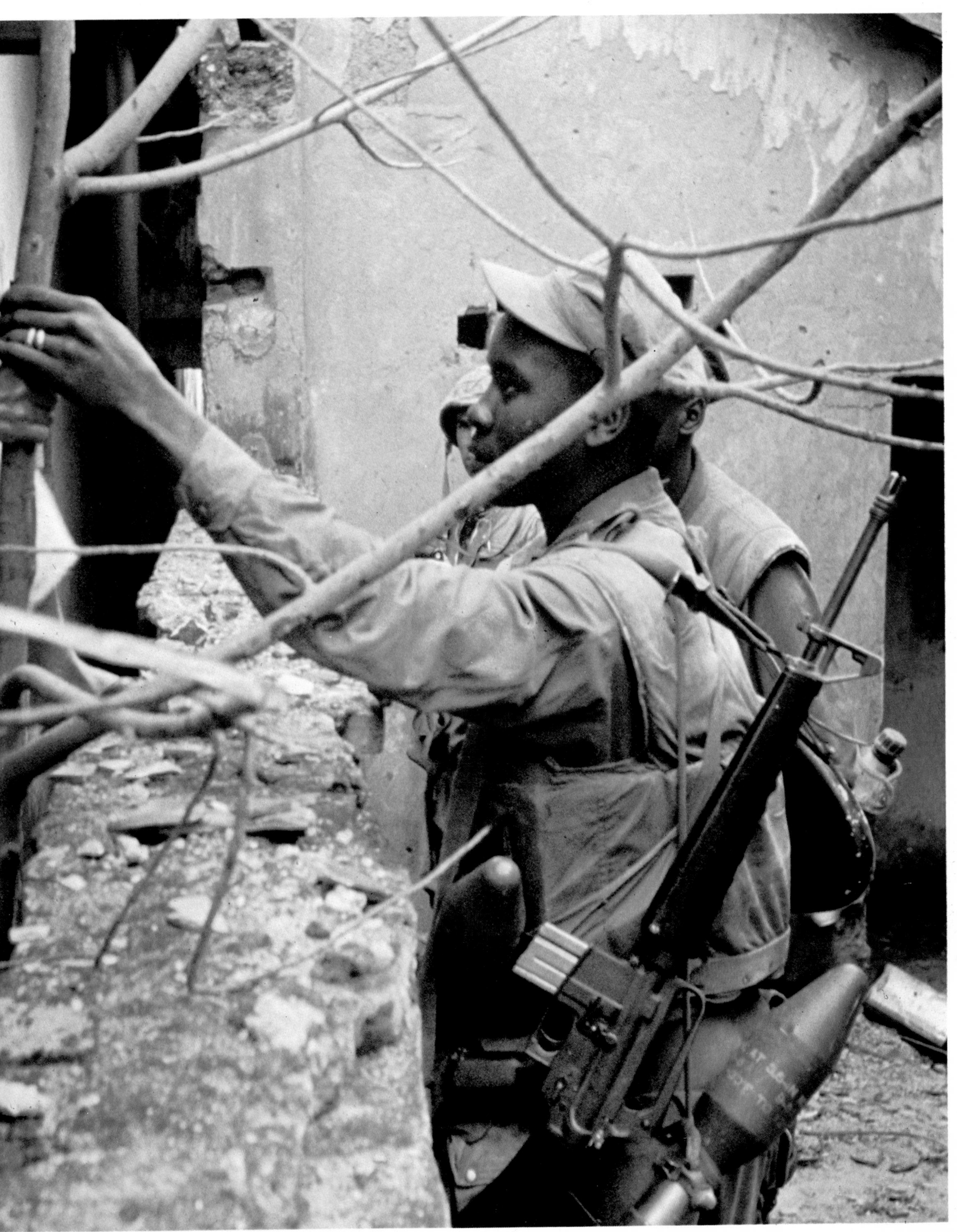

Right: A US Airforce F-100 Super Sabre from the 3rd Tactical Fighter Wing, operating from Bien Hoa Airbase, releases its bombs on enemy positions near the Bo Doc outpost in Phuoc Long, South Vietnam, in 1967.

hard to comprehend that a Phantom could carry a greater bomb load than the 'heavy bombers' sent against the Ruhr. However, between 1966-68 2,865,808 tons of bombs were dropped in South-East Asia; in World War II, in all theatres, 2,057,244 tons were dropped. One press comment in the United Kingdom was that each day more than enough earth was shifted in South Vietnam to cover the massive cathedral of St Paul's in the centre of London.

Harassment and Interdiction fire (H and I) was fired on unobserved locations (track junctions, fords, possible concentration areas) to disrupt enemy night-time movement. But H and I and the delivery of air and artillery strikes not only destroyed property and disrupted life, they gave the impression that the US forces and their allies were a vast, violent and uncaring organisation. A Rand analysis in 1969 gave the depressing comment that fire-power showed the GVN to be not only 'unintelligent and unpredictable' but also contemptible as well as hateful.

When arc-light (radar directed) B-52 bombing attacks hit jungle positions occupied by NVA or VC forces they were dauntingly effective. With a bomb load of 58,000 tons they would arrive too high to be heard over the target and defectors

Right: A 175 mm self-propelled gun from Bty 'B', 7th BN, 8 Artillery in action in 1967. The heavy fire power, either by artillery or aircraft, was one factor which made the pacification program harder to implement because the rural population sometimes saw little of the government except for incoming artillery fire and the destruction that resulted. The Viet Cong were quick to capitalise on this and would set up sniper positions on the fringes of villages in order to draw artillery fire onto these communities and further estrange the population from the government and American Forces.

Right: A Marine with a Combined Action Platoon bathes a group of Vietnamese children in the village to which he has been assigned. The conscription system was unfortunate in that it prevented the continuity of a relationship developing between the servicemen who had been assigned to a village. They were rotated home after they had completed their tour of 365 days and often the units in which they served would be pulled out of Combined Action Operations and used in Search and Destroy operations in the jungle or highlands adjoining the populated areas.

Left: C-130s on Operation Ranch Hand fly over the jungle spraying Agent Orange Defoliant to clear the jungle cover from areas likely to be used by the Viet Cong. Since the end of the Vietnam War, Agent Orange has proved to have been a controversial weapon, damaging both sides who came in contact with it. During the war it also destroyed agricultural areas and this forced the tough Vietnamese farmers to become refugees and further disrupt the social development of South Vietnam.

tated that the awesome blast and shock waves roduced fear and a sense of helplessness. Howev-r, they also gave the enemy a supply of high xplosive from the 5 per cent per month of bombs nat did not explode. This, combined with artil-ry shells that failed to explode, gave the enemy bout 800 tons of HE a month.

It should also be noted that the VC were keen to raw this fire-power on to villages so that they ould show that the government was not on the ide of the people. A few sniper rounds, or even he prospect of an advance across open paddy elds against an unknown village, prompted com-nanders keen to husband their men's lives to call own fire. As one US officer was to remark, 'It was xtremely difficult for a ground commander to econcile his tactical mission and a people-to-eople program.'

An extreme case for this was the 'free-fire ones'. These were areas which were designated as nfriendly where weapons could be used against nyone who was moving in them. In theory the opulation had been moved and re-housed out-ide. Of course the problem was not only to com-nunicate to the population that their family home vas now no longer a safe place to visit, but also that he vegetable plot, or ancestral grave, was also a langer area. The *Life* photographer Larry Bur-ows, who was killed in Vietnam at the close of the var, made a moving picture story of a young girl alled Tron who lost a leg when she ventured into free-fire zone.

Fire-power, as we have observed elsewhere, roduced a refugee problem, and though this night be seen by some as a move from VC control-ed areas, it was in fact a flight from death and lestruction. The defoliation programme was generally the final blow – men were prepared to stay on the land through high explosive and small arms fire, but with their crops destroyed they drifted to the town.

The effect of refugees on an already strained and inefficient government was to make things worse. The mass of unhappy people clustered on the edge of a city were ready for VC penetration – if the VC had not already come in with them. Vietnam, which had been a rice exporter, became an importer since her farmers were no longer at work. Rural intelligence sources dried up. As the tough Catholic communities had shown, a well organised hamlet or village with an honest and generous leadership was almost invulnerable to VC penetration. Creating refugees had the oppo-site effect. The refugee camps with their popula-tion of very old and very young were a pathetic advertisement for the failure of the GVN. Despite this there were those who thought that more re-fugees – or the relocation of the population – was an effective tactic in insurgent war.

It was only by 1966 that the US government, with the GVN, worked out a scheme that had the seeds of success. The CORDS scheme brought together all the agencies that had been working in Vietnam. It was unique since military men found themselves under the control of civilians from, say, the State Department or the CIA, while a White House official could come under military control as part of the scheme. By 1969 CORDS had peaked with 6,500 military and 1,100 civilians assigned to it. The scheme prompted the up-rating of Regional Forces, the rooting out of GVN corruption and the controversial Phoenix prog-ramme, launched against the infrastructure of the Viet Cong.

6. AN INDIGENOUS BUILD-UP

Overleaf: A Royal Australian UH-1H utility helicopter hovers over Centurion main battle tanks of the Australian army during operations in 1968. In the background is an Armoured Recovery Vehicle.

THE WAR THAT HAD BEGUN as a struggle between the north and south had by 1964 expanded to embrace more than the United States. Australia and Korea had each committed 200 men, while New Zealand had sent 30, the Philippines 17 and the Republic of China 20. A year later the figures had jumped from what were essentially advisor teams to battalion strength or greater. Australia had a battalion, Korea had sent 10. Thereafter the Korean figure remained stable at 22 battalions until withdrawal in 1970. Australia had two battalions and increased this to three between 1968 and 1970. New Zealand maintained a battalion between 1967 and 1970.

Incredibly there was some discussion about using men of the Brigade of Gurkhas, since the fate of the unique force in the British Army was a subject of debate in the late 1960s. In fact the Gurkhas were retained on the British Army strength and so the scheme never went beyond discussions.

One of the interesting groups that assisted the US and ARVN forces was the Royal Thai Army. It operated in an area of low level enemy action north-east of Saigon. The force, which reached a peak of six battalions with its own organic 105-mm and 155-mm artillery and air transport, had a strong volunteer element. Significantly it was ethnically the nearest to the Vietnamese and perhaps it was a sense of shared trials and troubles that made Thai senior officers reluctant to use air power to support their operations. One air strike a day was flown by the USAF on request by the Thais, but one US Air Force officer suggested that this was called for more in the spirit of good manners than tactical need.

Below: Mr Vinh Tho, Secretary General of the Vietnamese Ministry of Foreign Affairs, welcomes a Korean soldier to South Vietnam. In the background is General William C. Westmoreland, who commanded US Forces in Vietnam.

The Philippines peaked with over 2,000 men i 1967. The Philippines had been the setting of o of the great success stories of counter-guerilla o erations and it is significant therefore that t islands sent not a military-based contingent, but Civic Action Group. The organisation of t group included 60 men to man 105-mm artiller but the bulk were deployed under Medical an Dental, Engineer, Construction and Logistic support. Up to its withdrawal from Vietnam t Philippine group under the Engineering Civic A tion Programme constructed 116.4 km of road 11 bridges and 169 buildings. Other statistics i cluded 724,715 medical missions, 218,609 dent missions and 35,844 surgical missions. Sadl however, the US observers were to note that t Vietnamese were unhappy with the presence the Philippine group since they saw it as a patr nising gesture from a country with its own prob lems of internal security and corruption.

The Australian and New Zealand forces we most welcome to the US and ARVN. The calib of the Australians was demonstrated in a fierce fi fight that developed between Delta Company, 6t Battalion the Royal Australian Regiment, and a estimated force of 1,500 NVA and VC who clashe with the company during operations in a rubb plantation on 18 August 1966. For three hours i blinding monsoon rain the company fought th VC and NVA to a standstill. As ammunition ra low, Australian helicopter pilots flew through rai and winds to re-supply their forces. Using th noise of the rain, other Australian forces close with the enemy, who, pounded by artillery, wer forced to withdraw. The NVA and VC left behin 245 dead – in about four hours the Australians ha killed more enemy than they had in the previou 14 months.

Australia later increased her commitment wit HMAS *Hobart*, a guided missile destroyer, as we as eight Canberra bombers, and a civic actio team.

In a post-war study of allied participation in th war the US Army cites a survey made in Phuo Tuy province. The people respected the Austra lians for their fine soldiering and discipline. The commented on the fact that drivers observed th 10 miles per hour limit in built-up areas an helped the Vietnamese as well as paying fair wage for skilled and unskilled labour. However, th Australians and New Zealanders were noted fo their high volunteer element and the wealth o experience they could draw on from previous cam paigns in the jungle – the Malayan Emergenc being the classic example.

Just as the US Government followed by th GVN were keen to have these overt acts of assist ance to their operations in Vietnam, so too th NVA and VC drew on less obvious strength. It i erhaps worth killing one myth when discussing ıe NVA and even the VC. The popular idea was ıat they were a kind of self-sustaining organisa- on, and the long logistic tails were the reserve of Vestern' armies. When the Viet Minh fought the rench to defeat at Dien Bien Phu they had a vast rmy of porters to supply the men in the front line. y the time of the second Indo-Chinese War this ad altered to a more sophisticated load-carrying peration. However, after trucks had moved tores and, more importantly, ammunition down ıe Ho Chi Minh trail it had to be moved forward ɔ the front line in South Vietnam. The porters ould carry 55 lb at 15 miles a day in flat country or miles a day in the mountains. The war-winning veapon was still, however, the bicycle – it could be sed to get around stretches of the trail that had een bomb damaged, or were in the south. An rdinary bicycle was given an extension handle ar and an extension from the seat. The porter would load it up and then walk alongside, steering and controlling with the two extensions. In this way he could move 150 lb a day.

Supplies came from the Soviet Union and China, the most versatile weapons being the simple and rugged Kalishnikov small arms, the B40 rocket-propelled grenades and rockets up to 140 mm calibre that needed only a simple launching tripod. For the NVA the border of Cambodia offered a unique sanctuary in which to pause before attacks into the south and also a place where they could recover after an action. In places it reached close to Saigon and was to be a source of frustration to US ground force commanders who watched their battered enemy slip away into the secure jungle.

The Demilitarized Zone (DMZ), the provisional military line of demarcation laid down in 1954 between north and south, was another point where NVA troops could slip over the border.

Below: President Johnson with the South Vietnamese Premier Nguyen Van Thieu; to the right is General Westmoreland. The photograph was taken at Cam Ranh Bay in October 1966, when President Johnson toured South Vietnam.

Above: Captured North Vietnamese soldiers taken during joint American and South Vietnamese operations in May 1967. They can be distinguished from the Viet Cong by their simple khaki or olive-green uniforms.

Above right: Members of the 319th Artillery Battalion fire their 105 mm Howitzer in direct support of the second 2nd BN 503rd Inf, 173rd Artillery Division participating in Operation Greely near Dak To in August 1967.

They could also deliver shattering artillery fire from their Soviet-built 130-mm M-1954/M-46 field guns which, though carefully sited in isolated positions, could destroy ARVN and US fire bases close to the DMZ. The Soviet guns could outrange the 105-mm guns deployed by the US and ARVN and so remained almost immune to accurate counter-battery fire.

In order to counter infiltration across the DMZ and make the NVA journey south longer, Secretary McNamara authorised a project that came to be known as the McNamara Line. He had been convinced that a policy of defoliation and the erection of wire and sensors would, with mines and fortified bases, help to stem infiltration. To give the project its due, the French had operated a similar scheme in Algeria and there it had been most effective. However, the Morice Line was in open desert, its flanks anchored on the sea to th north and open desert to the south that was deat for all but the best equipped men. The McNamar line had the sea on one side, but the jungle on th other, and this was perfect cover for the enemy Moreover, while it was easy to maintain th Morice Line, jungle was a different problem Cleared areas quickly became overgrown an equipment defective through decay and rust. Th arrival of North Vietnamese 130-mm guns mad the project unworkable, although it was probabl doomed from the start since General Westmore land was unfavourable.

It was the Cambodian border that continued t plague both soldiers and politicians. In the earl 1960s the VC began to use the port of Kompon Som (then called Sihanoukville) to ship in arms an supplies. The travel time for these stores wa

elow: The heavy cruiser
ıe USS *St Paul* causes
ıperficial damage, while
ıelling the Cong Phu
ıilroad yard. She
ɛturned gunfire,
ccording to aerial
ɒotters, and destroyed
ne artillery site. She was
perating in conjunction
ith Her Majesty's
ustralian ship *Hobart*,
art of a three-ship group
ı Operation Sea Dragon
ff the coast of Vietnam
ı 1967.

quicker since they came by sea and then had a short journey to the front. This became the Sihanouk Trail. The base camps and stores areas were greatly expanded and by 1970 NVA and VC forces in Cambodia were estimated to be around 5,000 combat and 40,000 support troops. They controlled the bulk of eastern and north-eastern Cambodia.

In an attempt to keep his country out of the war that was devastating Vietnam, Prince Sihanouk, the urbane and cultured ruler of Cambodia, agreed to allow this NVA and VC presence as long as it was confined to unpopulated areas. Contacts between the NVA and Cambodian forces were few and in the ghastly bloodletting that was happening in Vietnam it was a strange fact that between 1963 and 1970 only 1,000 Cambodian troops were killed. In fact Sihanouk publicly stated that there were no VC or NVA forces in his country with base areas.

Because the area was so anonymous, the US intelligence officers adopted nicknames that passed into common usage. Between the cities of Phnom Pen (the capital of Cambodia) and Saigon the main feature was the so-called 'Parrot's Beak', a salient of land that jutted towards Saigon covering an area about 25 miles by 15. Route One passes through the area which also contains some small villages. To the north of the Parrot's Beak the border is covered by heavy jungle where it becomes the 'Dog's Face'. This feature is near the town of Krek; a smaller loop into South Vietnam was named the 'Fish Hook'. The Fish Hook and Parrot's Beak were both major NVA and VC concentration areas, with smaller camps along the border up to Laos. Opposite them were the US Special Forces camps in the highlands where local ethnic groups and Cambodian mercenaries were under US command.

In 1967 Sihanouk, still struggling to keep both the North Vietnamese and the United States happy, said that the NVA presence was not sanctioned

by his government and that 'hot pursuit' over the border was not unacceptable. In fact he was only putting a public gloss on a private truth. The United States admitted that before March 1970 3,630 B-52 attacks had been made on Cambodia.

While the United States equipped its allies with many of the weapons and equipment it deployed in the air and on the ground – the Thais, Koreans and Philippine troops might look identical with ARVN forces but at close range – the NVA and VC had many faces.

The US Army was to say of the NVA soldier:

> he is well trained and equipped; an expert at camouflage ... some even wear green head masks to blend in better with the surrounding vegetation. He is usually armed with an automatic assault rifle (AK47), carries a pouch filled with Chinese stick (potato-masher type) hand grenades, and has a lot of ammunition. He wears a khaki uniform and in a rucksack puts a clean uniform, a hammock, a nylon or light plastic poncho, a sack of rice, a ball of cooked rice, a small entrenching tool, sometimes a diary, pictures of his family or girlfriend and more ammunition.
>
> A number of NVA soldiers carry first aid ki which contain some US-manufactured drug while others carry metal boxes with mortar an rocket ammunition or machine-guns, or 40-mr rocket launchers, or 81-mm or 82-mm mortars.

Distinct from the NVA were the VC. The U analyst was to describe the VC as the poor relatio compared to the NVA. Dressed in peasant blac cotton working clothes:

> he is armed with any type of weapon he can pro cure. Usually it is of US manufacture – rifles carbines, automatic rifles, and submachine guns There is in his armory, too, a sprinkling of Frenc and communist bolt action weapons. He also car ries a couple of US fragmentation grenades, a U bayonet and, perhaps, a batch of panji stakes. H is good at concealing himself, and has a fantasti ability to perform his disappearing act and mi with the local people.

These men were farmers by day and guerillas b night and though they had been trained and edu cated politically they were not in the same leagu

Below: A stock of ammunition and napalm burns at the Bien Hoa airbase in South Vietnam after it was hit by Viet Cong rockets in November 1972. Airbases like Bien Hoa presented easy targets for the unguided rockets which were fired into them by Viet Cong or North Vietnamese infiltrators.

as the NVA regulars or even the hardcore Viet Cong. The standard of marksmanship and degree of motivation depended very much on the local leadership – but they could provide the screen behind which an operation could be launched. They provided the vital intelligence that went towards the very carefully planned attacks launched by the NVA and hardcore VC. Main force hardcore VC were well trained and dedicated. They had a wealth of experience of guerilla warfare to draw on and were organised into regiments, battalions, and separate companies.

The contrast between the 365-day conscript and the Vietnamese enemy was highlighted when US troops captured a lightly wounded battalion commander. Aged 37, he had been fighting since 1949, first the French and now as main force VC against the US. Showing no signs of defeat or anxiety, he insisted that the Viet Cong would emerge victorious.

Just as the soldiers fighting to support the Government of Vietnam had their hopes and fears – the greatest being the fear of death or injury during the short time before the rotation back home – so too the NVA and VC had theirs. The NVA had to cope with boring routines, jungle melancholia, home sickness, lack of family news, and at times a disillusionment with communism. Among his fears were the prospect of capture and how this would affect his family at home, a fear that was greater when he considered deserting or defecting. The fear that haunts any man who fights in the jungle is that of a severe wound that obliges his comrades to leave him alone to die like a hunted animal. The political officers within the units used this mix of fear and hope as well as the attitude to the US Army to keep morale at least at a workable level and high when operations were in the offing.

Among the journalists who were captured and later returned to ARVN and US lines, there was a respect for the order and discipline that existed among the main force VC. One West German TV team were impressed to find that the camera equipment that had been taken away from them had been wrapped in polythene and so kept in good order until it was returned to them. The political officer told the journalists that they could also listen to the BBC World Service 'because it told the truth'.

Below: South Vietnamese Marines flush out Viet Cong personnel from a village. The soldier is holding an M-1 sub-machine gun, commonly known as a Grease Gun, and is dressed in the typical black overalls with a bag of rice slung at his waist.

7. THE IN-COUNTRY WAR

Overleaf: The Mekong Delta; a French-built Vietnamese Navy Command Boat moves down a canal during a joint naval operation with the US Navy in 1967.

IT IS DANGEROUS to give the enemy nicknames that imply power or strength; their positions, too, can assume a potency that dominates the area if given dramatic names. One such place was the heavily-forested country close to Saigon that was dubbed 'the Iron Triangle'. It had been a Viet Minh concentration area and base during their struggle with the French and despite probes by ARVN troops and actions by the US 173rd Airborne Brigade with Australians and New Zealanders in late 1965, it remained a NVA and VC base.

During the 1965 allied operation, buildings had been destroyed, but the vast complex of tunnels that had been dug during many years remained an impossible target for the engineers set the problem of their destruction. Despite optimistic reports that the 'Iron Triangle was thoroughly searched and investigated, and all enemy troops and installations were destroyed...' it was soon back in use.

Earlier in 1965 the USAF had attempted to burn down the area with runs by cargo aircraft loaded with oil and gasoline, followed up by strike aircraft with napalm and incendiary bombs. The woods – dry before the monsoon – began to burn, but the massive thermal currents created by the updraft of heat caused their own atmospheric changes in the moisture-laden tropical air and suddenly local cloudbursts drenched the fires. They were further damped down by the monsoon that followed.

So it was that in early 1967 Operation Cedar Falls was set in motion to clear the Iron Triangle. This time the forces involved were greater – the 1st and 25th Infantry Divisions, the 173rd Airborne Brigade, and the 11th Cavalry Regiment. There were considerable helicopter assets available and artillery on call, and the operation began with the daunting impact of B-52 strikes on 4 January 1967.

Four days later the ground forces moved. An entire infantry battalion was dropped by helicopters on to the village of Ben Suc. The battalion – 1st Bn 26th Infantry – was commanded by Lieutenant-Colonel Alexander M. Haig, a soldier destined for new postings and responsibility. Other units moved into blocking positions around the jungle forest. Spearheaded by armour and tracks vehicles, the 25th Infantry Division commanded by Major-General Fred Weyand took up blocking positions along the Saigon River west of the Iron Triangle.

A day later the 1st Infantry Division, with the 173rd attached, made an airmobile assault with six battalions to block the northern exits. At this stage the south and east were screened by reconnaissance and air cavalry. The artillery was lifted in and registered; by the end of the second day an entire US Army corps was in position.

As the anvil of blocking forces was positioned, the hammer began to sweep westwards. The 11th Armoured Cavalry Regiment moved from Ben Cat, crossed the Tinh River and hit the jungle. Despite the danger from short range anti-tank weapons the leading squadrons made a 5-mile thrust to the Saigon River and so halved the triangle. The tanks and M113s then swung north to link up with the airmobile screen, and having cleared that position they swung south to clear the whole area.

However, the VC were not to be found – a few snipers to impede progress, but no large units. In the best guerilla tactics the enemy had melted away before a superior force.

This time the US forces set out to destroy the Iron Triangle with a vengeance. The Corps of Engineers not only set up helicopter LZs, but also cleared tracks. Their massive bulldozers carved one area into a gigantic copy of their 'three castles' corps insignia, while 'tunnel rats' began to search and clear the underground passages. The tunnel rats had one of the grimmest wars in Vietnam. In

Below: Troops of B Co, 1st Battalion, 3rd Marines on Operation Newton east of Con Thien.

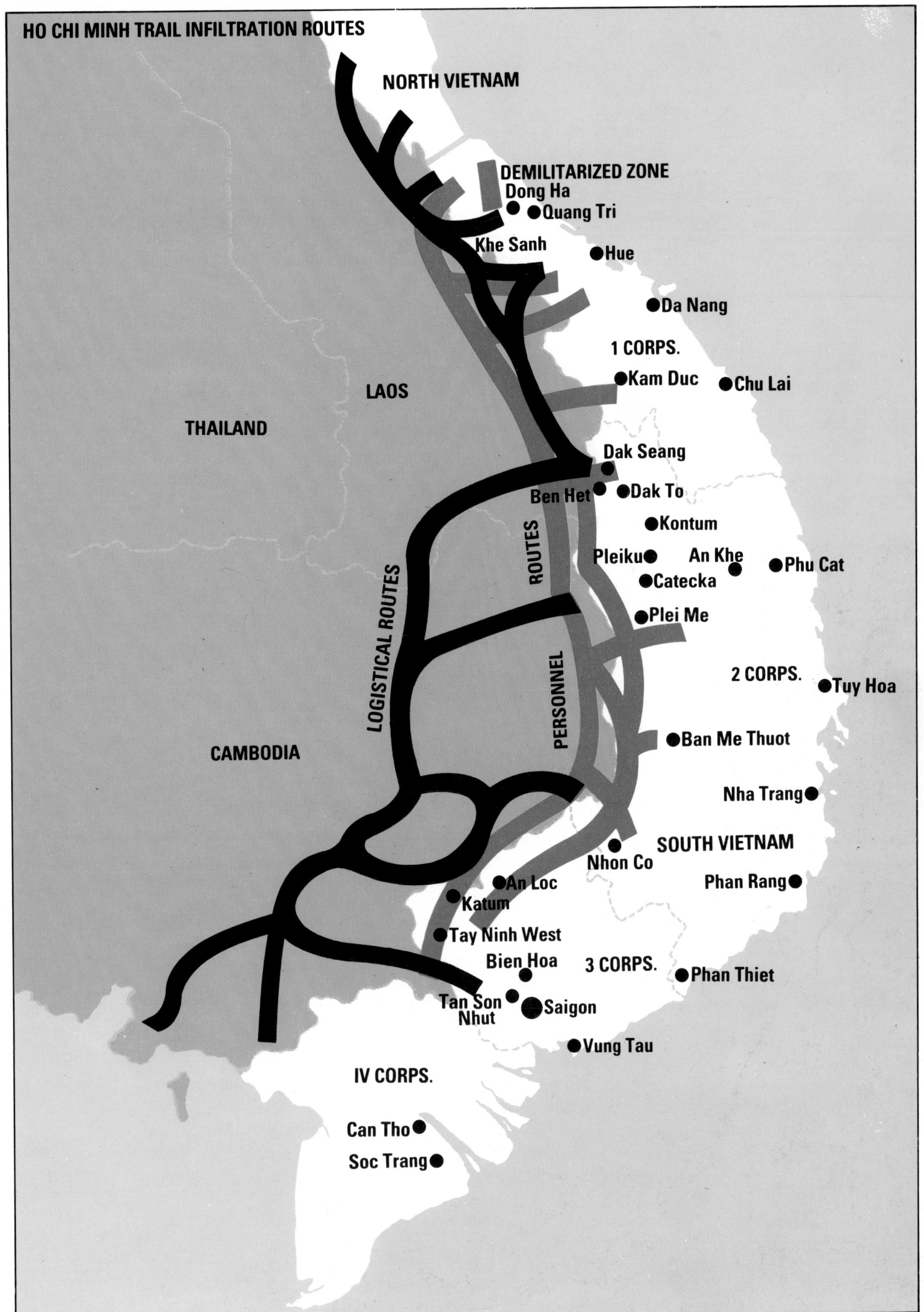
HO CHI MINH TRAIL INFILTRATION ROUTES
NORTH VIETNAM
DEMILITARIZED ZONE
Dong Ha
Quang Tri
Khe Sanh
Hue
Da Nang
1 CORPS.
Kam Duc
Chu Lai
LAOS
THAILAND
Dak Seang
Ben Het
Dak To
Kontum
ROUTES
Pleiku
An Khe
Phu Cat
Catecka
LOGISTICAL ROUTES
Plei Me
PERSONNEL
2 CORPS.
Tuy Hoa
CAMBODIA
Ban Me Thuot
Nha Trang
SOUTH VIETNAM
Nhon Co
An Loc
Phan Rang
Katum
Tay Ninh West
Bien Hoa
3 CORPS.
Phan Thiet
Tan Son Nhut
Saigon
Vung Tau
IV CORPS.
Can Tho
Soc Trang

narrow low-ceilinged passages they crawled forward armed with a flashlight and a ·45 Colt pistol. At the other end might be nothing, or a cornered, violent enemy soldier. Beneath the ground men fought and died, and 'tunnel rats' began to wear a complex armour made up of flak jackets. Underground there were various techniques that could be used. Smoke not only flushed out the enemy, it also gave an idea of where his exits might be, and also how complex the tunnel system was. In some cases the smoke would simply be lost in the multifloor systems, in others it would be seen to issue from various locations which could be sealed or guarded. CS gas, a non-lethal riot control agent, was used to drive out the enemy – and here the tunnel rats would have to make their forays equipped with respirators. When a tunnel had been cleared the major problem was how much explosive could be used for its destruction. In fact th
admitted that some systems were impossible
destroy since they ran for miles at different leve
Different methods of destruction were consider
and tried. The tunnels were filled with CS powc
in the hopes that this would make them unusal
for a long time; acetylene gas was pumped in a
detonated, but often the engineers had to be co
tent with destroying exits and tunnel workin
near the surface.

The engineers worked for three weeks. Wh
below ground they pulverised the tunnels, abo
ground the bulldozers uprooted trees and left th
muddy paths of destruction. At the end it seem
reasonable to think that the Iron Triangle w
useless. To confirm this destruction over 6,0
civilians who lived in or near the triangle we
moved to re-location camps.

Far right: M-113 APCs of the 2nd Battalion, 12th Infantry, prepare to engage North Vietnamese army units during operation Toan Thang in South Vietnam in 1968.

Below: Marines of F Co, 2nd Battalion, 9th Marines move through clearings guarded by tanks while CH-46 helicopters land to pick up casualties during operation Prairie II, north of Cam Lo.

When finally the US forces pulled out of the :ea they had suffered 72 killed and had killed a :w hundred VC and NVA. They had captured nd destroyed vast amounts of stores and a satis-·ing haul of documents. It seemed that Opera-on Cedar Falls had triumphed over the Iron 'riangle – but as the US forces withdrew, the ısurgents began to filter back.

While this war was fought in the south, the JVA brought pressure to bear along the DMZ.)n 20 March the NVA fired over 1,000 rounds at ıe ARVN and US Marines in the positions at Con 'hien and Gio Linh. The NVA ambushed a Iarine convoy a few days later, and then in late pril a series of actions known as 'the hill fights' egan when a Marine patrol 5 miles north-west of Khe Sanh tangled with a strong NVA force. The ills known by their heights as 861, 881 South and

881 North had been occupied by the NVA as a stage in their advance on the US Marine base at Khe Sanh. The US Marines fought their way up these hills supported by long range artillery fire and fighter ground attack, and thereafter held them as a ring of defences around the combat base at Khe Sanh.

For the US Marines in Con Thien there was the grim experience of suffering artillery fire similar in intensity to that delivered in World War II and the Korean war. It was a slugging match which was similar to the border battles at the beginning of the first Indo-Chinese war with the French. The Marines knew that if they evacuated the base the NVA would simply press forward to attack new positions, and also have greater freedom to hook around the DMZ and move southwards.

The US Marines' base was commanded by General Walt, who relinquished command with some regrets to Lieutenant-General Robert E. Cushman on 1 June. His regret was not due to any lack of confidence in his successor, but because he would not see the action through with the III MAF at Con Thien.

As the NVA continued their pressure, General William M. Momyer, commanding the US 7th Air Force, developed a system for co-ordinating air and artillery fire-power. He placed a forward

Below: General William C. Westmoreland (*left*) with Lieutenant-General Robert E. Cushman, jnr.

headquarters with the Marines which could direc both US Air Force and US Marine Corps tactica aircraft, naval gunfire and arc-light bombin attacks by B-52s. Directed against areas that wer likely staging posts for the NVA, they prevente the enemy from launching massed attacks. By th mid-autumn Con Thien was no longer unde pressure and the NVA withdrew to bring pressur on Khe Sanh. The 'siege' had been a useful pro ving ground for the men and equipment – and ha

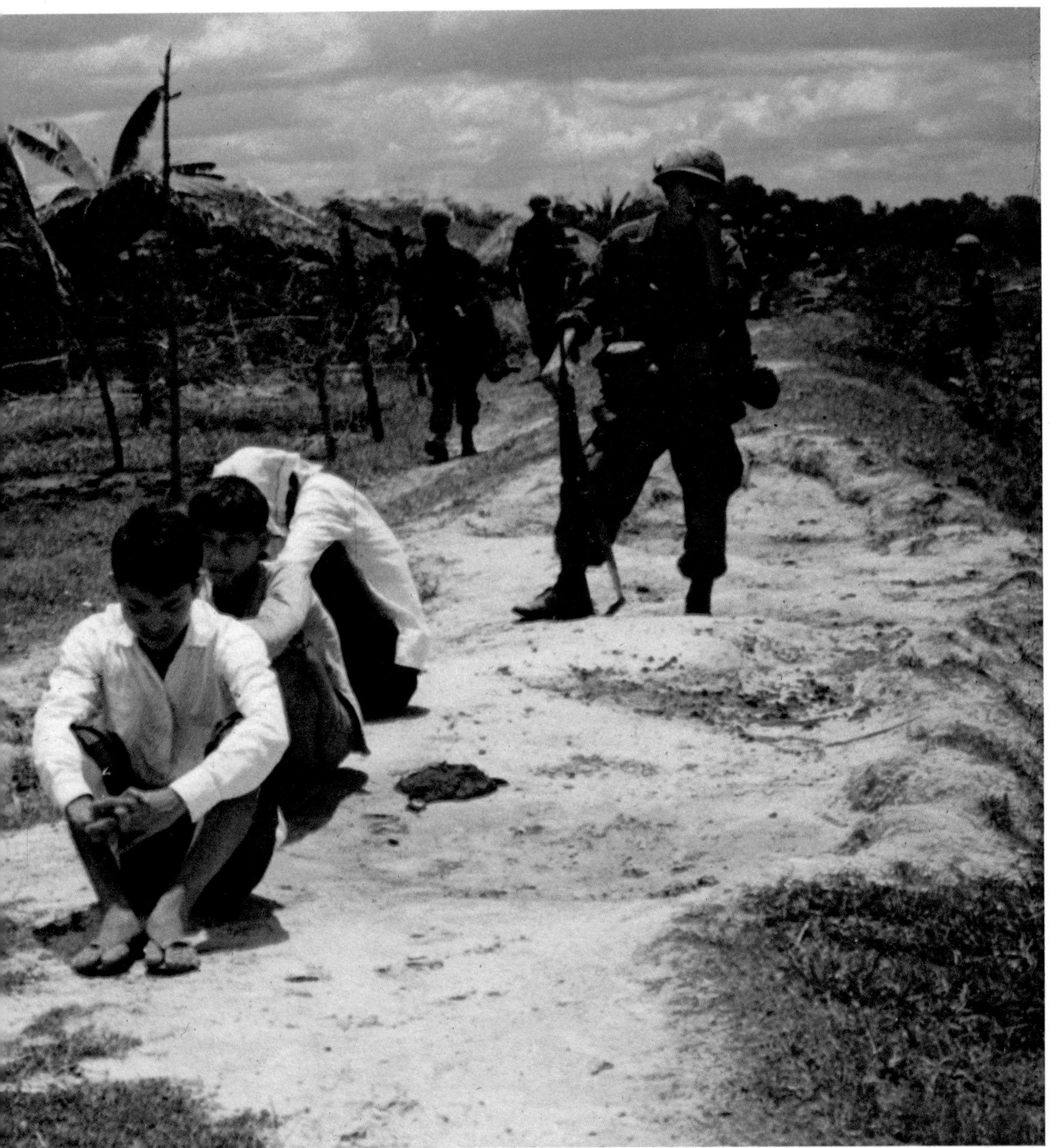

Above: During Operation Fairfax Viet Cong suspects are grouped on a trail outside the village of Long Trung, 8 km north-east of Saigon.

laid the ghost of Dien Bien Phu which was later to rise again at Khe Sanh.

Operation Fairfax which was conducted in early 1967 was aimed at reducing movement in the villages and hamlets around Saigon during the night. It had an open-ended date for its conclusion and a US brigade with an ARVN Ranger group patrolled and ambushed the area. The use of night fighting aids like the Starlight Scope made possible the identification of the enemy at a distance, even under poor light conditions, and therefore permitted ambushes to be sprung effectively.

However, the NVA leadership would accept casualties if these could be traded for US casualties that would make the war less popular at home. They were also drawing off the best troops to the north and diverting the attention of the command in Saigon and Washington away from the hinterland of Vietnam.

In Operation Junction City, which employed

22 US and four ARVN battalions – more than 25,000 troops – the aim was to clear an area in War Zone C in Tay Ninh province near the Cambodian border. It was an area rumoured to contain the headquarters of the Central Office for the South Vietnam Communist Party, or COSVN. As the operation got under way a battalion of the 173rd Airborne made the only large scale operational jump of the war when they dropped to seal off a perimeter at Katum. At the end of the operation in May some 3,000 enemy dead were claimed – but the evasive COSVN had slipped over the border into Cambodia. More importantly 282 Americans were killed and 1,576 wounded. A former US Intelligence officer was to write of Giaps's tactics: 'His is not an army that sends coffins north, it is by the traffic in homebound American coffins that Giap measures his success'.

In the Mekong delta the US resources were finding new outlets in a unique and very effective concept. The Riverine units were rather like the French Dinnasauts of the first Indo-Chinese war. The French had employed these river combat units in armoured landing craft and patrol boats to interdict Viet Minh movement. The United States with greater resources was able to improve on the original idea.

A base held the barracks and supply ships of the Mobile Afloat Force (MAF), which were anchored in a Mobile Riverine Base (MRB). US Navy assault patrol boats (ASPBs) and monitors gave floating protection and the US Army artillery backed up this fire-power. Operations were normally conducted about 30 miles from the base, the ASPBs covering the water routes, while gunships and tactical air power were deployed against the land targets. Artillery in flat-bottomed craft could be brought forward to give fire support. The Armoured troop carriers (ATCs) would land men to sweep through the enemy position, while others

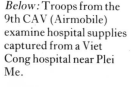

Below: Troops from the 9th CAV (Airmobile) examine hospital supplies captured from a Viet Cong hospital near Plei Me.

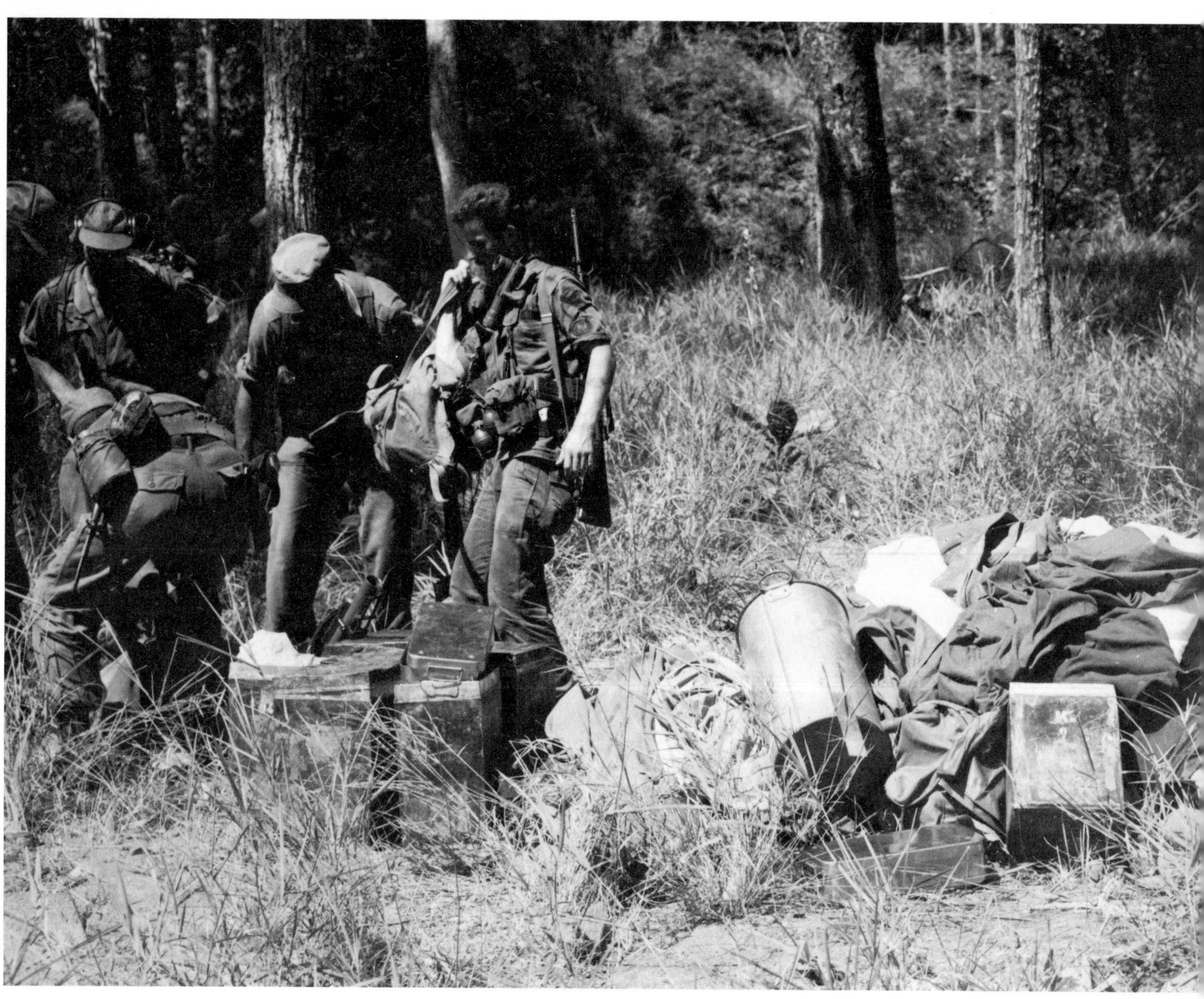

ould remain afloat with reserves.

It was reckoned that a battalion strength MAF uld conduct an operation over a period of four to x days and sweep an area of 15 square miles, fore it was withdrawn to re-arm and re-stock.

The main base for the Riverine Force had been edged out of the mud of the Mekong delta over vo years. One square mile of flooded paddy fields as filled with mud sucked up from the river bed. C Sappers sank one large and two small dredgers these operations but by the end the US Navy id US Army engineers had built an artificial land and secure anchorage for the force.

The vessels could carry 20-mm, 40-mm and -mm mortars, some were equipped with ·50-cal achine-guns and some even mounted flame rowers. Later operations in the swamp and arsh land were improved with the introduction hovercraft which allowed movement over terin that was impossible either for ships or vehicles. Designated a Patrol Air Cushion Vehicle (PACV), one sported a painted set of teeth with eyes to match, which made it look like a savage river monster.

Above: Members of Co A, 1st Battalion, 16th Infantry, 1st Infantry Division take a break during Operation Junction City, 15 miles north-west of Suoi Da. The sergeant on the radio has a snap link clipped to his webbing harness to allow extraction by helicopter if necessary, while the man on the left has his C-ration tin stowed in a sock tied to his webbing harness.

The US Navy also deployed its own Special Forces, the Sea, Air, Land (SEAL) force which was arguably the best specialist unit in Vietnam. SEALs were employed both in intelligence gathering and also in attacks on point targets of high value. One US Army officer monitored the air traffic as SEALs put in an attck on a small isolated hut which contained several VC senior officers. The only land zone was the thatched roof of the hut, so the SEALs jumped straight out of the helicopter through the roof – an exercise made more hazardous by the fact that the inmates were firing upwards at the helicopter. SEALs were the only units in Vietnam to employ the Stoner small arms weapon system.

However, while the war was fought for the

Right: The USS *Harnett County* (LST 821) used as a base for Detachment 1, Light Helicopter Attack Squadron on Bassac River, South Vietnam in 1968.

Below: Salvaging parts of a downed UH-1B helicopter on a PACV (Patrol Air Cushion Vehicle) in the Mekong Delta near Vinh Long.

Above: A UH-1 Helicopter supporting Riverine Patrol Boats along the Mekong Delta in 1967.

Top: PBRs fire into VC positions on Tan Sinh island on the Mekong Delta in 1968.

Above: Operation MacArthur: men of the 1st Battalion, 173rd Airborne Brigade cross the stream near Hill 800 close to Dak To in November 1967.

mountains of the north and the swamps and paddy fields of the south, a different struggle was being waged at home in America.

President Lyndon Johnson, who had taken office after the assassination of President Kennedy, had hoped to lead America into a 'new society'. His plans for reform had to be shelved as the war took more time and resources, but despite vilification by the left wing press and eastern bloc, he was a man troubled not only by the moral issues of the war, but by the growing public dissent.

Therefore in April 1967 the President ordered General Westmoreland home to explain the war to Congress and the people. Unfortunately the soldier, unversed in the attitudes of the media, managed to offend them by stating at a dinner given by the Associated Press in New York that 'through a clever combination of psychological and political warfare' the enemy had gained popular support in the world 'which gives him hope that he can win politically that which he cannot accomplish militarily'. A later comment about anti-war demonstrators who burned the Stars and Stripes angered the 'Doves' who were becoming a major force in US politics.

It was during this visit to Washington that Westmoreland told the President and his advisors that with a minimum force of 550,000 men he could end the war in five years and with 670,000 men he could end it in about three years. This was disturbing news for Johnson, Secretaries McNamara and Rusk and the Chairman of the Joint Chiefs of Staff, General Wheeler. Johnson agonised over these requests and in July told Westmoreland that he could have an extra 47,000 men. This would give a total of 525,000 which was less than the minimum that Westmoreland had considered essential for continued operations in Vietnam.

During October 35,000 anti-war protestors besieged the Pentagon. The event produced some striking film and still pictures which seemed to complement the grim TV viewing from Vietnam ıat was becoming a regular part of US television.

In an attempt to make the war more acceptable ıd to give the people more hope, Westmoreland ıd the newly appointed ambassador to Vietnam, llsworth Bunker, appeared several times on TV. Vestmoreland, with his iron grey hair and heavy yebrows, had considerable presence and on 21 November he spoke to the National Press Club, ıying, 'We have reached an important point when ıe end begins to come into view'. He was later to ıy that by November 1969 or perhaps earlier, oops would be withdrawn by stages as the RVN took over the prosecution of the war.

The last days of 1967 passed with fighting along ıe borders as the NVA attacked Song Be in Phuoc ong province, this being followed by actions gainst Loc Ninh in Binh Long province. In these tacks the NVA suffered heavily, and at Loc Ninh RVN and US reinforcements strengthened the arrison. By the end of the fighting, on 2 November, the NVA had lost 900 men to the allies, 60 ead.

At Dak To US, ARVN and NVA units fought a ng drawn-out action that produced over 1,400 IVA dead – more than had been killed in the Ia rang in 1966. It looked as if Westmoreland's words might come true. However, intelligence had reported an increase in traffic on the Ho Chi Minh trail and a fall-off in defectors. Something was in the offing and most people's attention was turned north to the DMZ.

Above: The 2nd Battalion 173rd Abn Brigade destroy enemy bunkers on Hill 875 in November 1967.

Left: A 'Dustoff' as the 173rd Abn Brigade loads wounded men into a UH-1D helicopter after the Battle on Hill 815.

TU THUC THANH

8. KHE SANH AND THE TET OFFENSIVE

AT THE END OF JANUARY in the Gregorian Calendar the Vietnamese celebrate Tet – the Chinese New Year. It is a time when the family gathers together, special food is prepared and fireworks set off. Tet is a combination of the Fourth of July, Thankgiving and Christmas all rolled into one. But Tet of 1968 was to become an infamous date in the history of the second Indo-Chinese war.

However, before considering Tet, and the VC and NVA offensive, a glance northwards to the Marine combat base at Khe Sanh will show where Saigon and Washington were most interested. Close to the DMZ and the Laotian border, Khe Sanh had been a French military outpost and then with the second Indo-Chinese war had become a small base for Special Forces (the Green Berets) and local tribesmen. Here the Special Forces monitored the movement of supplies down the Ho Chi Minh trail. By 1967 the signs were that the NVA would use the French-built Route 9 to hook round the DMZ for a foray into the northern areas of South Vietnam. A Marine garrison was to be moved in and when Colonel John Lanigan's 3rd Marines arrived, the Special Forces moved to the village of Lang Vei. Seabee engineers built a 1,500 foot runway with pierced steel planking; the runway was to be so heavily used by C-130s that it later had to be closed while repairs were made. The lighter de Havilland C-7A Caribous were too small for the loads that were needed for the build up, therefore at Khe Sanh a method was developed of delivering pallets of stores with a very low level pass over the airfield. Parachute extraction used a parachute to pull the cargo out of the open rear ramp of a C-130 and dump it on the runway after a free flight fall of a few feet.

By December 1967 it seemed clear that the NVA were planning an assault. Oblique com ments from General Giap and later leaked new that two NVA divisions, the 325C and the 304th were moving towards the base served to confir fears in Washington that this could be anoth Dien Bien Phu. The 304th was a guards divisio that had been the victor of Dien Bien Phu. Th battle which was about to start was to so obses Johnson that he had a scale model built in th White House and followed the action in grea detail.

The action began on 21 January 1968 when th NVA made an unsuccessful attack across the rive It was this river that supplied water for the bas and it was a constant fear that the NVA migh pollute it. The attack was followed by artillery fir that ripped up the runway and set off secondar explosions in the main ammunition dump. Th Marines suffered 18 dead and following this attac they closed into their defences and evacuated th civilian population of the village.

A massive re-supply operation using smalle Fairchild Providers began to replace the ammuni tion losses and Lieutenant-General Robert E Cushman Jr, Commanding the III MAF, autho rised the reinforcement of the garrison with the 1s Battalion 9th Marines. Colonel Lownds, com manding the garrison at Khe Sanh, had one artil lery and four infantry battalions and later receive the 37th ARVN Ranger Battalion which booste the garrison to 6,000 by the end of January.

The estimate of how many NVA forces wer deployed against Khe Sanh varies; some author ities put it as low as 15,000 and others up t 50,000. However the US Air Force using UGS (unattended ground sensors) and ADSIDS (ai delivered seismic intrusion devices) were able t build up a picture of movement around the base After the war one intelligence expert was to say that each night they plugged in the electroni monitoring system to their radio receivers an computers and played it like a giant pinbal machine. The pinball machine provided vital in telligence of enemy movements in terrain that wa totally hostile. It was these sensors that gave th garrison warning that their outpost at Hill 881 would come under attack in early February. Before dawn on the 5th a heavy artillery barrage neutralised the planned attack.

Elsewhere, however, at 861A an advance that had not been detected put the NVA in a position to launch a surprise attack that ended with savage hand-to-hand fighting. Marines equipped with armoured vests were able to survive short range fire and fragmentation wounds that killed or wounded their assailants. In fact the Marines used their hand grenades at point blank range – taking the blast with their flak jackets.

Though the Tet Offensive had begun, slightly off schedule, the pressure on the Khe Sanh base

Overleaf: ARVN Rangers take aim on suspected Viet Cong positions in a ruined building during street fighting in the Cholon district of Saigon during the Tet offensive.

Below: ADSIDs (Air Delivered Seismic Intrusion Devices) on a pylon of a USN OP-2E during Operation Igloo White over Laos in June 1968.

did not slacken. The Special Forces' camp at Lang Vei was attacked before first light on 7 February by 10 Soviet built PT 76 light tanks. The PT 76 was generally regarded as an older AFV, but the shock value of the cry 'Armour on the wire!' and the noise of the tank tracks with their head lights blazing was more than enough compensation. Added to this some of the defenders had the terrifying experience of finding that their short range anti-tank weapons did not seem to have any effect against the armour. However, in confused fighting the 24 Green Berets and 900 local troops knocked out three tanks and damaged others.

For the Marines in Khe Sanh there was the grim experience of monitoring the battle, but there was also the knowledge that an attempt to reach the small garrison would without doubt have been stopped by an ambush on the route. However, artillery and air strikes hit NVA men and vehicles and with the confusion of these strikes Captain Frank C. Willoughby of the Green Berets rallied 13 men and 60 local troops and made his way to Khe Sanh.

A day after Lang Vei the NVA attacked a position held by the 1st Battalion 9th Marines to the west of the combat base. With mortar and artillery fire covering their advance the NVA breached the wire obstacles with bangalore torpedoes and with heavy mats that they placed over the wire. Using satchel charges and Chinese potato-masher hand grenades they worked their way through the bunkers. When they had captured 50 per cent of the position it looked as if they would gain a local victory, but a relief force commanded by Captain Henry Radcliffe and backed with armour, artillery and air strikes returned to the position. One man

Above: An ADSID in position. It was designed to be camouflaged as natural vegetation and therefore be hard to detect where it had landed along the Viet Cong and North Vietnamese jungle trails. It only had a limited life with its own batteries built into the system.

who had a unique tale was Marine Lance Corporal R. Wiley who was taken for dead by the NVA when they came upon him temporarily paralysed but still conscious. They searched him, but left him unharmed.

The difference between Khe Sanh and Dien Bien Phu was chiefly that the US forces had a

Below: The remains of a KC-130 shot down at Khe Sanh. It was to be the backdrop of many TV news broadcasts.

assive superiority in air and artillery fire-power. uring the siege they dropped 53,600 tons of palm alone in four weeks. However, like Dien ien Phu, the NVA began to move in anti-aircraft ins to cover the approaches to the airfield and rrison. On 11 February a KC-130 Hercules fuel nker was hit as it flew in. It landed but burst into flames – incredibly eight crewmen survived though six died. The burned hulk was to become, as one commentator put it, 'The most photographed aircraft wreck in Vietnam' and was later to be a backdrop for TV journalists doing quick 'on the spot' presentations. It was damage to other C-130s, aircraft that cost $2·5 million each, that persuaded General William Momyer, commanding the 7th Air Force, that re-supply should be done by the smaller C-123K Provider. It could turn round in 1,400 feet in contrast to the C-130's 2,000 feet – so it was on the ground for less time and also presented a smaller target to NVA gunners.

Two C-123s were lost to ground fire. One wa hit by a mortar bomb as it began to take off on March, but the crew escaped. Enemy fire damaged another aircraft on the ground and it was late further damaged beyond local repair by subsequent fire. On 6 March, however, disaster fel when AA fire hit a C-123 as it was starting it approach run. It crashed in the hills and 48 mer died.

Re-supply to the hill-top positions around th base was done by CH-46 Sea Knight helicopter with fighter ground attack escorts. Loads woul

Below: A USA C-130 taxies to a halt at Khe Sanh. A US Marine waits to be evacuated out of the base – his entrenching tool and water bottle have been given to the men who have remained in the garrison but he retains his M16 rifle.

Above: The 'super gaggle' in action. A CH-46DC Night helicopter of the Marine Medium Helicopter Squadron 364 carries an underslung load of 3,000 lb of ammunition to Hill 881 near Khe Sanh. This helicopter was one of eight used by the Squadron based at Phu Bai.

e slung in cargo nets and the sight of the helicop-
rs clattering off to their objectives became
nown as a 'super gaggle'. Among the supplies
ken to the Marines in their isolated positions was
e cream. While it was not an essential store, the
ttle luxury was a welcome boost for morale. Sup-
ies were also parachuted from C-130s. Using the
ar ramp, loads could be dropped on pin-point
rets in a cluster rather than the older method of
hing them out through a side door with the problem of drifting parachutes.

For the Marines on the ground, life in Khe Sanh was sometimes muddy, sometimes dusty, nearly always dangerous, but also boring. On some days they would take more than 1,000 rounds of 'incoming' fire and they grew to recognise the sound of shell fire and look out for places to take cover as they moved around the base. Dien Bien Phu had been strangled by a combination of assaults on outposts and by trenches and tunnels

Below: Evacuating the dead from a CH-52 helicopter hit by North Vietnamese Army mortar fire at Khe Sanh. Though incoming rocket and artillery fire hit the Marine base the NVA were unable to prevent resupply by air.

that had closed in on the garrison. This time tunnels were a lesser threat to the Marines, but trenches were seen to zig-zag their way nearer. Air reconnaissance gave timely warning of these activities and napalm and delayed-action bombs made the work of the NVA troops very hazardous. Despite this there were nights when the enemy could dig 1,000 feet.

Patrols sent out to attack the enemy work parties and keep their listening posts off balance were sometimes bloody affairs. In one the Marine patrol was caught in an ambush and as a second patrol went out to rescue it the fighting became more intense – by the end, the extrication cost 25 lives.

There was a much smaller private war also fought at Khe Sanh between NVA and Marine snipers. The US Marines deployed teams of three – an officer and two snipers – with Winchester sporting rifles and Match quality ammunition. Each team would claim a kill if one of the two men killed an NVA soldier. It required patience and good eyesight. The NVA also deployed snipers, who had a slight advantage since they were operating from the jungle fringes. However, when the location of an enemy sniper had been confirmed, a 106-mm recoilless rifle would be brought forward by the Americans to blast him out of his position. In one area of the camp the Marines decided that they would not attempt to eliminate the new sniper who had replaced a man just killed in this way; the newcomer was so incompetent that he posed no threat to the garrison.

One final attack was launched by the NVA on 29 February. Alerted by their electronic equipment the Marines called in fire-power that included

Right: Smoke rises from a fuel dump hit by NVA mortar fire at Khe Sanh in March 1968.

Below: A US Marine goes for a pallet of stores, dropped by the US Air Force at Khe Sanh.

Right: The Khe Sanh perimeter. Many military commentators drew parallels with the French defeat at Dien Bien Phu but the Marines were quick to assure General Westmoreland, who in turn assured President Johnson that no defeat would follow at Khe Sanh.

Far right: The Tet offensive in South Vietnam. Though the press and public in the United States were surprised, astute intelligence operators in Vietnam were aware of the possibility of a Viet Cong and NVA assault on the country. Though it achieved political success, it was to cost the NVA and Viet Cong heavy casualties.

KHE SANH TACTICAL DISPOSITIONS

Water point
Landing strip
GCA
Control tower
Ammo dump
MATU
DROP ZONE
HQ & SVC Coy
TAFDS
USMC
155mm battery
HQ 1/13
4.2in mortar battery
FSCC
DASC
105mm mortar battery
ASRT
Forward operating base – 3

Below: Smoke and dust billow up as rockets hit Khe Sanh during a Viet Cong bombardment. Marines became quickly adept at recognising incoming and outgoing artillery and rocket fire.

strikes by B-52s, and the attack petered out before it reached the barbed wire in front of the ARVN Rangers' position.

After Con Thien and during the siege of Khe Sanh the Marines, Air Force and US Army developed a technique for co-ordinating their fire-power. If an attack was expected the Marine 105-mm howitzers would box it in with creeping fire so that it was pushed towards the direct fire weapons at the base perimeter. While the three 105-mm batteries were firing, the fourth would move up and down the box, sweeping the area. An outer box was formed by the 175-mm guns based at the Rockpile and Camp Carol firebases. These guns would walk their fire inwards from the flanks of the area; finally, air strikes by B-52s would block off the third side of the box to prevent any reinforcements from reaching the attack and the enemy from escaping this meat grinder. It used fire-power which had never been available to the French at Dien Bien Phu and expended it at hourly rates that would have been thought of as weekly or even monthly rates by the French. By the close of the action 100,000 tons of bombs had been dropped in support of Khe Sanh, which made it the most heavily bombed target in the history of warfare.

It was relieved on 6 April, after Major-General John J. Tolson had launched Operation Pegasus with the 1st Air Cavalry and an ARVN airborne battalion. Clearing operations continued through mid-April, though the Route 9 land communications were open by the 12th. These clearing operations produced a low body count, which led some US military commentators to wonder if the siege had been quite the high priority operation for the NVA they had assumed it was at the beginning of the action.

What it most certainly was on the other hand

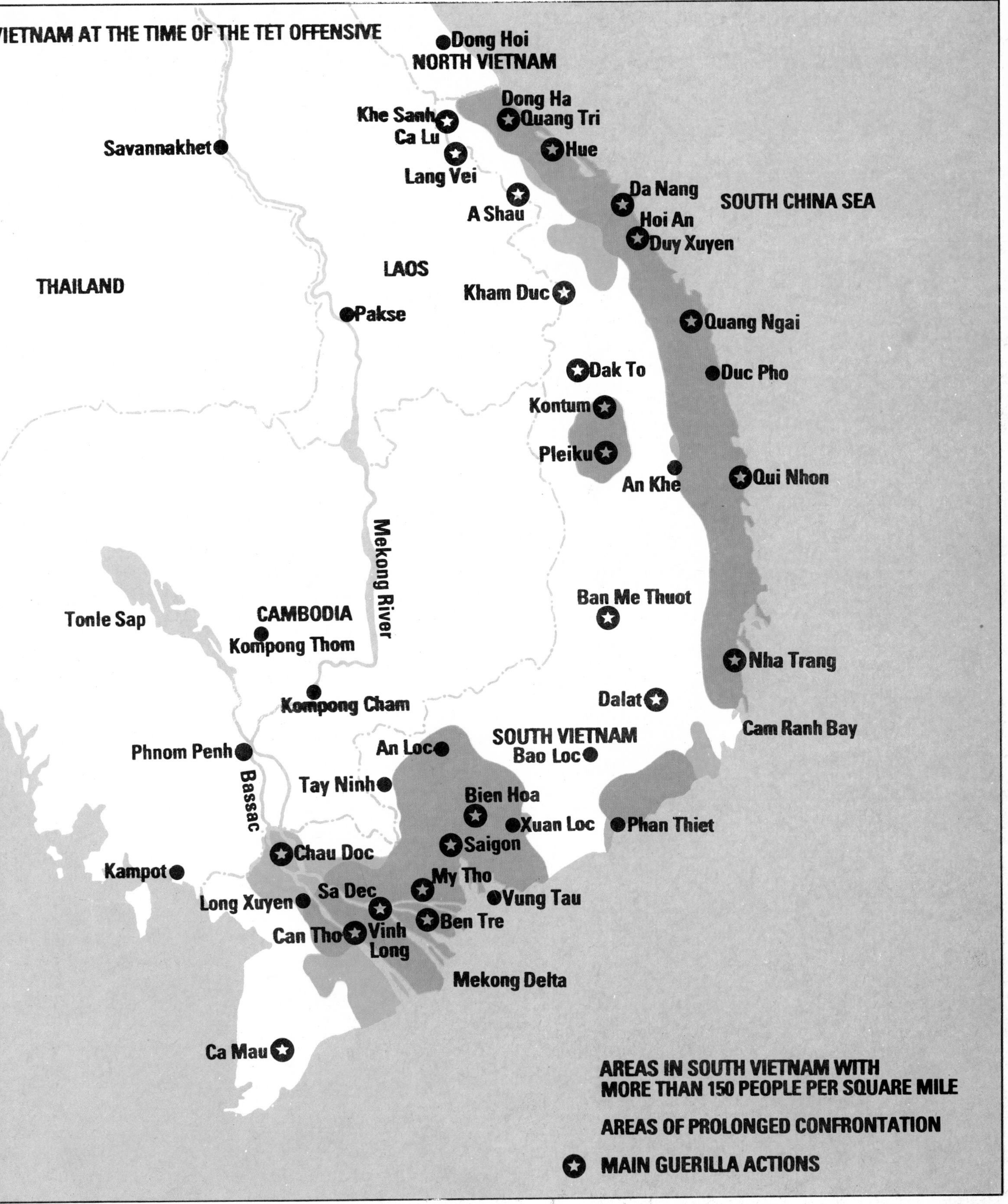
VIETNAM AT THE TIME OF THE TET OFFENSIVE
Dong Hoi
NORTH VIETNAM
Dong Ha
Khe Sanh
Quang Tri
Ca Lu
Savannakhet
Hue
Lang Vei
Da Nang
A Shau
SOUTH CHINA SEA
Hoi An
Duy Xuyen
LAOS
THAILAND
Kham Duc
Pakse
Quang Ngai
Dak To
Duc Pho
Kontum
Pleiku
An Khe
Qui Nhon
Mekong River
Ban Me Thuot
Tonle Sap
CAMBODIA
Kompong Thom
Nha Trang
Kompong Cham
Dalat
Cam Ranh Bay
SOUTH VIETNAM
An Loc
Bao Loc
Phnom Penh
Tay Ninh
Bassac
Bien Hoa
Xuan Loc
Phan Thiet
Saigon
Chau Doc
Kampot
My Tho
Sa Dec
Vung Tau
Long Xuyen
Ben Tre
Can Tho
Vinh Long
Mekong Delta
Ca Mau
AREAS IN SOUTH VIETNAM WITH MORE THAN 150 PEOPLE PER SQUARE MILE
AREAS OF PROLONGED CONFRONTATION
MAIN GUERILLA ACTIONS

was a major distraction for Washington and Saigon. The press corps too thought that the Marine base was where the war was being fought. No one assumed that it would come right into the streets of Saigon and as far as the ambassador's front door.

The Tet Offensive

The idea that, when the circumstances were right, a general uprising would turn the country against the US imperialists and their lackeys the Saigon puppet government, remained a firmly held article of faith for the Viet Cong and also the NVA. It was also part of revolutionary warfare doctrine. In 1968 Giap planned a series of attacks throughout Vietnam that wuld trigger this uprising. He code named it TCK-TKN (*Tong Cong Kich-Tong Khoi Nghia*) or 'General Offensive – General Uprising'.

In planning TCK-TKN Giap and his staff recognised that they could not beat the US armed forces in a stand-up fight; they also recognised that the NVA should not be seen as spearheading the attack since this would be less politically acceptable to the South Vietnamese; finally they knew that the attacks would have to stun the Saigon government and with it the people of South Vietnam.

The NVA was therefore deployed in the battle zones on the borders where they fought the best of the US Army and Marines. Meanwhile the Viet Cong began to filter into the cities. Close to the cities they began to train with new Soviet-made weapons and to prepare propaganda and exhortations. The plans assumed that if the VC could get into the cities and hold certain key points they would be able to show that the Saigon government did not exercise control. Offers of amnesty to the ARVN, plus the popular support of the people, would put pressure on President Johnson to withdraw his forces. There was an optimism and hope among the cadres that this was what they had lived for and planned for many years. The VC had been re-organised in the summer of 1967 so that they were cohesive larger groups more suitable for these more conventional operations.

The US intelligence offiicers were aware that something was in the offing, but some were inclined to dismiss some of these indicators as propaganda and mis-information. Not only did Giap and the northern press speak of a great new offensive, but at a more covert level there were other signs: captured documents, prisoners, a fall-off in men defecting from the NVA and VC – a sure sign of greater political control and optimism – and an increase in activity in urban areas and clear lack of success in the pacification programme.

While this was happening the US Command in Saigon set in motion 'Operation Moose' – a programme to reduce the number of servicemen in larger cities. It also released a translation of a captured document which, one month before Tet, predicted the way the campaign would be fought:

> Using very strong military attacks in coordination with the local population to take over towns and cities. Troops should flood the lowlands. They should move toward liberating the capital city, take power and try to rally enemy brigades and regiments to our side one by one. Propaganda should be broadly disseminated among the population in general, and leaflets should be used to reach enemy officers and enlisted men.

The handout said it all: 'Captured Document Indicates Final Phase of Revolution at Hand'.

The infiltration into the cities of South Vietnam

Right: A B-52 Heavy Bomber takes off. It could carry 12,750 lb bombs under each wing and 21 bombs inside its bomb bay. Attacks by B-52 bombers were to decimate NVA forming up positions and supply routes in the northern battle around Khe Sanh. The Marines evolved a system of concerted artillery fire and air attacks which prevented NVA assaults reaching the perimeter of the base at Khe Sanh.

Below: During Operation Pegasus the 1st Cav Division (Air Mobile) uses a field tractor to dig a gun pit for a 105 mm Howitzer as the Air Cavalry start the operation to relieve the Marines at Khe Sanh.

U.S. AIR FORCE

Left: A former Viet Cong Sapper platoon leader shows how he was trained to work his way through the thick barbed wire defences that were placed around American and South Vietnamese positions.

was made easier by the general population movement around the Tet holiday. VC arrived in civilian clothes, dressed as ARVN soldiers, as fruit and flower merchants with weapons concealed under carts laden with seasonal goods. There were even funerals with the casket containing weapons and a larger number of male mourners than usual. Though some were captured, US intelligence officers assumed that these were men who had decided to come home for Tet before returning to the jungle.

Though many senior US officers might have been caught wrong-footed by the TCK-TKN operation, General Fred Weyand, field commander in the Saigon sector, sensed that something was in the offing and pursuaded Westmoreland to move 15 battalions back from the Cambodian border. This meant that 27 US battalions were within striking distance of Saigon when the attacks began.

A final propaganda ploy by Hanoi was the announcement of a Tet truce of seven days. Saigon, less trusting, said that it would observe a 36-hour truce between 29 and 31 January. Saigon gave about half its armed forces passes to go home and the tempo of action slowed down.

On the US and South Vietnamese side the peace of Tet was interrupted shortly after midnight on 30 January. Though fire crackers were exploding to greet the new year other grimly familiar explosions awoke sleepers in the cities.

However, due to the excessive secrecy of the VC command structure, there was confusion about the launch date for the attacks. On the first day of Tet the VC hit Kontum, Pleiku, Binh Dinh, Darlac, Khanh Hoa and Quang Nam. These attacks served to alert the US and ARVN that something serious was afoot, but not until the following night did they realise that it was much bigger than they had anticipated – despite the warnings.

In essence the story of Tet is one of surprise and shock followed by reaction and the deployment of technology and fire-power to defeat the enemy. Everyone who fought in Tet had their own story. For some it was a night disturbed by incoming mortar rounds and rockets, for others it was days of bloody fighting which at times resembled the grim street fighting in Germany and the Philippines during World War II.

The bulk of the attacks on the second night fell

on Saigon, and the provinces of Quang Tri, Thua Thien, Quang Tin, Quang Ngai, Binh Thuan, Vinh Long and Phong Dinh. A day later, eight more provinces – Tuyen Duc, Binh Duong, Kien Tuong, Bien Hoa, Dinh Tuong, Kien Hoa, Vinh Binh and Kian Giang – suffered assaults. There were others, the last being Bac Lieu, which was attacked 12 days after the beginning of the offensive. The Viet Cong attacked or shelled 36 of the 44 provincial capitals, five of six autonomous cities, 64 of 242 district capitals and 50 hamlets. These actions were supported by moves against almost all the airfields in Vietnam in an attempt to neutralise the most effective arm of the ARVN and US Army.

As will be described later, in Hue the NVA and VC hung on until 25 February, while parts of the highland town of Dalat were still in enemy hands until 9 February. In the warrens of Cholon in Saigon the VC were still a problem in mid-February.

Perhaps the two incidents that remain most firmly in people's memory are the assault on the US Embassy in Saigon and the execution of a

Below: Marine Corporal R. J. Strick employs his flame thrower during operations at Khe Sanh.

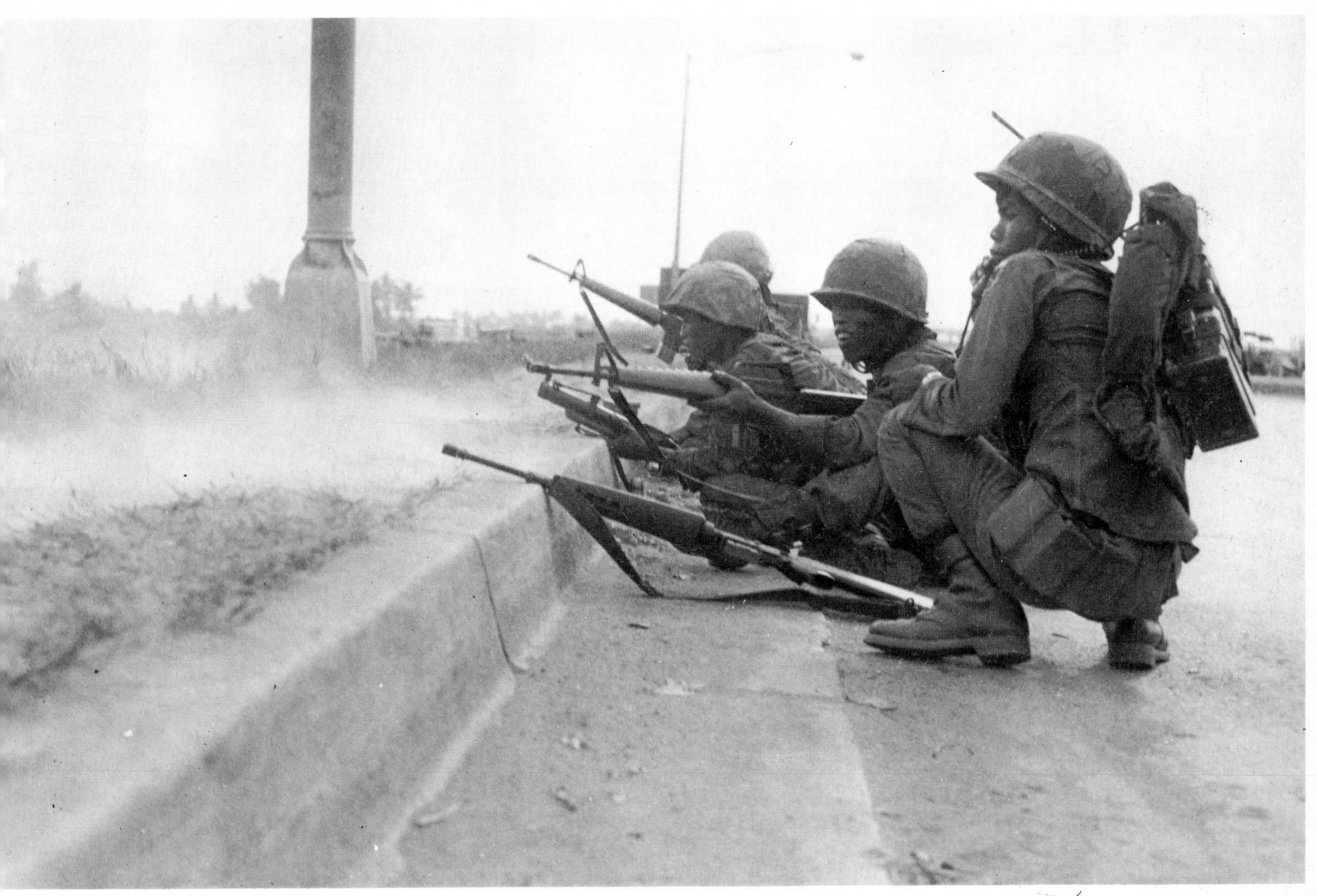

:apured VC officer by the Saigon police chief Nguyen Ngoc Loan. The captured VC stood in he open street and Loan drew his snub-barrelled evolver and shot him in the head – the incident vas filmed and photographed by US and Western newsmen. Many of the Viet Cong executions were only discovered after the offensive was over when nass graves were discovered outside Hue. Curiously, too, the media have forgotten the leaths of three of their number machine-gunned n their civilian jeep in Saigon.

However, the battle of the 'bunker' a play of vords on the name of the new US ambassador in Vietnam, Ellsworth Bunker, was the most dramaic story of the offensive. About 20 men of the VC Sapper Battalion C-10 had gathered in a garage not far from the embassy. They had moved in veapons and explosives and with these stowed in an old taxi and a truck they made their way tovards the building. Their orders were to break in and cause as much damage as possible. They eached the embassy at 2.45 am and the men in the axi opened fire on the guards at the gate. These nilitary policemen returned the fire and closed the nassive gates. Two minutes later they had radioed he emergency code to request assistance and warn hey were under attack. The VC sappers blew a nole in the wall, but in the fire fight that followed heir platoon leader was killed. Deprived of orders, they remained in the grounds and did not attempt to blast their way through the big teak doors that had been locked. More military police arrived at dawn, and airborne troopers landed by helicopter on the heli-pad on the embassy roof. By 7.00 am the fight was over. In all the attack had killed five Americans and caused some minor damage to the embassy. Its political impact was greater.

Newsmen at one point were reporting that the VC were in the embassy, and even after the fighting had ended the photographs of the blood soaked bodies of the sappers – all dressed in bright check shirts – scattered in the embassy grounds still made dramatic pictures. It was the idea that the embassy had been entered by the enemy that made the most lasting impact – even after the news of street fighting in Hue and country-wide operations had started to come in.

The VC had other targets in Saigon and the newsmen struggled to grasp what was happening at the presidential palace, the ARVN Joint General Staff compound, the airbase at Bien Hoa and the civil and military air base of Tan Son Nhut. At Tan Son Nhut four NVA/VC infantry battalions and a sapper battalion put in attacks that cost then 962 killed with nine prisoners. The US losses were 19 US Army and four USAF personnel killed, with 74 US Army and 11 USAF men wounded. Some 13 aircraft were significantly damaged. The ARVN suffered 32 killed and 79 wounded.

Left: Amid the formal gardens of the US Embassy in Saigon a Viet Cong Sapper lies dead. The ability of the Viet Cong to penetrate the American Embassy was one of the political victories scored during the Tet offensive, though it achieved nothing of military significance.

Above: Members of Company A, 30th Ranger Battalion maintain radio contact as they move against the Viet Cong near Saigon during the Tet offensive. The fighting by the ARVN was to come as a happy surprise to American forces who had wondered if the ARVN could be relied on as allies in battle, particularly in one as demanding as that fought during Tet.

Below: American and South Vietnamese troops examine a captured 12.75 mm heavy machine gun. These weapons firing tracer ammunition were widely used in Vietnam against helicopters and high performance aircraft.

Right: Viet Cong infiltrators captured during street fighting in Cholon are loaded into a truck by ARVN Rangers. The check shirts worn by some of the VC were an identification feature during the Tet offensive.

At Bien Hoa two NVA/VC battalions with a reinforced company destroyed two aircraft and damaged 20. They killed four USAF and wounded 26 personnel. The NVA/VC suffered 139 killed and 25 prisoners at the base and in follow-up operations a further 1,164 were killed with 98 prisoners.

President Thieu declared martial law on 31 January, but had withdrawn this decree by 5 February. Elsewhere in Saigon the enemy seized the French cemetery and the race track and defended them in battalion strength against the ARVN. The cemetery was built to last, with concrete headstones which gave the defenders excellent cover. Happily for the population of Saigon the enemy did not remain long. Viet Cong Political Officers were found to be carrying death certificates with blanks for the name, date and crime; clearly, executions were planned in the city.

Hue to the north was to suffer occupation and street fighting. However, as Peter Braestrup in his excellent book *Big Story* was to explain, the press and television concentrated on images that were those of destruction and drama – which gave a misleading picture of what happened to the city. Hue is located on the Suong Hong, or Perfume River; on the left bank the Citadel is surrounded by a moat and a thick brick wall. The Citadel and the left bank of the town are linked by two bridges, one of which carried two lanes of traffic.

The Citadel was once the residence for Annamese emperors and the town was the ancient capital of Vietnam. Inside it is a smaller version of the Imperial City of Peking. Two miles square, it has some vestige of nineteenth-century angled fortifications. But the real strength was the 16 foot high wall which at places was 60 to 100 feet thick.

On 30 January Brigadier-General Ngo Quang Truong commanding the ARVN 1st Division had held a flag raising ceremony in the Citadel. Since reports were already coming in of VC and NVA actions he decided to keep his HQ staff together at the Citadel. In the town VC sappers were awaiting the arrival of the 4th NVA Regiment commanded by Lieutenant-Colonel Nguyen Van and the 6th commanded by Lieutenant-Colonel Nguyen Trong Dan. Hue was about to be attacked by a total of 10 battalions, 4 NVA and 6 VC, with

Above: Vietnamese homes destroyed during the Tet offensive in Bien Hoa. Scenes such as this made excellent film and still photography for the news agencies in the United States but were not entirely representative of the material damage caused by the offensive.

drafts moved in to take the place of men who had been killed, and with their arrival tensions between northerners and southeners bubbled up and had to be suppressed by political officers.

However, victory and defeat in revolutionary war is a different experience compared to conventional war. The military defeat of Tet had the seeds of political victory for the north. The coffins that had gone home to the USA were now followed by news coverage that asked the question, 'If we were told that we were winning the war – how have we suffered attacks like this?'

Few of the TV and press journalists had either military training or had studied military history. Tet, to them, was a defeat and this was the way they reported it. As was seen at Hue, the natural temptation was to film or photograph the ruins, the fighting and the soldiers. With these pictures went written accounts that used emotive language and conveyed an impression of widespread damage. The most quoted statement on the physical destruction was about the town of Ben Tre. A US officer said, 'It became necessary to destroy the town to save it'; the tortured logic of the statement was seized on and repeated. In fact Ben Tre suffered 25 per cent severe damage. In *Big Story*, Braestrup comments:

. . . repeatedly, informative TV film was marred by sloppy, sometimes simple-minded narration. Most of the explanatory commentary was overblown – partly because TV correspondents had lacked time to probe to any degree into the meaning of filmed material. The idea, as always, was to get 'good' film first.

Moreover, it was clear here as anywhere, other factors aside, that as 'processing' – rewriting and editing – increased, accuracy tended to decrease.

Though public opinion polls in the USA reported the bulk of the population still supported the war, the news coverage was reaching the middle level civilian bureaucrats and Congress. Significantly many did not ask why the damage had been caused, but blamed it on the ARVN and US forces – not the NVA and VC who had occupied buildings in the centre of cities.

The pressure generated by the media and the anti-war movement began to tell on Johnson. General Westmoreland, who had been in Vietnam for four and a half years, was promoted to Chief of Staff, and replaced by his deputy, General Creighton W. Abrams. The decision had been made before Tet, but critics of the war said that it was a rebuff to Westmoreland. Johnson was persuaded however to call another halt to bombing in the north and make an appeal to the North Vietnamese to negotiate. Perhaps the most memorable outcome of Tet was the President's TV talk to the nation which closed with his announcement that in order to be free to give all his efforts to peace he would not stand for President in 1968.

The north agreed to talk. Paris was chosen as the venue, but the Hanoi government stalled with pointless discussions about the shape of the table. For four years they used the ploy of talks to heap pressure on the United States. It would give them a way of talking the US out of the war and leave them free to launch their massive conventional assault on the south.

9. VIETNAMISATION

ONE OUTCOME OF THE post-Tet discussions was the decision to press forward with a policy of Vietnamisation. This meant the re-equipping and re-arming of the ARVN so that they could not only take the load of the war on their shoulders, but that US forces would have less combat commitments. The US planners had been encouraged by the performance of ARVN forces during the Tet actions, but after the war had ended one senior Vietnamese officer said that the programme should have begun in 1965, rather than 1968. By the time the US forces withdrew the ARVN were not fully ready to resist NVA assaults, for although they were able to carry out operations against the Viet Cong in the country, the well trained and motivated NVA was another matter.

With President Richard Nixon in power the USA was committed to withdrawal from Vietnam. On 8 June 1969 he met Thieu at Midway Island and announced that an initial 25,000 troops would be withdrawn. The whole withdrawal policy was a pragmatic exercise to see if this would placate the doves and anti-war activists in the US – if it worked then other military options were still available like B-52 strikes into Cambodia. On 16 September a cut of a further 25,000 men was announced and on 15 December another 50,000 men.

While the US armed forces were shrinking in Vietnam, the ARVN were growing. Between 1965 and 1968 they had risen from 250,000 to 393,000 men. Some of the structures had changed, but the four corps headquarters were retained with 10 infantry divisions of three regiments of four battalions.

It was the supporting arms that saw the major expansion. By 1968 the divisional mortar battalions had been replaced by two 105-mm howitzer battalions, an armoured cavalry squadron with light tanks and M113 APCs; the divisional engineer, signal, logistic and other combat support arms had been added or expanded.

Under command of the corps' HQs were 155-mm artillery battalions, 20 'Ranger' light infantry battalions as well as signal and engineer units. In addition there were area logistical commands with their own ordnance, quartermaster, transportation and depot units. Reserve forces were commanded directly by the Joint General Staff and consisted of airborne and marine units that had been expanded from brigade to division strength.

By April 1969 all ARVN units were equipped with the M16 rifle (previously they had the M1 rifle which was not only unwieldy but had a

Overleaf: Men of the 9th Marines board a USAF C-130 to fly to Da Nang in July 1969.

Below: The 12 men of an ARVN machine gun squadron, combat-equipped with their ammunition, stand by a Huey prior to operations in Vietnam in 1962. Though most of their equipment is World War II vintage, the M1 Carbine, Browning Automatic Rifle and .30 machine gun are of 1940s vintage. The squadron leader has an M16 rifle.

powerful recoil for a small Asian soldier).

The South Vietnamese Navy had 43,000 sailors operating 1,680 naval craft and 51,000 airmen flying well over 1,000 aircraft including about 500 helicopters. Territorial forces had stabilised at 300,000 Regional Forces (RF) and 250,000 Popular Forces (PF). Between 1970 and 1971 the ARVN trebled the number of operations that they had undertaken in the period 1966-67 and therefore suffered twice as many killed. They also undertook operations with the US Army which were intended to give them greater confidence and act as a training vehicle. It must also have been good to have the US fire-power on call – a report in 1968 had shown the GI was supported by 10 times

s much artillery fire and air attack sorties as an RVN soldier.

In order to release the ARVN forces for opera-ions against the VC and NVA the regional forces nd police were expanded and modernised. By 972 there was a police force of 116,000 men. On he western border the CIDGs (Civilian Irregular)efense Groups) of Montagnards would cover the nfiltration routes.

The expansion programme was backed by mas-ive re-equipment. From the M16 upwards RVN received new weapons and equipment. Known as CRIMP – Consolidated Improvement nd Modernization Program – it took into account mploying civilian contractors to operate long ange communications links, maintain equip-nent, and cover logistic tasks that would eventual-y be filled by Vietnamese. ARVN began to re-eive M113 APCs, 175-mm SP guns, M48 tanks, nti-tank missiles and jet fighters.

The effectiveness of CRIMP and Vietnamisa-ion depended on whether the ARVN could rely n US air power to neutralise strong enemy posi-ions or stop ground attacks.

The optimism that infected the Vietnamisation rogramme reflected the US desire to encourage he Vietnamese. Advisors also faced the fact that oo negative a report on their units would affect heir careers in the US Army. In a report after the war Brigadier-General James I. Collins Jr wrote:

> Too often advisors did not take firm stands with heir counterparts on key issues nor recommend he relief of unsatisfactory commanders for fear hat such recommendations would reflect badly n their own abilities... In any future hostile con-litions, the emphasis should be on getting the job lone, not merely on getting along with the indi-vidual being advised.

Though there were faults with the advisor system here were greater problems with the leadership within the ARVN forces. Part of the problem was hat commissions were awarded to men with satis-actory academic qualifications. Battlefield com-missions only became a feature in the latter stages f the war. The officers with ability, and there were some outstanding ARVN commanders, found themselves overworked and without the resources that would allow them to prosecute the war.

The most bitter comment by the US was the contrast with the VC; 'Charlie [VC] doesn't need advisors when he conducts a sapper attack. He doesn't need Tac air or gunships or artillery. He's hungry and he's got a cause and he's motivated. Therein lies the difference. On our side nobody is hungry and few are motivated because leadership is lacking'.

The lack of leadership also showed itself with the level of desertion. The ARVN soldiers who had been called up knew that the only way out for them was either death, injury or desertion, since they were in service for the duration of the war. The poor pay, concern for their families and the sight of officers who were making money from legal and illegal sources conspired to lower morale and motivation.

One way that Saigon and Washington hoped that the ARVN would become more effective was by the uprating of the RF and PF – forces that became known as the 'RuffPuffs'. By 1971 these unpaid militia had reached more than four million. Membership was compulsory for men above or below the draft age.

However as Guenter Lewy was to say in his valuable book *American in Vietnam*:

> ARVN was less a national army than a federation of semi-autonomous corps: there was little flexibility in deployment and the dispatch of a division from one region to another could create major problems. Each division commander believed that only he knew how to fight the war and resisted outside direction.

Though the ARVN had problems, the US Army too was suffering. Following the Tet offensive and the decision to withdraw from Vietnam there was a growing disenchantment with the war. It showed itself in many forms. The ready availability of marijuana made the use of soft drugs both easy and also acceptable among the US conscripts.

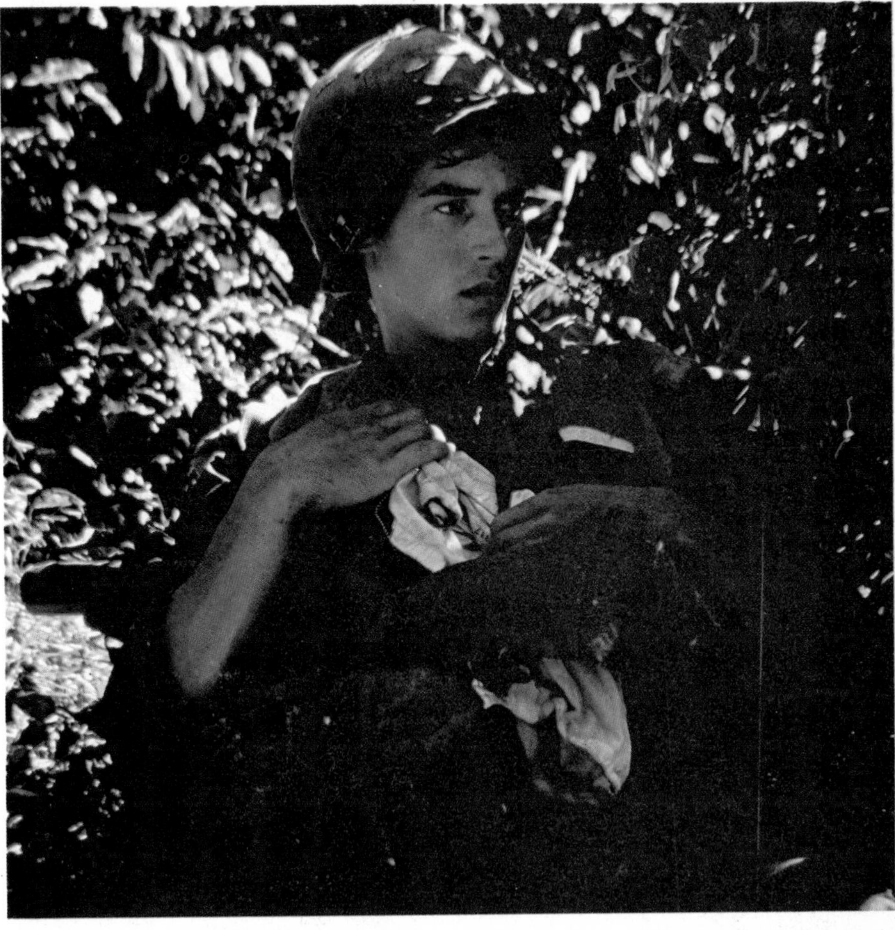

Above: This photograph, though taken in 1968, shows the strain of operations which had begun to sap the morale and commitment of American forces in Vietnam. As they were withdrawn from the country it became increasingly important that ARVN troops take over the war against the North Vietnamese and Viet Cong.

Above left: Vietnamese troops at the ARVN armour school at Thu Duc repair recently-acquired M-48 tanks for operational training in November 1971.

Below left: Airburst shell fire in support of a US position near the Cambodian border explodes in the distance, causing dust clouds as the shell fragments hit the ground. It was fire power like this that US forces had on call for their operations beyond the capability of the South Vietnamese military resources.

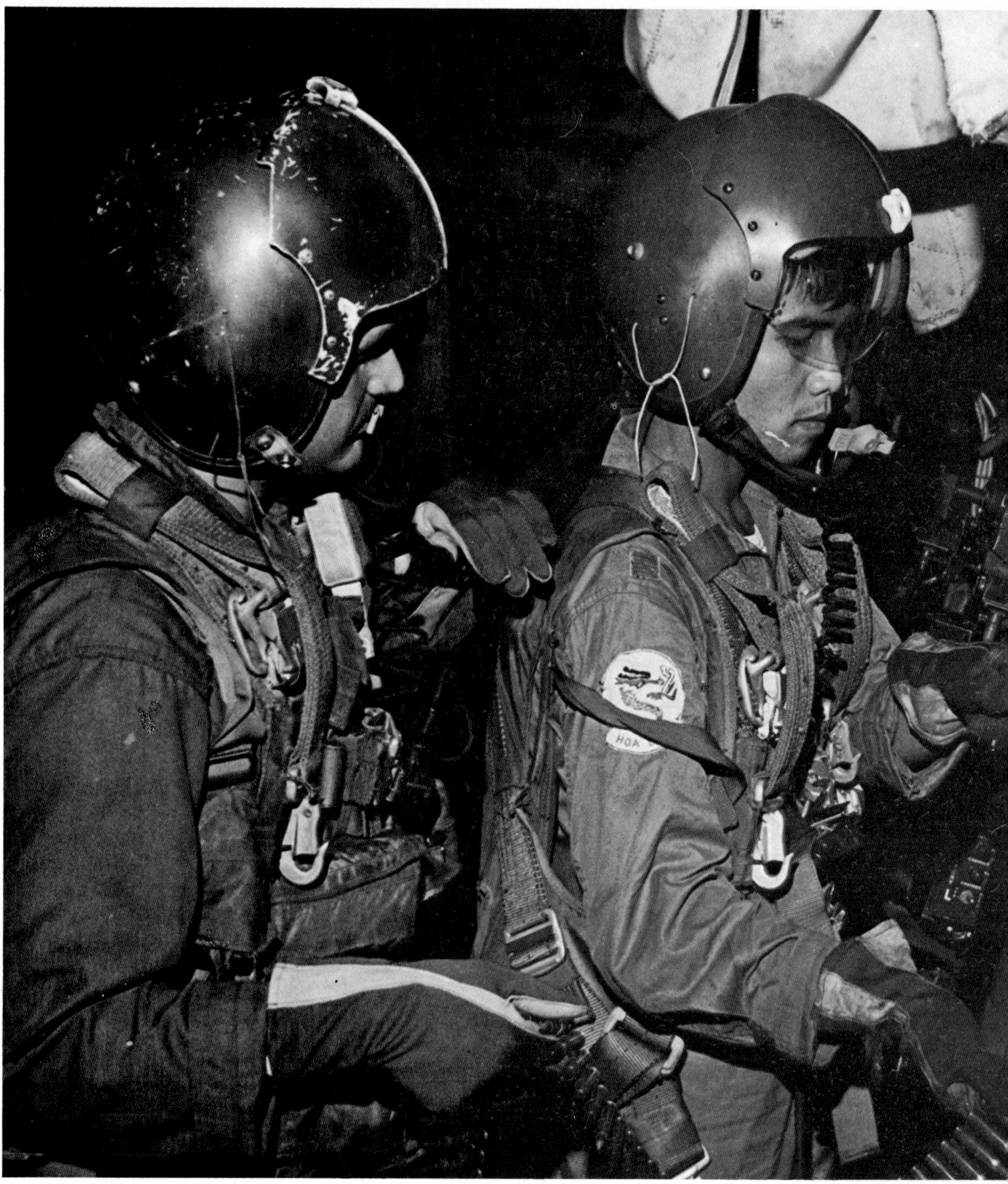

Right: A USAF Staff Sergeant assists a Vietnamese Sergeant Nguyen Van Heip in the loading of a Minigun with live ammunition aboard an AC-119 gunship at Phan Rang airbase in South Vietnam. By the time the United States Armed Forces had withdrawn from South Vietnam, the Saigon government had one of the most powerful airforces in South-East Asia.

The 'Lifers', men who had signed up as regular soldiers, favoured alcohol and received the pejorative name of 'juicers', while men who used drugs became 'heads'.

Though soft drugs might help to relieve the boredom and involve a social group, hard drugs like heroin began to pose a major health and morale problem. Prior to their return to the United States conscripts would give urine samples to see if they had become drug-dependent. Severe cases would be hospitalised and receive psychiatric care and counselling. Nevertheless the heroin plague returned to the United States where it was fostered by supplies from the Central American and South American countries.

One of the problems with a conscript army was that men were not in uniform because they wanted to be – they had not volunteered. With this went the fact that they were, in their own parlance, i Nam for a year – just 365 days. For most men th aim was to get through this experience and ge back to the world, the real world of the Unite States. As their days in Vietnam became fewe they became short-term soldiers and with thi came the feeling that you owed survival to your self. It was not worth risking life or limb when in few days you would be going home.

Therefore an officer or NCO who was commit ted to closing with the enemy or getting his forc involved in operations that were thought by th men to present a higher risk of death or injury, wa seen by his men as a severe threat to their chance of survival. 'Gung Ho' (aggressive) officers, o merely those who were unpopular, began to ru the threat of 'fragging'. This was murder by thei own men using a fragmentation grenade. The us

of a grenade was less personal than small arms fire, and could be mistaken for enemy action. If it killed or even merely crippled, fragging took the man away from the men who felt threatened.

Though men will fight better when they are supported by some level of creature comforts – even hot food on a regular basis will make for greater combat efficiency – there might be a limit to these efforts. The US armed forces with the vast logistic resources of their nation were able to bring recreation and entertainment almost into the front line. In a television interview one GI was proud to say that he had managed to build the most forward front line swimming pool in Vietnam. The priorities were becoming confused. Was the army in Vietnam to win a war, or to get a year's draft of conscripts through with the least disruption and distress?

Junior level leadership also presented a problem. Bright men who had been conscripted were able to make some steps up the promotion ladder as junior NCOs. However, this had the effect of putting these conscripts into a position where instead of supporting and assisting their seniors 'all they wanted to do was go down town bopping with the boys'. Who can blame them? They were not career sergeants.

The anti-war movement spilled into Vietnam and with it also came an increasing feeling among black Americans, that they were being used to fight a 'white man's war'.

One incident that made the war even less acceptable had happened a year earlier. The 'My Lai Massacre' was made public in 1969, but in 1968 the press had largely ignored the American Division and had relied instead on the press releases from MACV (Military Assistance Command Vietnam). Peter Braestrup in his book *Big Story* cites the news stories that were produced from these press handouts about the action at 'Pinkville'. These accounts were imaginative improvements on the less than full description of US operations.

Discussing the massacre, in which between 175 and 200 Vietnamese men, women and children were murdered by American soldiers, Guenter Lewy writes:

Probably the most important single element, present in almost all incidents, was weak leadership. Strong and effective commanders managed to keep their subordinates under control even in situations of great stress; but such leaders were often in short supply, especially at platoon and company level.

Company C 'Charlie' of Task Force Baker, a battalion-sized unit of the Americal Division, were ordered to search and destroy an area of hamlets in a zone controlled by the 48th VC Battalion, but clear orders and effective leadership were lacking. The defects of the draft system had led to men with higher than average intelligence avoiding the draft through educational deferment. Poor orders, weak leadership and the lack of proper training that both officers and men had received, on top of the stress of casualties from booby traps all contributed to the state of mind which led the men to commit these excesses which were unforgivable.

Some observers were keen to suggest that a policy of genocide and excessive use of fire-power were a regular feature of operations in Vietnam and to this was added the natural temptation to exaggerate in letters home. Neither side in the war was guiltless, but nothing approaching the mass killings at Hue can be laid to the charge of the US or ARVN forces.

10. ACROSS THE BORDER

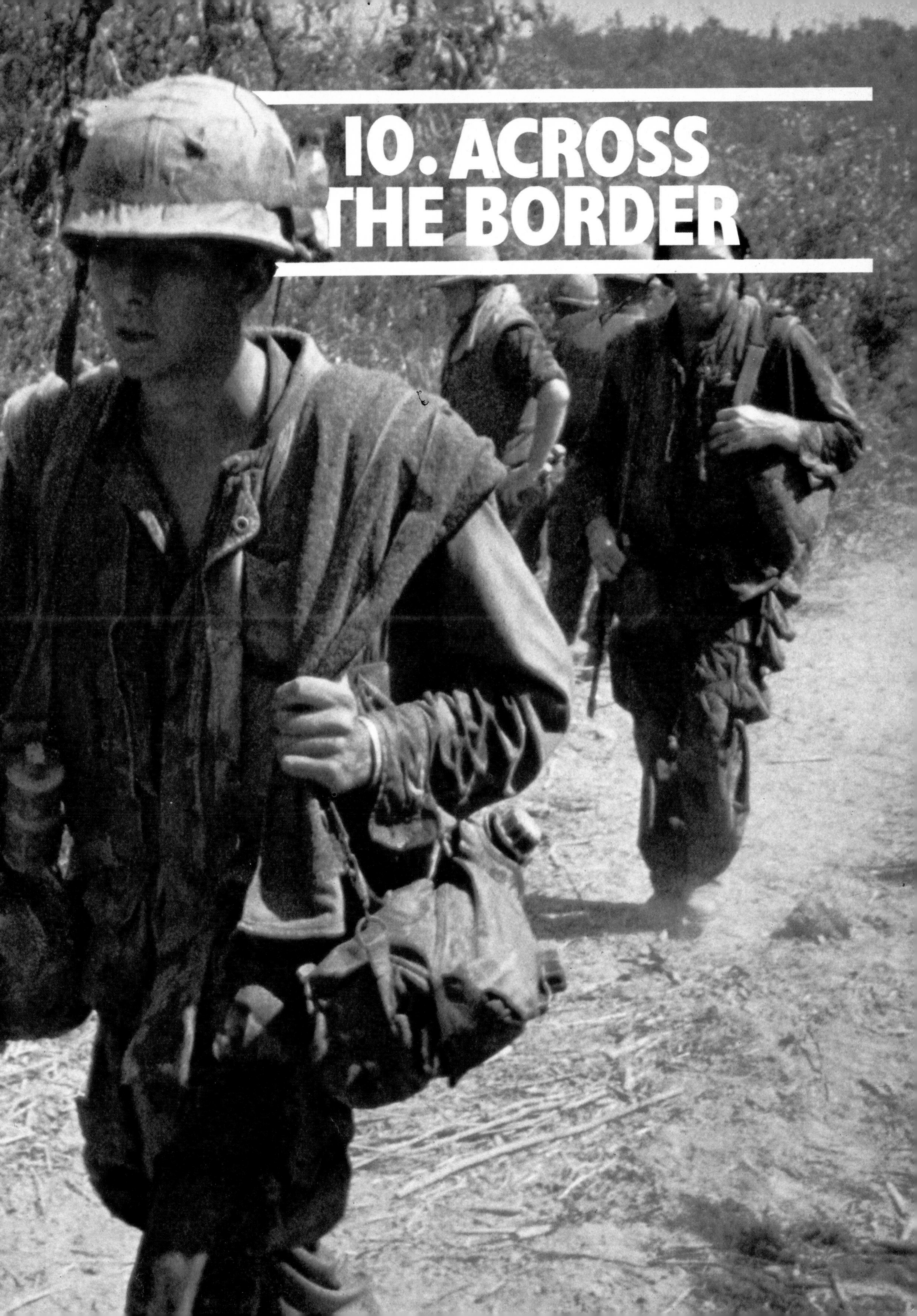

Overleaf: US Marines moves out on operations in the summer. Heat exhaustion was another enemy that men faced during the war in Vietnam.

Left; Soldiers of the 2nd Battalion, 49th Regiment, 25th ARVN Division move out from the Parrot's Beak after being relieved by soldiers of the 46th Regiment ARVN. They were attached to Task Force 255 which also contained M-113 Armoured Personnel Carriers from the 10th Armoured CAV, ARVN.

THE CAMBODIAN SANCTUARIES had always tempted the planners in Washington. It was therefore ironic that Nixon, the President who had been voted to power on a withdrawal-from-Vietnam ticket, was the one who would sanction entry into a neighbouring country that was in name 'neutral'.

The US armed forces had been sending clandestine teams over the border earlier in the war. Normally men from ethnic groups who would be unnoticed, they were armed and equipped with weapons and stores that were 'sanitised' – in other words they could not be traced back to the US armed forces. Some weapons were Communist-made or left-overs from the French involvement in Indo-China. Uniforms were simple olive-green or black. The teams would gather intelligence, direct air attacks on the Ho Chi Minh trail and take prisoners for intelligence.

The irritation of VC and NVA cross border raids was highlighted by a series of attacks in mid-1969. On 11 August, for example, 179 widely scattered bases were hit by artillery, rocket or mortar fire and in some cases these attacks were followed up with infantry assaults.

Sweeps to reduce these actions had in mid-1969 taken US forces into the Michelin Rubber Plantation north of Saigon, and the coast of Quang Nam south of Da Nang. On 10 May men of the 101st Airborne entered the A Shau Valley near the border with Laos. On 14 May they clashed with VC forces that had dug in on Hill 937, Ap Bia Mountain or, as the press named it, 'Hamburger Hill'. The first attacks fell back under fire from well entrenched VC positions. Artillery and air-power were called in and the battle became a grim infantry action with the ARVN and airborne forces working their way up the hill. After nine assaults over six days the hill was captured. It was abandoned soon afterwards and observers asked why it had been fought for – and if the VC were located there why had not greater use been made of B-52 strikes and artillery fire rather than the men of the 101st Airborne?

In the light of this criticism it seemed better to take the war to the enemy and enter their sanctuaries in force. Intelligence had located 14 major NVA bases inside Cambodia. Three adjoined the 4th Corps' area and seven the 3rd Corps' area. Some were only 35 miles from Saigon.

The decision to go into Cambodia was coloured by events within the country. The monarch and national leader, Prince Norodom Sihanouk, was ousted in his absence by General Lon Nol who dedicated his country to the task of removing foreigners. The coup had taken place in early March when Sihanouk was away in Russia and within the month the NVA had launched operations to secure the border. They drove the small Cambodian Army from a strip to 15 kilometres wide and on 13 April 1970 they expanded operations to clear their communications links from this strip.

Under pressure Lon Nol turned to Washington for help, and so Nixon had a politically acceptable reason for a foray across the border. On 14 April the ARVN went into Cambodia on a three-day raid. The NVA, who had thought they were secure from attack from the east, were caught and suffered heavy casualties as well as losing large stocks of ammunition and stores. The US domestic reaction was mild. After all US troops were not involved – yet.

There had in fact been plans for American attacks as far back as January 1970 so General Abrams was able to order Lieutenant-General Michael S. Davison to start planning for an attack on 30 April, within six days of receipt of orders. The attack was to be on the Fish Hook where besides NVA logistics bases there was reported to be the National Liberation Front's Central Office for South Vietnam, or COSVN. It was an objective that was to haunt planners throughout the war in Vietnam.

The US force had a strong emphasis on mobility: it included the 1st Cavalry Division, the 11th and ARVN 1st Armored Cavalry Regiments while the ARVN 3rd Airborne Brigade gave air mobility; finally, the tanks and APCs of the US 25th Division were to give the weight of armour and infantry. In all there were over 10,000 US and

00 ARVN forces in the operation.

The man who led the operation was General bert Shoemaker and though he thought that it uld be like the earlier ARVN attack, a short ust into the sanctuaries, he was to learn when operation was under way that it would mean a -month stay in Cambodia.

The operation had been given the name Toan ang 43 in respect to the ARVN role and as a lection of Vietnamisation. Sadly, because of a ay between the commitment of US troops, the VN attack that went in on 29 April only served warn the NVA that the Parrot's Beak was no ger secure.

Attacks by B-52 bombers, artillery fire and air ikes prepared the way. The plan was to launch ARVN 3rd Brigade into blocking positions to north while the US 11th Armored Cavalry giment swept up from the south. To the west armour would advance to cover the flank and ve on the town of Mimot.

Ground fog caused delays in the helicopter lifts, t once it cleared the 5th Battalion was off by d-morning, followed by the 3rd and the 9th. e ARVN armour moving from An Loc velled steadily, encountering only sporadic re- tance. By 2 May the US armour had cut the road to Mimot and the ARVN and US troops began to close in.

The slight delays had been enough to enable the NVA to slip out of the net, but they had been forced to go only with their rucksacks and weapons. The vast amounts of stores that they left behind in camouflaged bunkers and huts earned the nickname from the GIs of 'The City'. The quantities were so great that army engineers built temporary roads to allow the booty to be removed.

While these operations were under way the air and armoured elements pushed further into Cambodia. They were working against two deadines, the monsoon that would make further movement difficult by the beginning of July and massive domestic pressure from the United States. The civilian population was horrified by the extension of the war, and the men on the ground found that they were subject to a politically imposed restriction of 20 miles.

On 4 May a smaller operation had been launched near Pleiku where ARVN and US troops crossed the border into the Se Sam valley. On 6 May three more attacks were launched, the Dog's Face to the north of the Parrot's Beak; north-east of the Fish Hook above the town of Loc Ninh; and north of the provincial capital of Phuoc Binh. On 8

Below: A US soldier examines assorted weapons captured in 'The City' in the Fish Hook area near the South Vietnamese border. The camp was staffed by the Communist 50th Rear Service Group and seen in this photograph are a variety of weapons including 82 mm mortars and 75 mm recoilless rifles, as well as medium machine guns, sub-machine guns and magazines for automatic weapons.

Inset: A rocket expl
a can of diesel fuel n
US Marine Corps 1
mm Howitzer batter
position. It was to de
the Viet Cong and N
the supply of artiller
ammunition and roc
which would allow s
bombardments, that
South Vietnamese a
US Armed Forces
crossed over the
Cambodian border a
captured or destroye
stocks of ammunitio
stores.

Below: Napalm cannisters tumble from a F-100 Super Sabre. It was the valuable close air support that made the cross-border operations possible as they softened up potential enemy opposition.

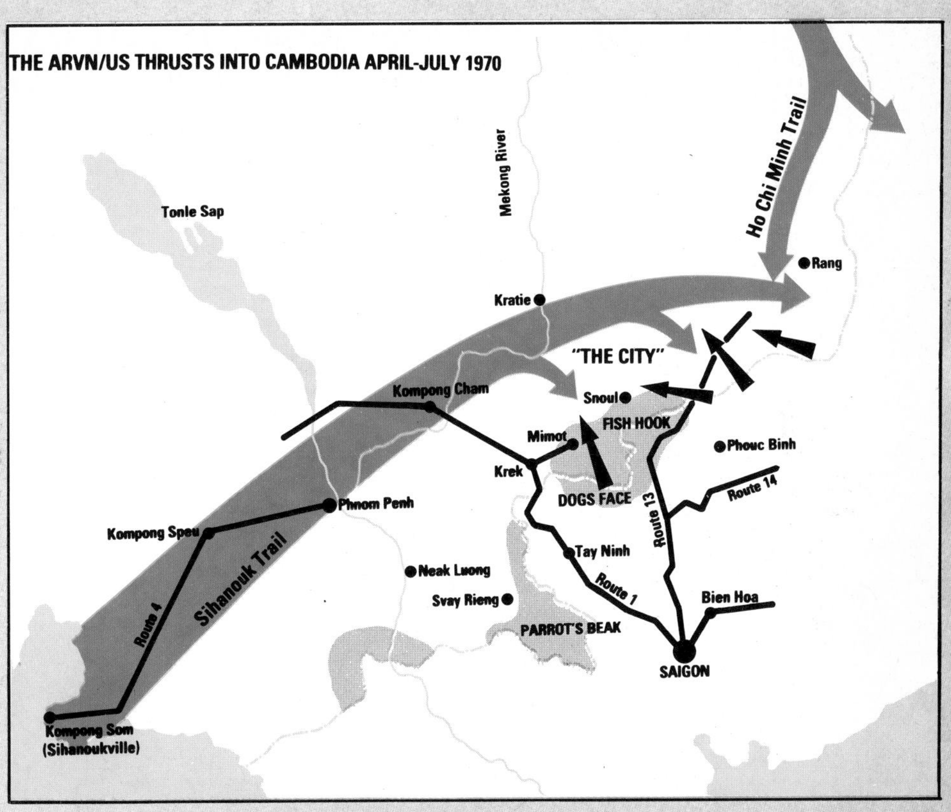

Below: Soldiers of the 2nd Battalion, 49th Regiment, 25th ARVN Division stand guard over P-o-Ws from the D30 NVA Battalion captured after a fire fight in the Parrot's Beak area in May 1970. Each of the P-o-Ws has a label attached indicating where he was captured and other details of his name, rank etc. Prisoners are tied to prevent escape and blindfolded to prevent them observing any military installation or equipment.

May ARVN troops crossed into Cambodia along the Mekong River, entering the Parrot's Beak from the south.

When the intelligence analysts had sifted through the captured stores in 'The City' they established that it had been the storage depot for the NVA 7th Division. It had 182 large storage bunkers as well as 18 mess halls, barracks, training and classroom facilities. There was even a small farm. Among the captured weapons were 1,282 individual and 202 crew-served weapons – enough small arms for 55 battalions and enough crew-served weapons for 33. There were also more than 1·5 million rounds of small arms ammunition, 58,000 lb of plastic explosives, 22 cases of anti-personnel mines, 30 tons of rice and 16,000 lb of corn.

Over 300 vehicles were located. They were largely trucks, but had the unlikely addition of a Porsche sports car and a Mercedes-Benz sedan, cars that did not fit with the image of the ascetic NVA political soldier.

Further stocks were captured by the US 1st Cavalry's 2nd Brigade at a base nicknamed 'Rock Island East', to the north-east of the Fish Hook. Here, among other booty, 329 tons of munitions were located on 8 May.

The anti-war movement that had seen Nixon as an almost acceptable candidate now saw him in a new light. Demonstrations in cities and universities were generally peaceful, but at Kent State University, Ohio, panicky National Guardsmen killed four students. In Congress the Gulf of Tonkin Resolution was withdrawn and the President was required to withdraw troops from Cambodia by 30 June.

The peace talks that had been dragging on in Paris were a constant hope for the United States. If an acceptable solution could be found there, then the US could get out of Vietnam. As mentioned in Chapter 8 they had begun in 1968 when President Johnson had accepted a North Viet-

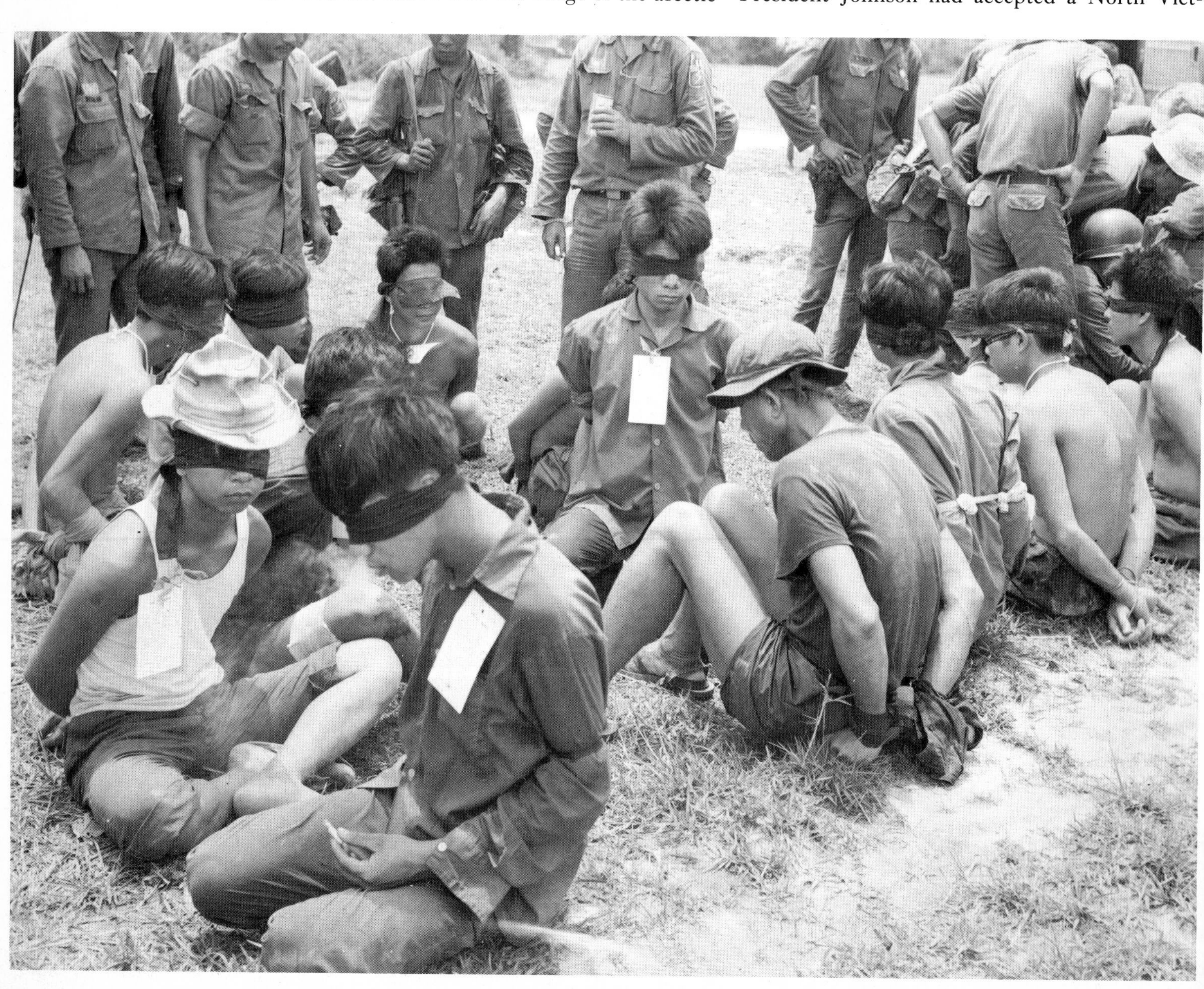

namese offer to start talking on 3 May. The first formal meeting was held on 13 May that year but it was not until 25 January 1969 that the negotiations got under way in Paris. On 15 November 1969, life in the United States was temporarily halted by the Moratorium, a massive nationwide peace demonstration. Some troops in Vietnam also participated. However the protests that followed the incursions into Cambodia produced an estimated 75-100,000 demonstrators in Washington alone. After the Kent State shootings, demonstrations continued at some 400 other colleges.

It was not until 1971, however, that the greatest anti-war demonstrations paralysed Washington. On 24 April, 500,000 protestors came to Washington and 150,000 took part in similar demonstrations in San Francisco, California.

With the increased peace pressure at home, Washington placed greater hope in the effectiveness of Vietnamisation. US troops were already being withdrawn and so it was essential that the ARVN should be better able to look after itself. In Cambodia US observers had noted that the ARVN commanders had been able to run an efficient truck-borne logistic link, but that artillery support had been laid on by US Army gunners. Some of the ARVN senior officers were reluctant to call in artillery and favoured marking their positions with smoke and withdrawing to allow air strikes to reduce enemy opposition. The ARVN incursion into Laos, with US fire support, helicopter and logistic back-up was to be the real test of Vietnamisation.

The operation was named Lam Son 719 by President Thieu. Lam Son was a village in North Vietnam where a Vietnamese national hero Le Loi inflicted a major defeat on the Chinese in 1427. Planning was done by Lieutenant-General Hoang Xuan Lam who commanded the I Corps area. His task was to penetrate into Laos to take and hold the NVA Base Area 604 centred on the town of Tchepone. Here intelligence analysts had established that large stocks of ammunition and stores had been massed. Backed by these the NVA could either push across the border and attack Quang Tri or with a short march via the Laotian Base Area 611 they could attack Hue. By February and March the logistic bases would be fully stocked. So it was that February was chosen for the attack and planning was completed by 16 January 1971.

Lam was assisted by Lieutenant-General James W. Sutherland, commanding the US XXIV Corps. Sutherland committed several units to the operation, including an engineer group, an artillery group, a combat aviation battalion, and a military police battalion; the 101st Airborne Division (Airmobile) provided two brigades of airborne infantry, three battalions of divisional artillery and a combat aviation group; the 1st Brigade of the 5th US Division and the 11th Brigade of the 23rd US Infantry Division (Americal) also participated. The total US force was 10,000 men with 2,000 fixed-wing aircraft and 600 helicopters in support. However, after the protests in the USA, only the aircraft crossed the border.

The operation, which was code named Dewey Canyon II by the US Army, was in four phases. On 30 January ARVN and US forces would clear NVA ambush sites and mines on Highway 9 from central Quang Tri province to the Laotian border. This would allow ARVN troops to concentrate near the former Marine base of Khe Sanh. In the second phase on 8 February 16,000 ARVN would advance with M113 APCs, armour, trucks and helicopters towards Tchepone. During the next two days the area would be secured against counter-attacks and the stores there would be destroyed. Then would follow the difficult phase of withdrawal which would begin on 10 March or later, depending on the strength of NVA reaction.

There would be three axes for the advance: the ARVN 1st Armored Brigade would move along Highway 9, the Airborne and Ranger Battalions would be lifted by helicopter along the ridge lines north of Highway 9 and the 1st Infantry Division would also be heli-lifted along the 1,000 foot high escarpment south of Xe Pon River to the south of Highway 9. The Marine Brigade would be a reserve. These ARVN units represented the élite of the South Vietnamese Army and the nation's general reserve.

This operation was especially important since not only would no US troops cross the border on foot into Laos, but neither would the advisors who were attached to ARVN units. The NVA too realised that an operation like this would be important since not only did it threaten their bases – almost on their own front door – but defeat for the ARVN

Below: South Vietnamese soldiers move along past the Ho Chi Minh trail in Laos in 1971. Visible in the photograph are trucks M-113 Armoured Personnel Carriers and jeeps. The area appears to have been subjected to bombing attacks before Vietnamese ground forces entered the area.

would deal a severe blow to their morale. Hanoi had massed nearly 20,000 men in the area, of whom 13,000 were first line combat troops. While the ARVN would be bringing their stores and ammunition forward, the NVA would have their stocks where they would be fighting. They had also positioned AA guns in the valleys that would be the most likely axes for air attacks and helicopter missions.

At one minute after midnight on 30 January the 1st Brigade of the US 5th Infantry started the advance towards Khe Sanh. Though a six-day news blackout had been imposed by General Abrams, the NVA were alert. By 1 February, before the border had been crossed, there were complaints about an 'imperial war of aggression' in Laos.

The second phase of Lam Son began on 8 February with armour and APCs crossing the border. The Ranger and Airborne forces established their fire bases on the hill tops to the north of Highway 9, while the 1st Infantry Division constructed theirs along the escarpment by the Xe Pon River. All seemed to be going according to the plan as the armoured column reached the Laotian village of Aloui by 9 February.

The NVA had first to establish whether this advance was a diversion or the main attack. The US 101st Airborne had already fired a series of artillery barrage around Base Area 611 at the be-

Below: The ubiquitous Huey – these troop-carrying helicopters gave the Americans and Vietnamese essential mobility. During the cross-border attacks into Laos they were invaluable for placing troops along the high ground and later evacuating troops.

Below: A door gunner in Huey gunship observes the surrounding jungle. Though no Americans were involved on the ground in the attacks on the Ho Chi Minh trail, helicopters and fixed wing aircraft crossed the border to attack targets and lift troops. During the course of these operations some machines were lost and the crews were obliged to operate on the ground.

Below centre: Bunkers in Laos, under attack by A-1E Aircraft of the USAF.

ginning of Phase I while the ARVN 1st Division had moved up Highway 1 towards the DMZ as part of the deception plan.

The 12 February saw the first fire fights with NVA troops and gave a taste of what was to come. The NVA 70B Corps committed three divisions to battle, the first to make contact being the 308th. With fighting closely mixed, air power was of less value than has been expected. The weight of the first attacks hit the Airborne and Ranger bases, where artillery fire was followed by sapper attacks and infantry assaults. In the morning the haze plus the smoke from burning scrub hindered the air strikes and helicopter operations. By 22 February the NVA had surrounded Ranger Base South and AA fire was preventing re-supply of Ranger Base North. Under this pressure the Rangers withdrew leaving behind over 600 enemy dead for 298 of their own men.

On 25 February 7 miles north-west of Aloui, 20 Soviet-built PT-76 light tanks with 2,000 infantry assaulted Airborne Objective 31. Backed up by air strikes the 500 paratroops held their ground and killed an estimated 1,000 NVA troops. After fighting for three days the paratroops began the grim battle southwards. During this action the NVA captured 120 ARVN including a battalion commander.

By 1 March it became clear that the NVA were attempting to cut off the head of the ARVN advance by attacking the fire bases covering the flanks. Two fire bases had been lost and General Lam realised that he could not push as far as Tchepone with his armour. Three NVA divisions were set on cutting off Highway 9 behind him. Deploying the Armor, Airborne and Ranger units on the defensive, he brought the 1st Infantry Division in by helicopter to make landings along the escarpment south of Aloui to Tchepone.

Three landing zones were established and it was

Below: A scene in the Vietnam war that was becoming part of the past, Marines of the 1st Battalion, 5th Marines try and pinpoint a sniper in the late 1960s, American forces would no longer be caught up in the complex and grim business of ground fighting as President Nixon's promised withdrawals became a reality.

reported that they bore the names Lollo, Liz and Sophia – after Gina Lollobrigida, Elizabeth Taylor and Sophia Loren. It was suggested this was an indication that the US Army had become involved in an operation that was meant to be exclusively ARVN.

On 6 March, a month after the operation had begun, the ARVN reached their objective. The NVA base at Tchepone was hit by arc-light raids using B-52 bombers. Then an enormous airborne assault went in. Some 120 Huey troop-carrying helicopters left Khe Sanh lifting two ARVN battalions up to 48 miles. This was to be the longest and largest combat assault by helicopters during the Vietnam war. The 'slicks' – troop carriers – were supported by 'gunships' and HueyCobras, the armed helicopters which attacked the AA positions along the route and prepared the landing zones before the slicks went in. Two days after these landings Lam Son was hailed as a success – and so it was, up to that point. The Ho Chi Minh trail had been cut, the NVA had been brought to battle and suffered heavy losses, but several of the 34 ARVN battalions involved had been so heavily mauled that they were no longer effective. As with the French operations in the first Indo-Chinese war, the moment of truth was when the order came to withdraw. By now the NVA were out for revenge.

At the peak of the NVA attacks some 36,000 men with two regiments of tanks were hammering the exhausted ARVN units. For Giap this was a battle that he had to win and he was prepared to take high casualties to achieve. The NVA had a quite material loss to avenge. At Tchepone they lost 76 artillery pieces, 106 tanks, 405 trucks, 1,934 crew-served weapons, 5,066 small arms, 12,000 tons of rice and 800 tons of ammunition. This represented enough rice to feed 159 battalions for 30 days, enough small arms to equip eight NVA infantry battalions and enough crew-served weapons for nine infantry battalions.

The extraction of the ARVN units was not assisted by the arrival of the seasonal rains and attacks by reinforced units of the NVA 70B Corps. The helicopter pilots were magnificent under the most testing of conditions. Flying into AA fire they packed as many ARVN troops aboard as possible. However, some of the South Vietnamese, fearing that this might be the last helicopter, attempted to ride home hanging on to the skids. About 10 miles south-east of Aloui the ARVN 147th Marine Battalion at Fire Base Delta fought for four hours before they were obliged to call for helicopter evacuation. It was the last battle of Lam Son 719.

In all, American pilots flew 160,000 helicopter sorties losing 107 helicopters. There were over 8,000 tactical air strikes and 1,358 sorties by B-52s. The big bombers dropped 46,000 tons of bombs.

Among the helicopters shot down was one carrying the *Life* photographer Larry Burrows; he was killed along with the crew and with his death photo-journalism lost one of its great men. He had

covered Vietnam from the earliest days of US involvement and had the dream that he would one day be able to do a picture story of the country at peace.

When Lam Son 719 came to a close estimates were that US fire-power had killed 8,900 NVA and the ARVN had killed over 10,000. The ARVN had lost 1,483 killed, 5,420 wounded and 691 missing. Each side – Hanoi and Saigon – claimed a victory.

Left: A US Air Force F-100 Super Sabre releases a bomb during operation Lam Son 719. The US Air Force flew over 8,000 tactical airstrikes against North Vietnamese positions and units attacking the South Vietnamese. The North Vietnamese made every effort to close with their enemies and present a far harder target to the high-performance bombers that were seeking to destroy them.

II. THE LAST THROW

Overleaf: A B-52 comes in to land at U-Tapao airfield, Thailand after a mission over South Vietnam. US and Thai troops man the guard bunker in the foreground.

Top right: The USS *Ticonderoga* underway in the South China Sea in 1966.

Centre right: North Vietnamese railroad cars blasted by two A-4 Skyhawks from the 7th Fleet in two operations. Some 20 of the 25 railroad cars were destroyed with 500-lb bombs.

Below: US Airforce HH-3E Helicopter of the 37th Aerospace Rescue and Recovery Squadron (ARAS) on a rescue mission over the waters of South-East Asia.

AMERICAN EMPLOYMENT OF AIR POWER over North Vietnam had begun with the hope that by escalating its pressure the USAF and Washington would show Hanoi that they could paralyse North Vietnam – but that they were holding back. As with so many other bombing campaigns the Rolling Thunder operations did not achieve this aim. Bombing can have the effect of uniting a nation and giving them a common enemy. It also allows a government to explain to the people why they are not receiving the butter today; it must be guns today to give butter tomorrow. So it was for North Vietnam. Local militias manned AA guns, and even fired on USAF aircraft with small arms. Sacrifices were demanded of the people and were given. Some NVA soldiers were found to have tattoos which read 'Born in the North to Die in the South', and like the Japanese in World War II there was a philosophical acceptance that if a man was sent south he was not likely to return alive.

As already mentioned, the bombing campaign had gone through a series of self-imposed stops and starts. It had begun on 5 August 1964 and after separate attacks had been designated Rolling Thunder when raids began as a programme on 2 March 1965. On 18 June B-52s, 'Big Ugly Fellows' as they were known to the press – the servicemen had a less printable name for them – hit their first targets in South Vietnam. There was a 37 days pause in bombing which ended on 31 January 1966 and then on 12 April that year B-52s made their first attacks in North Vietnam. Washington was quick to point out that these were directed against the Mu Gia Pass on the Ho Chi Minh Trail and were simply doing with bigger bombers what was already being done with tactical bombers.

Following his decision in 1968 not to run again for the Presidency, Johnson ordered that bombing of North Vietnam should be restricted to the so-called 'Pan Handle', the narrow strip running from the DMZ up to Vinh. On 31 October that year he announced that bombing would end over North Vietnam, though reconnaissance flights would continue.

With Richard Nixon as President it seemed that the war would wind down, but on 5 June 1969 bombing was resumed after a reconnaissance aircraft had been shot down. Raids like this recurred from time to time. Bombing of the Ho Chi Minh trail and in support of the neutralist forces in Laos continued, but it was not until 26-30 December 1971 that bombers were back over North Vietnam

n numbers. They hit NVA airfields and other nilitary targets to frustrate the build-up of forces. n 1972 the arrival of the USS *Kitty Hawk* in-reased the number of carriers in the South China ea to three. Three more later joined those on tation. It was this year that was to mark the most ntense air activity over the north.

Though these attacks did frustrate Hanoi's roop build-ups and restricted her war-making otential, they also produced the unhappy prop-ganda asset of prisoners-of-war. For Hanoi these ilots and crewmen were 'air pirates' and were araded, photographed and interviewed by jour-alists. They were confined in various prisons in nd around Hanoi. Among the most notorious was he Hanoi Hilton, the former civilian prison where nen were locked in individual cells. The triumph f personal courage over adversity was only re-ealed after the war was over and the men returned o the United States. They were, however, all men f a particularly high calibre to have passed the election and training as air crew.

During interrogation they learned to keep their tories as simple as possible. Tell a complex tale nd the relays of interrogators will catch you out. But there were lighter moments even in the horror of the P-o-W cells. The North Vietnamese could not imagine how the crew of a major warship like an aircraft-carrier could be fed while they were on station and in a moment of inspiration a pilot suggested that they had a farm aboard which supplied their needs. When this was put to another pilot he agreed and gave more details of the farm programme. Another small triumph was the naming of men who had refused to fly on operations against North Vietnam; it was an idea that would appeal to the Hanoi propagandists. These men were of course fictional, and were called after characters out of the world of comic books like Clark Kent and Casey Jones – convincing enough American names.

The grim travail of the P-o-Ws changed in November 1970 when the Son Tay road exploded in the north. This was the only publicly known raid into North Vietnam by US forces. It had been launched after intelligence became available that 61 US P-o-Ws were being held in a hutted compound at Son Tay, only 23 miles from Hanoi. Using helicopters and specialised equipment and headed by the redoubtable Colonel Arthur D.

Below: A B-52 of the Strategic Air Command's 91st Bomb Wing in Thailand prepares for its 100th mission in Vietnam. The aircraft has not yet been loaded with bombs which will be slung underneath the wings and in the fuselage bomb bay.

Right: Yen Bai Airfield in North Vietnam photographed by an F-4 which was on its way to attack Huudo ammunition plant during Operation Linebacker in September 1982.

'Bull' Simons, the raiders hit the camp in a controlled demonstration of massive fire-power. As they raced to cut open the locks of the prison cells they found to their horror that the American prisoners had been moved. The raiders left minutes later without suffering a single serious casualty. In five minutes the 22 raiders killed between 100 and 200 NVA – and clashed with some unknown strangers who did not wear NVA dress, but tee-shirts and fitted dark undershorts. They may have been Chinese or Russians.

Though they left without the prisoners, the effect of the raid was dramatic. The North Vietnamese began to bring in all the P-o-Ws who had been held in small compounds around Hanoi. Concentrated together, the pilots were at last able to meet and talk and so build up a structure of command and support. No longer on their own, the men could counsel one another and give support under the stress of confinement. One man recalled how a P-o-W gave his fellow prisoners their first 'viewing' of a popular Western movie. As a student the pilot had worked in a cinema and, with excellent recall of the films he had seen, he

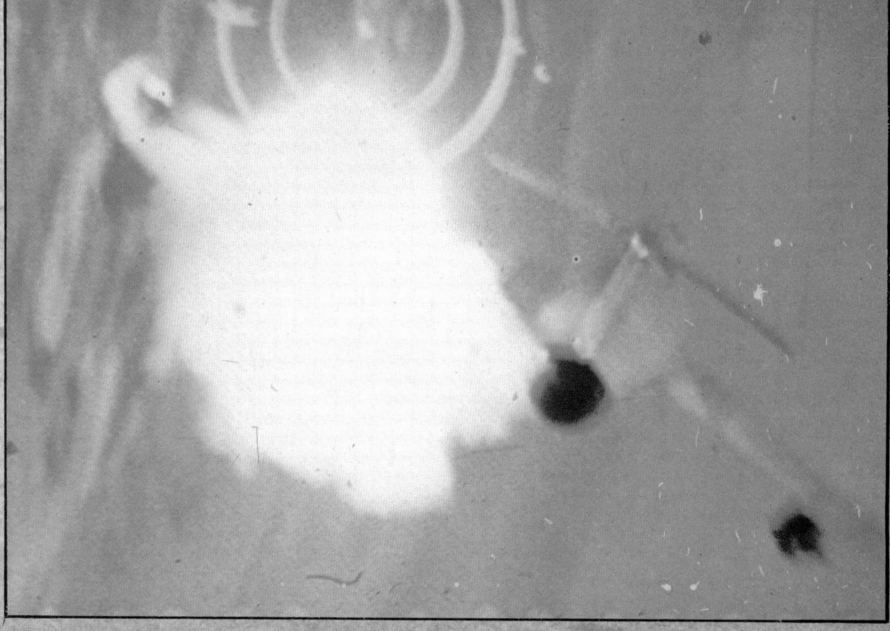

Right: A MiG-17 is shot down north of Hanoi by aircraft of the 469 Tactical Fighter Squadron.

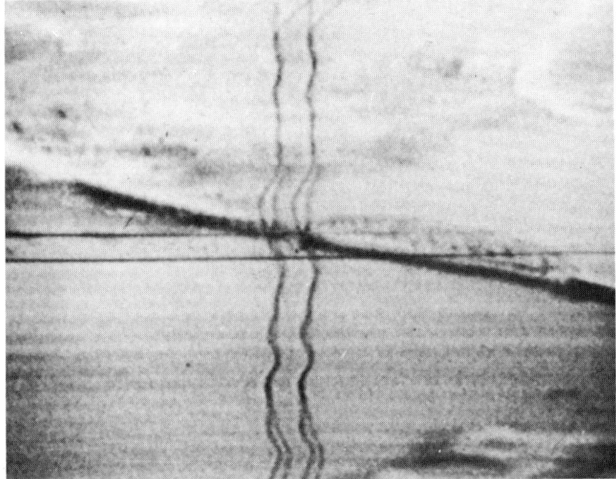

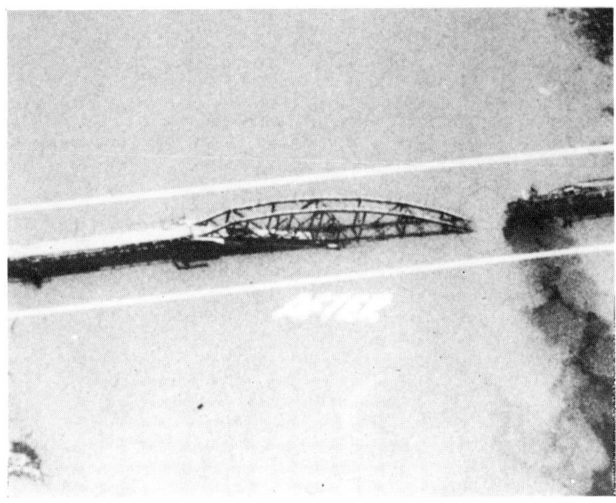

The destruction of the Ninh Binh railroad bridge. The bridge was hit by a Walleye TV-guided bomb, and the photographs show the path of the bomb as it approached its target. The bottom picture shows the damage afterwards.

described in vivid detail to his audience the incidents and scenes.

The pilots had the strange experience of being on the receiving end of USAF attacks on Hanoi. As the dust swirled and even cracks appeared in the walls of their cells they at least had the satisfaction of knowing that their guards were as terrified as they were.

Air power was, and is, a powerful asset in the land battle. In 1972 it was to be a vital factor in the NVA invasion of the south. In 1971 the Soviet Union had delivered the weapons and equipment to enable the north to launch their attack. Trucks, T-54 tanks and SAM missiles began to arrive.

In the early hours of 30 March 1972 three NVA Divisions pushed into South Vietnam. They crossed the DMZ and also hooked eastward along the much disputed Highway 9 through the A Shau valley towards Hue. They had deployed 200 T-54 tanks and large numbers of 130-mm guns. The fire bases of Camp Carrol and the Rockpile that had been vital in the Marines' battle for Khe Sanh fell quickly to these powerful NVA forces. After only a week they had captured a 10-mile strip between the DMZ and the Cua Viet River. Three NVA divisions then moved into Binh Long province to attack the town of Loc Ninh close to the Cambodian border. The next objective for this thrust was An Loc on Highway 13 – the road to Saigon. By 13 April Loc Ninh was surrounded and could only be supplied by parachute drops.

On 23 April the Central Highlands came under attack. It had been expected, but the ARVN 22nd Division fell back and it needed the 23rd to hold Kontum. While this fighting was under way the NVA had committed a new division in Binh Dinh province and after capturing three coastal towns threatened to cut the country in two.

Within three days of the NVA attacks President Nixon had given authority to bomb targets in North Vietnam 25 miles above the DMZ. Code named Freedom Train, they were extended to the 19th Parallel on 9 April. A month later Nixon

Below: The Thanh Hoa railroad and highway bridge, three miles north of Phan Hoa city in North Vietnam, which was destroyed by F-4s using 'smart bombs'.

ordered offensive operations throughout North Vietnam with the exception of a 25-30 mile zone around the Chinese border and areas 10 miles from the centre of Hanoi and Haiphong. In these cities specific strikes had to be authorised. The mining of Haiphong and the blockade of the coast were also ordered and intended to restrict the flow of war equipment. It was a crucial move.

Significantly, Nixon had also started overtures to the Chinese and so Communist reaction was reduced to verbal complaints. The full scale air attack on the north was code named Linebacker. It was a more flexible operation than the controlled Rolling Thunder and began at last to approach the use of air power advocated by the theorists. When Linebacker I ended on 22 October 10 fighter bases had been attacked, six thermal power stations and almost all the fixed petrol and oil storage farms; some strikes had been put in on plants in the centre of Hanoi. However a new generation of air-delivered weapons had allowed pilots of tactical bombers to hit point targets like bridges. 'Smart bombs' in contrast to 'dumb', or 'iron bombs' were TV- or laser-guided. The old dumb bombs had been free-flight, the new smart bombs could be guided down to their target and allowed pilots to hit a railway tunnel near the Chinese border. On 13 May the Thanh Hoa bridge was hit by several laser-guided bombs. Its destruction was a boost for USAF morale, since it had survived many attacks during the Rolling Thunder operations.

The new weapons had an added spin-off; greater accuracy meant that success could be achieved with a lower tonnage and less sorties. With this went a lower loss rate. Attacks had been launched with a complex electronic counter-measures back-up. Aircraft equipped with instruments to locate and analyse the radar frequencies of SAM sites were also supported by tactical bombers armed with missiles designed to ride down the radar beam and destroy them. In addition to these measures AA sites were hit with Flak suppression missions and the North Vietnamese radio and radar clogged with false signals. In this the United States was assisted by a raid launched by the

Right: Smoke billows from a North Vietnamese steel mill hit by F-105 Thunderchief Fighter Bombers in April 1967. These were part of the Rolling Thunder bombing operations against the north.

Below: An F-105 of the 57th Tactical Weapons Wing testing radar countermeasures equipment. These aircraft were used to evaluate North Vietnamese radar directed guns and missiles and employ methods to jam or defeat them.

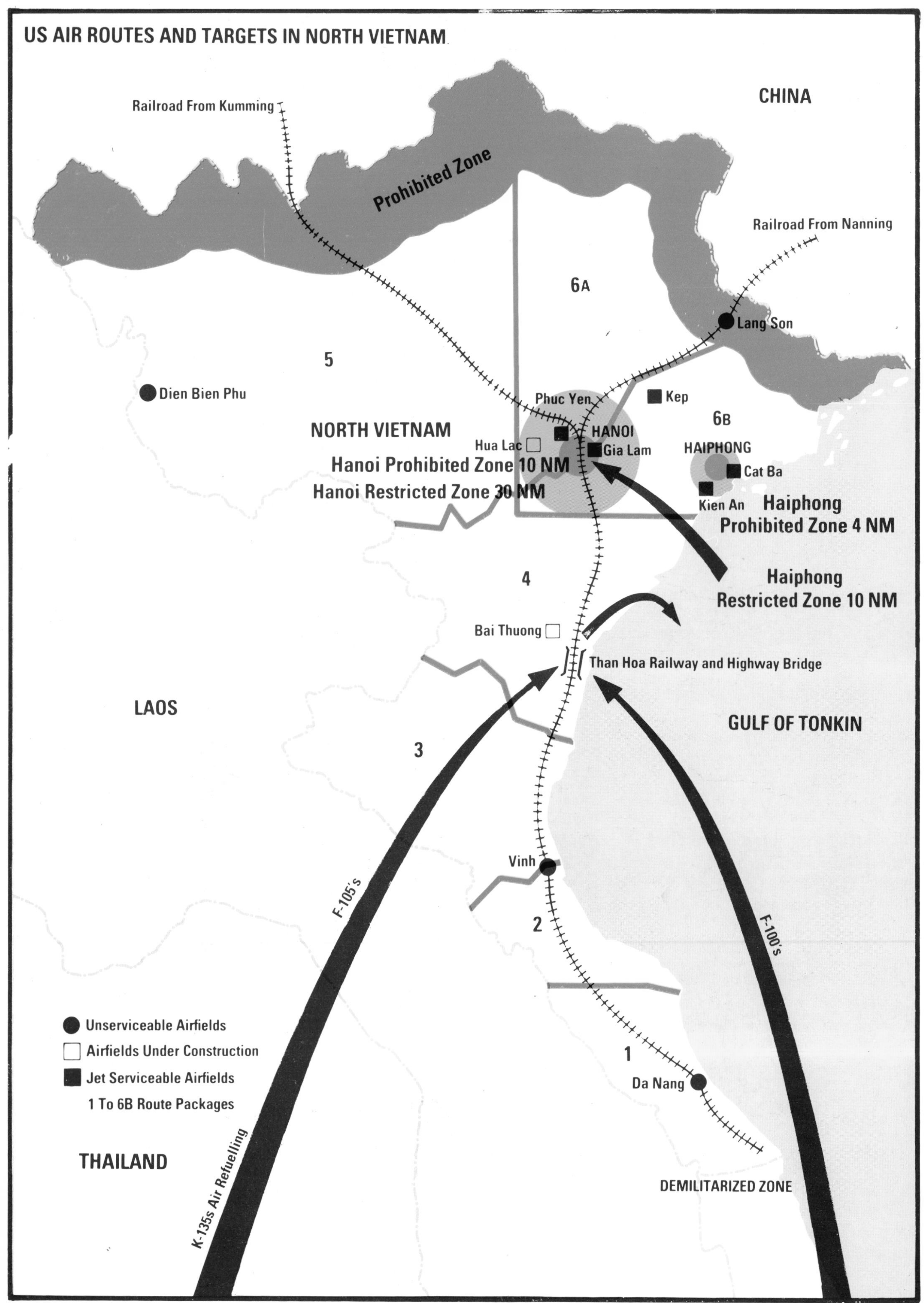
US AIR ROUTES AND TARGETS IN NORTH VIETNAM
CHINA
Railroad From Kumming
Prohibited Zone
Railroad From Nanning
6A
Lang Son
5
Dien Bien Phu
Phuc Yen
Kep
6B
NORTH VIETNAM
HANOI
Hua Lac
Gia Lam
HAIPHONG
Hanoi Prohibited Zone 10 NM
Cat Ba
Hanoi Restricted Zone 30 NM
Kien An
Haiphong
Prohibited Zone 4 NM
4
Haiphong
Restricted Zone 10 NM
Bai Thuong
Than Hoa Railway and Highway Bridge
LAOS
GULF OF TONKIN
3
Vinh
F-105's
2
F-100's
Unserviceable Airfields
Airfields Under Construction
Jet Serviceable Airfields
1 To 6B Route Packages
1
Da Nang
THAILAND
K-135s Air Refuelling
DEMILITARIZED ZONE

Left: A Minigun fires from the side of an AC-47 as it attacks targets at night in Vietnam. The aircraft had many names, some were known as Spooky others such as this one as 'Puff the Magic Dragon'.

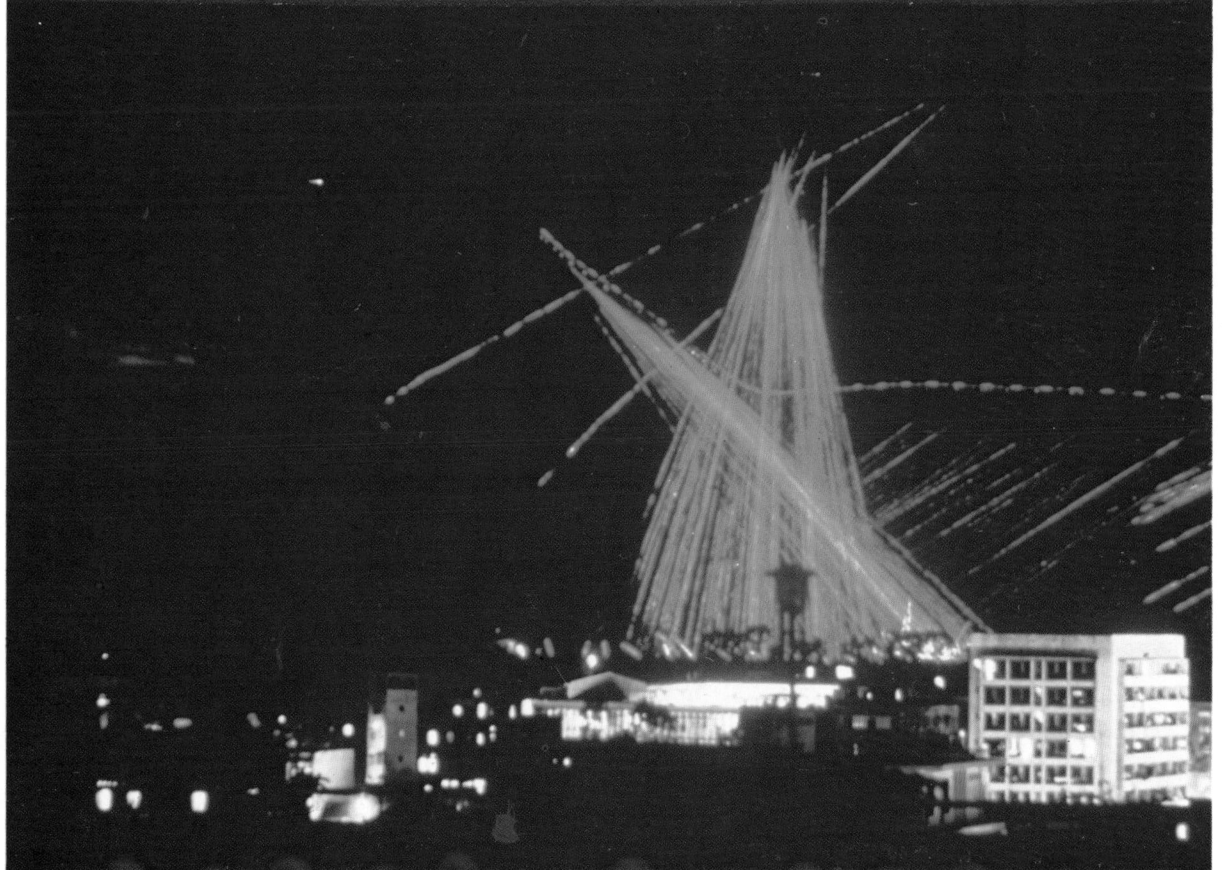

Left: Two AC-47s and an armed helicopter engage targets near Saigon. The traces from the Miniguns gave a characteristic fan of light which leads upwards to the aircraft. The sound of these guns firing was not that normally associated with automatic weapons but a continuous roar. During demonstrations in the US, a rabbit would be released onto a football pitch and would not be able to make it to the edge of the football pitch and escape before the entire pitch and the rabbit had been devastated by fire from an AC-47.

Israelis across the Suez canal; they had captured and brought back for analysis a Russian built SAM mobile radar unit.

The North Vietnamese cranked up their propaganda machine with the new attacks. They accused the USAF and US Navy of attacking civilian targets, and did not admit that many stores were deliberately placed in populated areas.

The attacks began to achieve two aims. The NVA actions in the south were coming under control and the Hanoi government dropped its insistance that Thieu should resign and that a coalition government be formed. The peace talks looked as if they were back in business. Nixon suspended all bombing north of the 20th parallel on 23 October 1972 and three days later Secretary

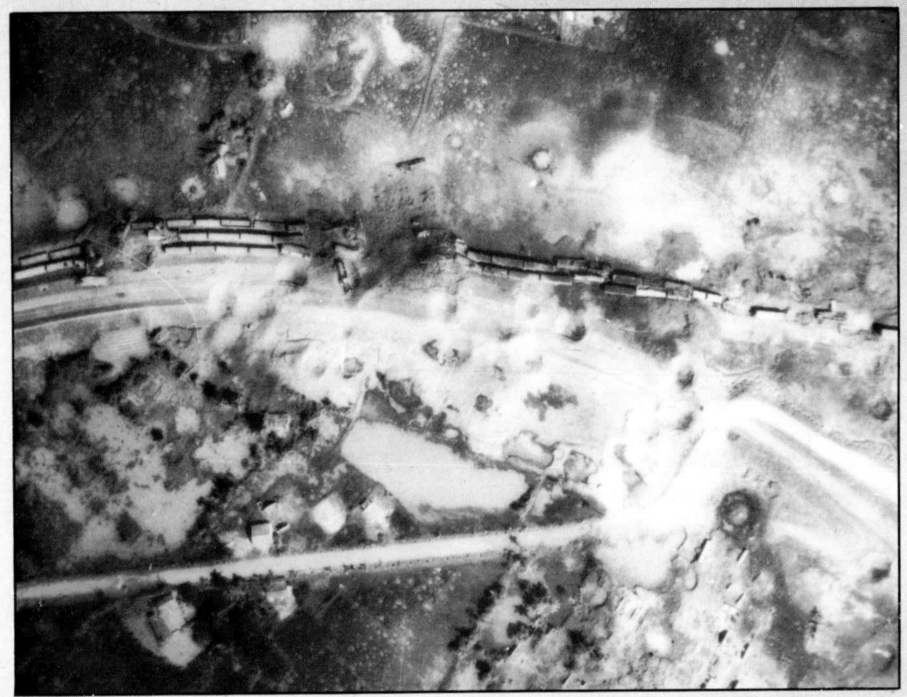

Above: part of the railroad system north-east of Thanh Hoa which was attacked by A-4 Skyhawks and A-6 Intruders in September 1966. Despite the devastation, the North Vietnamese were adept at improvising transport around bottlenecks caused by air attacks and managed to keep their supplies moving.

Below: An AC-47 gunship over Vietnam. The AC-47 was the veteran Dakota which had been troop transport throughout World War II.

of State Henry Kissinger announced 'peace is at hand'. It was a premature statement.

The peace negotiations were deadlocked by late December and Linebacker II was ordered. It lasted only 12 days, but in just under two weeks North Vietnam came under an intensity of attack never previously experienced. There were 729 B-52 sorties and about 1,000 fighter-bomber attacks. Though 20,370 tons of bombs were dropped 26 aircraft including 15 B-52s were lost. The main weight of the attacks fell on the road and rail communications between Hanoi and Haiphong as well as storage areas, power stations and airfields.

From North Vietnam and from peace groups in the United States and Europe came accusations of terror bombing. During B-52 attacks it was estimated that 90 per cent of the missions had one or two bombs that fell outside the target area.

One of the sites that the North Vietnamese made much of was the Bach Mai hospital in Hanoi. The shattered wards and operating theatre were shown as examples of US terror bombing. The Hanoi authorities did not however show that the hospital was about 1,000 yards from Bach Mai airfield and barracks.

Though the bombing of North Vietnam reduced Hanoi's war-making capability and forced it to the negotiating table it did not prevent the final campaign against the south in 1973.

Elsewhere in the South air power had other roles. Perhaps the most unusual was 'Puff the Magic Dragon' or 'Spooky', the C-47, the venerable Dakota, re-equipped as a gunship. The idea had been proposed by Captain Ronald Terry of the USAF who had read of the technique of flying tight circles over a fixed point on the ground; the method had been used to lower stores to small clearings in South America. Armed with three multi-barrel 7·62-mm Gatling type machine-guns which fired through two of the windows and the door, Spooky could fire 18,000 rounds a minute and devastate a target the size of a football pitch. One veteran of the war in Vietnam recalled a USO show that was forced to come to a temporary stop when the audience became more interested in the activities of Spooky in the hills behind the base.

Above: A C-130 Hercules armed with a 105 mm Howitzer. This gunship and others like it were used for attacking transport along the Ho Chi Minh trail where hits by this weapon were more than capable of destroying North Vietnamese trucks.

The flares floating down and the noise of the aircraft engines were interrupted by the long roar of the guns firing and the arcs of tracer hosing down to the ground.

However, Vietnam will be remembered as a helicopter war. The early US involvement saw the deployment of Sikorsky H-34 Choctaw, but the almost universal Huey – or Bell UH-1 Iroquois – remains the trademark of airmobile operations in the war. It arrived in the country in November 1962. By the end of the war it had been used for troop lift as a 'slick', casualty evacuation (dustoff), and as an armed attack helicopter (gunship). In the latter role it could carry four M60 7·62 mm machine-guns, a 40-mm grenade launcher, 48 2·75-in rockets, or an M22 guided missile. The Huey could lift 11 to 14 troops – but with weapons and kit this was normally about eight – six litters with an attendant as a dustoff, or 3,880 lb of freight.

An officer of the 82nd Airborne who worked with helicopters in the Delta recalled that as the gunships began their 'prepping' run (attacking likely enemy positions before a landing) sparks streamed out of the back of the rocket pods when they fired. 'I had always thought the sparks in Flash Gordon were rather unconvincing when the rockets were fired in the movies, but then I realised that they were true!'

One development of the gunship which was to be invaluable in stemming the NVA attacks was the HueyCobra. This helicopter mounted a six-barrelled minigun with 8,000 rounds of 7·62-mm ammunition, two 40-mm grenade launchers, and as external stores 78 2·75-in rockets.

However, the now venerable Huey was back as a tank killer with the TOW (Tube-Launched Optically-tracked Weapon). At Kontum city,

massed attacks by T-54 tanks were halted by the first helicopter-versus-tank action in history. The ability of the helicopter to 'shoot and scoot' made it a hard target, and the tank was exposed on the streets of the city.

While Linebacker I was pounding the north, fighting continued in the south. On 27 April 1972 the NVA used bad weather to cover their advance and pushed towards Dong Ha, which they captured. The ARVN units fell back towards Quang Tri combat base, but as the situation became worse the base was evacuated and the fight moved to the city. On 1 May, under heavy fire from 130-mm artillery and with another NVA attack in the offing, the ARVN troops panicked and began to stream south. Tanks, artillery, trucks and

Top: A UH-1B of the Helicopter Attack Squadron 3, Detachment 7.

Above: The doorman looks out of a 'Dustoff' Huey as it comes into land. The 'Dustoff' was a casualty evacuation helicopter.

Left: A US Marine trains a South Vietnamese to operate a M-60 machine gun. Co-operation was essential to allow the Vietnamese to take over the modern American hardware.

APCs were left undamaged and only one Marine brigade remained in good order. The line stabilised on the southern bank of the Tach Ma River and the ARVN regrouped for a counter-attack in June.

The second NVA thrust from the A Shau valley began on 30 March. Here the 1st Division of the ARVN fought hard at the fire bases Bastogne and Checkmate. When these fell after nearly a month of fighting the ARVN forces fell back to fire support base Birmingham.

The fight for Hue began on 1 May – International Labour Day. Saigon had made efforts to reorganise their command structure to cope with this conventional attack. The northern and eastern approaches to Hue were the responsibility of the newly-formed Marine Division, while the battle-hardened 1st Division covered the southern and western approaches. A strong reserve had been formed and the Regional and Popular forces were placed under the operational control of 1 Corps.

An airborne brigade, which had fought hard in the Kontum area, had arrived with a battalion of artillery and were taken under command of the Marine Division. Four days later they launched a brigade attack across the Thac Ma River. The Marines made an amphibious attack behind NVA lines and the 1st Division re-captured fire base Bastogne on 15 May and followed that with Checkmate.

The ARVN forces had been assisted with arc-light raids by B-52s. On 28 June the South Vietnamese launched a general counter-offensive. This was intended not only to liberate areas captured by the NVA, but also to restore confidence in the Saigon leadership. It took two months before Quang Tri was liberated by South Vietnamese Marines, on 16 September.

Meanwhile, in Military Region III around Saigon, an NVA and two VC divisions were given the task of capturing the southern capital. However, before this they would have to take An Loc and hoped to set up a provisional capital by late April.

The US intelligence assessment was that though there would be activity in MR III it would not involve anything greater than the usual ambush, sabotage and propaganda activities. The first indication that in fact it was to be a major battleground came when fire support base Lac Long, north-east of Tay Ninh on the Cambodian border, was overrun by a regimental strength force with armour and artillery. When the base at Thien Ngon fell the ARVN assumed that the threat was to Tay Ninh city. Here, however, they fell for the NVA deception plan. The NVA paused

Below: An A-4F Skyhawk unloads its 500 lb bombs over Vietnam. US firepower was essential to the South Vietnamese when they fought the regular North Vietnamese forces to a standstill but both sides knew that it would not remain forever on call to the ARVN as America withdrew from South-East Asia.

Above: During the early days in Vietnam, men of the 3rd Reconnaissance Battalion, 3rd Marine Division carry captured North Vietnamese 12.7 mm anti-aircraft guns to the rear. These Soviet designed and built heavy machine guns were used against helicopters and fixed wing aircraft and proved to be most effective.

and then on 5 April they smashed through Loc Ninh in 24 hours. It seems to have been a fight to the death, with an NVA division against an ARVN regiment with armour and a Ranger battalion attached. The enemy was thrown back from the wire on several occasions, but despite air strikes close to the perimeter the ARVN defenders were swamped by sheer numbers, backed with armour and artillery.

There was a pause as each side regrouped and between the 8th and the 12th the ARVN relocated their forces to cover the NVA axis of advance through Binh Long province rather than Tay Ninh. The town of An Loc was the next obvious objective for the NVA. Holding it would prevent any movement south-eastwards to Saigon. It was therefore reinforced with the 21st Division and an airborne brigade from the general reserve. The 21st made the move northwards from the delta area of MR IV along Highway 13. Indications that the next phase of the NVA attack was coming were given to the Saigon leadership when a screening force 9 miles north of An Loc came under heavy attack. It suffered badly and was forced to destroy its equipment and make its way south on foot to reinforce the garrison of An Loc.

As reconnaissance probes were made by the NVA around the city, the 'Big Ugly Fellows' – B-52s – made arc-light attacks on suspected enemy concentration areas. Attacks in depth around the city hit the NVA forces as they prepared for the first phase of their attack on 13 April.

The battle raged for three days. There were conflicting reports about the 66-mm M72 Light Anti-tank Weapon (LAW). Some sources said that the ARVN were keen tank hunters with this one-shot portable weapon, others that despite the LAW's proven effectiveness it was hard to motivate men to go out against NVA armour.

By 16 April only the northern part of the city ammunition storage area was in NVA and VC hands. Again there was a pause and then, preceded by heavy artillery fire, the NVA put in new attacks on the 19th. It was reported that they had set a deadline of the 20th to capture the city. Having failed to achieve this they moved to an

Right: An aircraft is silhouetted against a backdrop of exploding shells and ammunition as NVA fire falls on a base in South Vietnam.

Below: A US Marine Corps fire base: a CH-47 Chinook helicopter can be seen the guns grouped behind sand bag and earth parapets to protect them from shell fire. This style of base had been developed by the Americans in Vietnam and was in turn taught to the South Vietnamese. It required air mobility and of course a substantial supply of ammunition to make it effective. Both these commodities were in short supply in South Vietnam after the Americans withdrew.

artillery bombardment and siege phase. AA artillery was moved in to prevent helicopter re-supply and reinforcement and the 4,000 defenders came under an average of 1,000 rounds a day.

On 10 May the NVA and VC had re-deployed for another assault. Sir Robert Thompson, the British counter-insurgency expert whose advice and writings on Vietnam had coloured thinking in Washington, described the Hanoi leaders as 'old men in a hurry'. Certainly they had set a deadline and were pushing their forces to achieve victory. Thompson explained that the Hanoi leaders had seen the death of Ho Chi Minh on 4 September 1969 as a sign that they too had a limited time in which to 'unify' Vietnam.

The NVA attacks ended by 12 May, pounded by massive air attacks and by the stubbornness of the exhausted defenders. By last light on the 15th the enemy was withdrawing. The US advisors with the ARVN units assumed that the withdrawal was prompted by the approach of the 21st Division from MR IV and other ARVN units closing in on the siege.

Between mid-May and June the ARVN mopped up the remaining enemy forces around An Loc and the NVA regrouped over the border. They had not only to replace ammunition stocks, but also bring in fresh troops to make up losses from the combined ground and air actions.

An Loc was a triumph of ARVN resistance and also of the logistic and attack missions of the USAF, US Army and Vietnamese Air Force. As the strength of enemy AA fire increased so the re-supply tactics changed. From helicopter missions the move was to parachute drops, and as these became too hazardous the USAF introduced high altitude systems. Many of these methods had been pioneered at Khe Sanh and they made a dramatic contrast to the haphazard re-supply missions flown by the French at Dien Bien Phu. There, AA fire forced aircraft high and when parachute drops were made the loads often ended up in Viet Minh lines.

The Central Highlands had also been attracting attention. Military Region II had been quiet, but with air reconnaissance reports of enemy armour and the arrival of 122-mm and 130-mm guns in the Cambodian and Laotian border areas, Saigon began to move troops in anticipation of NVA action. The Central Highlands were always an attractive place for an attack, since a concerted thrust would take the NVA to the sea and sever north-south communications.

An ARVN airborne brigade was sent to reinforce the fire support bases on Rocket Ridge to the west of Kontum. A second airborne brigade followed in March with the Division HQ. They covered the southern area of the province. Aggressive air and ground actions delayed the NVA plans for the Central Highlands and the two enemy divisions now in position were not ready for action until 23 April.

The first objective for the NVA was Tan Canh on Route 14. Pushing to the north of Kontum they captured the fire support bases Charlie and Delta on Rocket Ridge and with their capture the NVA were able to dominate Highway 14 from the west. While these actions were in progress ARVN troops were committed to Tan Canh.

NVA observers began to call down accurate fire on the town for a day and then on 24 April the ground assault began. The five M41 tanks that made up the defensive armour at Tan Canh were destroyed by artillery fire. With the heavy shelling the ARVN defenders took to their bunkers and after the ammunition dump had been hit the NVA pressed their attack and despite heavy air counter-attacks were able to take the town by the dawn of the 25th.

As the fighting was under way at Tan Canh, Dak To II also came under attack. Here an ARVN

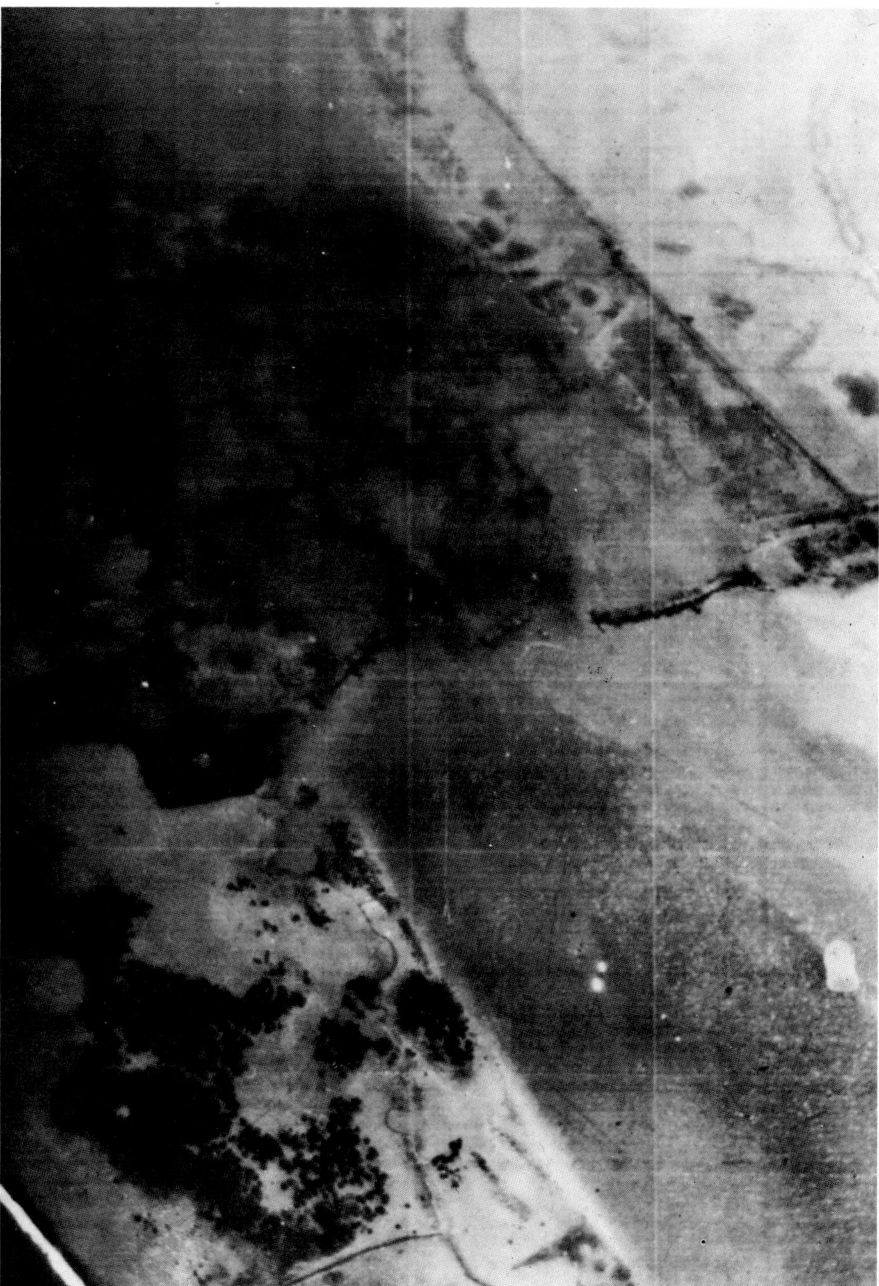

Above: A reconnaissance photograph of a pontoon bridge destroyed on Route 1A, 15 miles southwest of Than Hoa in North Vietnam. It was destroyed during air attacks in April 1972.

regimental HQ and the airfield were subjected to artillery and ground assault. An armoured counter-attack by ARVN forces pushed back the NVA, but the US advisors were in grave danger. Here, as at Quang Tri, a collapse of morale led to desertion and retreat by ARVN troops. Kontum was threatened from the north; on 4 May fire base November fell. While this ground pressure was sustained the NVA also shelled Ranger camps up in the high land to the west of Kontum. Of the two that suffered most, Ben Het survived, but Polei Kleng was neutralised by shell fire.

Kontum's agony began on 14 May. A massed armour attack by T-54s was launched from the north and north-west. By mid-morning it was at an end, broken by long range TOW missile attacks, tactical air-strikes and Cobra passes, and the Vietnamese in the rubble with their LAWs. In hand-to-hand counter-attacks the ARVN pushed back the NVA to restore their line by nightfall. The NVA were back after dark and in fierce fighting the ARVN used a tactic that dated back to World War I – except modified to new fire-power. They pulled back from their positions and called for close-in strikes by B-52s. Two days of inactivity were followed by increased artillery fire and NVA attacks on 20 May. Attacks a day later were stopped by B-52 strikes.

Aggressive patrolling and counter-attacks by the ARVN attempted to keep the NVsionA off-

Above: A Chinook helicopter lifts a 105 mm Howitzer with its underslung load of ammunition to a new firing position. The American helicopter lift capability allowed them to employ fast and flexible tactics to block likely enemy withdrawal or attack routes. These tactics were harder for the South Vietnamese to employ with their more restricted resources.

balance, but on 25 May the NVA made extensive penetrations into the defences of Kontum. As 122-mm and 130-mm fire increased, the ARVN called for all available air power – helicopters and fixed-wing aircraft. In the dawn of the 26th, the US Army pilots, USAF and Vietnamese Air Force found targets in the streets of Kontum; the tanks which had pushed through the ARVN lines were now exposed on open roads.

The battle was still in the balance when President Thieu flew into the city on the 30th. He ordered that it should be held; and, as at An Loc, as South Vietnamese reinforcements moved closer the besiegers were in danger of becoming besieged. Tanks were captured intact – some with their engines still running as the crews realised that they were priority targets.

As the Kontum battle raged, VC main forces joined an NVA division in attacks in the coastal Binh Dinh province. This had been part of the strategic plan that would cut South Vietnam in half, but here B-52 attacks and aggressive ARVN action turned back the NVA and VC. However, for a time it looked serious as the Communists cut Highway 1 and held several district capitals.

In Military Region II ARVN forces began operations to re-open Highway 14 in the mountains between Kontum and Pleiku. Fighting continued, but less intensely until the cease-fire in January 1973.

12. THE COLLAPSE OF THE SOUTH

PRESIDENT NIXON HAD PREDICTED that Linebacker I and II meant 'the bastards are going to be bombed like they have never been bombed before'. The air attacks on the north coupled with the mining of Haiphong Harbour, as well as the failure of the conventional attacks in the south, obliged Hanoi to return to negotiations in Paris. However, if they could not take South Vietnam by force they would talk their way into it. Each side knew that the United States was war-weary and seeking a way out of South-East Asia. For the north this meant that they must content themselves with waiting another year or two before attempting attacks on the south. By then the bombers would be gone.

Ironically it was Nixon who showed political awareness of the value of the peace talks. As the NVA forces shelled and smashed their way into the south, he ordered a boycott of the talks and for the first time the NVA and VC delegations found their tactics turned against them. Nixon was determined to quit Vietnam, but with honour, and this would not be achieved if the NVA were obviously still holding gains made in battle. Hanoi watchers were interested to see new men in the politburo: General Van Tien Dun, the chief of staff of the NVA and Tran Quoc Hoan, the minister of public security. This seemed to show that the north was taking a new interest in its internal affairs, and official publications began to talk of building Socialism in the north while the south 'must directly fulfil the duty of liberating itself'. It

Above: Evidence of air attacks on targets in the north: gasoline tanks in Haiphong billow with smoke, April 1972.

Previous page: Part of Operation Lancaster II.

Right: Haiphong oil storage depots after an attack by A-4 aircraft in June 1966. During these early missions over North Vietnam air crew were shot down and held as P-o-Ws by the north.

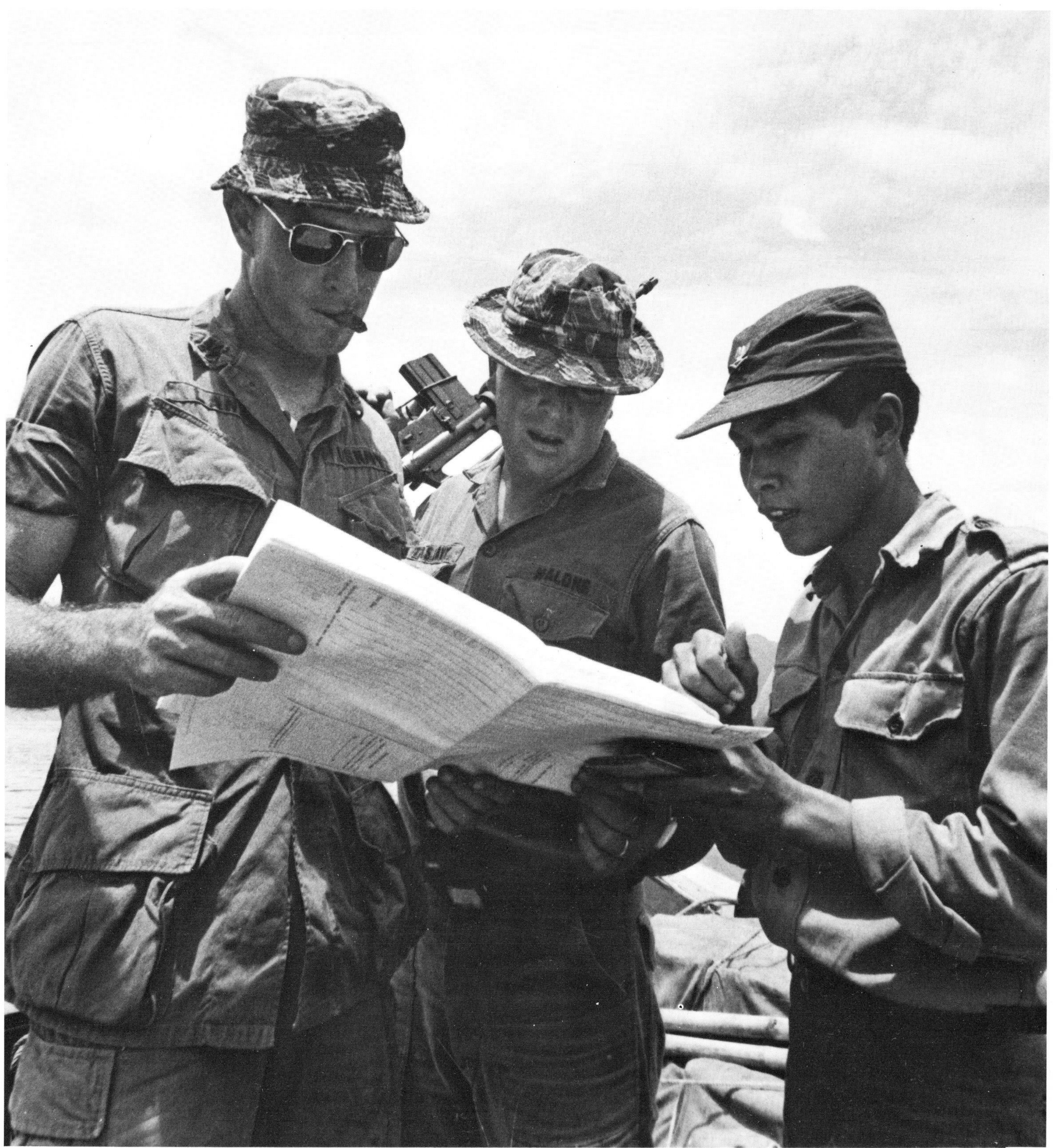

Above: Two US advisors and a Vietnamese sailor check the papers of a civilian junk as they search for VC supplies. The Viet Cong used civilian junks to move men and supplies by sea.

was significant that both Peking and Moscow seemed to be tired of the long war, while the predictions of planners in Hanoi that their attacks would crush the newly armed and re-formed ARVN units had only proved true in some areas. The public talks in Paris were also accompanied by private contacts. Linebacker II had interrupted the negotiations and then Hanoi was back talking seriously.

Even though the United States was negotiating its way out of the war, while pressing Hanoi with air power in the north and the south, it was also withdrawing troops steadily. By July 1972 there were less than 49,000 men in Vietnam, and ARVN units were back in action with advisors – much as they had been in the early days. However, it was not the withdrawal of troops that mattered for domestic American opinion, but the knowledge that if US armed forces were not involved at all in South-East Asia, then they could not be drawn

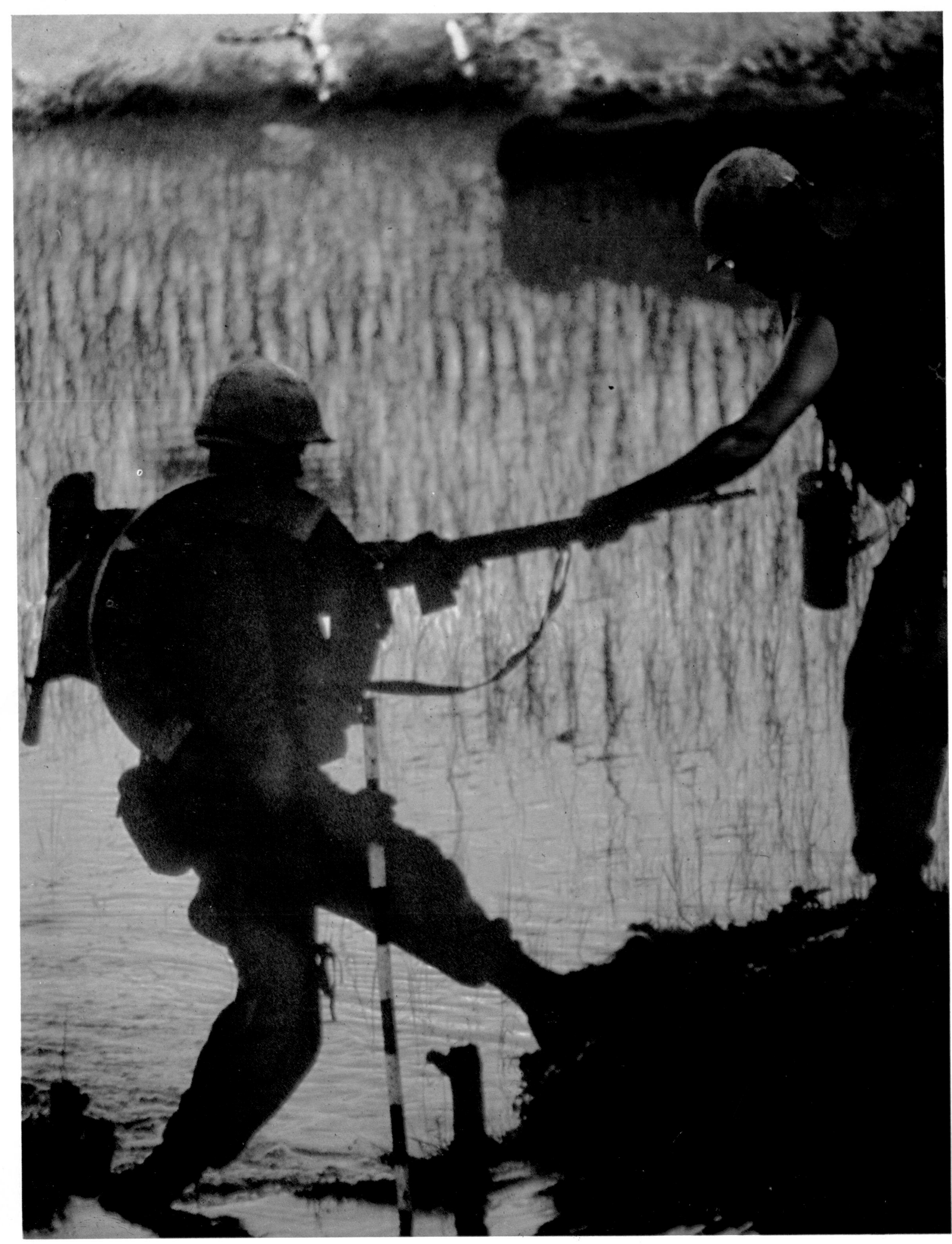

back into the fighting. They wanted out.

The talks between Kissinger and the representative of the north, Le Duc Tho, hinged on the US desire to see that the south had a chance to find its feet without interference from Hanoi. The north wanted to unite both countries. Following the end of Linebacker II, Thò and Kissinger signed a cease-fire agreement on 23 January 1973. A formal signature followed on the 27th. With this the final US forces started to withdraw and the release of ARVN and US prisoners began.

The prisoners of war were an emotional issue for the United States. Some of the pilots had been held since the first raids over North Vietnam in 1966 and even though information was scarce there was enough to indicate that they were being held under harsh conditions. The wives of US Air Force and Navy officers formed an effective and tireless lobby.

Among the first P-o-Ws to be released was Lieutenant Commander Everett Alvarez Jr, the first man to be captured. He spoke for many of the men when he said, 'God bless the President and God bless you, Mr and Mrs America. You did not forget us.' The returning men were released as part of Operation Homecoming, and it was here that Hanoi produced 512 men. Controversy still exists about the number of men who were listed as either missing or captured. At the Peace Accords of January 1973 the US Department of Defence listed 591 P-o-Ws in South-East Asia, 1,380 missing and 1,929 unaccounted for.

Of the 512 men released, 53 were men who had been listed as missing and one who had been listed killed. Three years later the Department of Defence still listed 36 men as P-o-Ws and 795 as missing. A House Select Committee on Missing Persons stated the 'live sightings' had been reported of captive US servicemen and also of 21 journalists. They added that insufficient effort had been made to follow up these reports. In the early 1980s pressure to locate and bring home any men still imprisoned spawned freelance civilian operations across the Thai border.

Remembering the trauma of the P-o-Ws from Korea, the United States went to great efforts to make the returned men feel that they were appreciated. They were flown via Hawaii and checked by teams of doctors. TV documentaries which included the US moon missions were prepared to allow them to catch up with the news they had missed while in prison. Film of the men, still in their plain prison overalls, showed them taking their first breaths of freedom, one man leaning back in the aircraft seat and taking long happy pulls at a large cigar. The homecomings in the United States were watched by millions on TV whose hearts went out to the wives and children who ran across the tarmac to embrace the returning men.

Far left: Marines of 2nd Battalion, 5th Regiment, move through flooded paddy fields during Operation Colorado, August 1966. During the last years of US involvement US forces were less involved in ground operations.

Below: Marines of 3rd Battalion, 4th Marines Division, wait to board the USS *Tripoli* for Okinawa on 29 December 1969. President Nixon kept his promise 'to bring our boys home'.

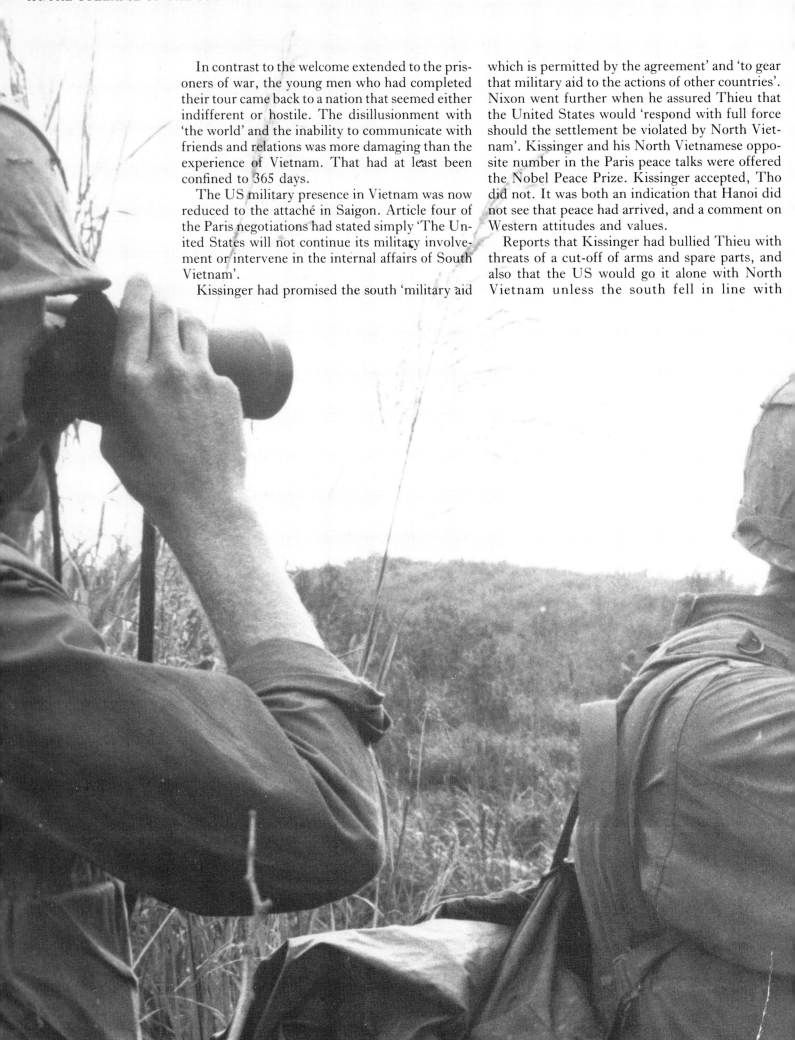

In contrast to the welcome extended to the prisoners of war, the young men who had completed their tour came back to a nation that seemed either indifferent or hostile. The disillusionment with 'the world' and the inability to communicate with friends and relations was more damaging than the experience of Vietnam. That had at least been confined to 365 days.

The US military presence in Vietnam was now reduced to the attaché in Saigon. Article four of the Paris negotiations had stated simply 'The United States will not continue its military involvement or intervene in the internal affairs of South Vietnam'.

Kissinger had promised the south 'military aid which is permitted by the agreement' and 'to gear that military aid to the actions of other countries'. Nixon went further when he assured Thieu that the United States would 'respond with full force should the settlement be violated by North Vietnam'. Kissinger and his North Vietnamese opposite number in the Paris peace talks were offered the Nobel Peace Prize. Kissinger accepted, Tho did not. It was both an indication that Hanoi did not see that peace had arrived, and a comment on Western attitudes and values.

Reports that Kissinger had bullied Thieu with threats of a cut-off of arms and spare parts, and also that the US would go it alone with North Vietnam unless the south fell in line with

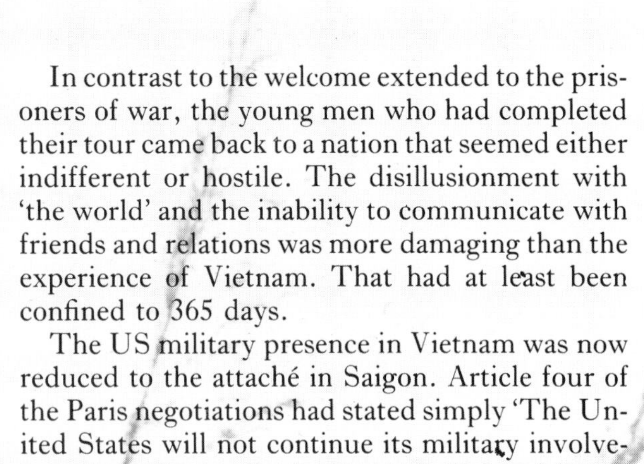

Washington's plans, give a ring of truth to the comment of Tom Lehrer, the satirist, that 'satire was dead after Kissinger accepted the Nobel Peace Prize'.

As soon as the Accords were signed, the north began new preparations for offensives in the south. Troops moved south through Cambodia and Laos, and SAM-2 sites were installed at Khe Sanh. Informed of these actions Nixon said:

we have informed the North Vietnamese of our concern about this violation...and I would only suggest, based on my actions over the past four years, that the North Vietnamese should not lightly disregard such expressions of concern, when

Left: An artillery officer spots a target for a Marine firing an M16 rifle, during Operation Prairie.

Above: Aerial photograph of 10 SAM missile sites, almost hidden by camouflage, 50 miles south-west of Hanoi. The Soviet Union continued to supply the north following the US withdrawal from South-East Asia.

Far right: A reconnaissance photograph reveals enemy surface-to-air missiles and equipment under attack by F-4s, four miles north of the DMZ, August 1972.

Far right, below: NVA artillery men in Laos. They are equipped with Soviet-built guns, ammunition, and even helmets and small arms from the USSR.

they are made with regard to a violation.

The threat of a Linebacker III was reinforced as reconnaissance flights began again over the north. In March as the last P-o-Ws acknowledged by Hanoi left the north, the last US troops left Vietnam.

It was the Watergate scandal that rang the death knell for South Vietnam. As Nixon fought for his political survival the north pressed ahead with its build-up of troops and the VC kept a guerilla war bubbling in the south. Congress, sensing that the President could not defend himself, voted on 10 June to cut off all funds for US military activity in and over Indo-China. On 7 November 1973 the War Powers Resolution confirmed Congressional oversight over the President's use of US troops abroad and gave further indications that the United States wanted to stay clear of South-East Asia.

Observing these decisions in Washington, with the President powerless as Watergate became his private struggle, Hanoi knew that they could move from the political war fought in Paris to open hostilities. In the spring of 1974 the Politburo and NVA General Staff began to formulate plans for an offensive in 1975.

As with the smallest operation, the preparations were extensive. The Soviet Union, which had indicated that it would keep out of the Vietnamese struggle, began again to send weapons and equipment. It included T-54 tanks; the feared 130-mm artillery; SAM-7, the portable anti-aircraft missiles, as well as the modern SAM-2, SAM-3 and SAM-6; the ZSU-23-4 tracked AA guns; and the re-loads and ammunition necessary to keep this hardware operational. These AA systems were to balance the considerable air power available to the South Vietnamese. With 2,000 aircraft they were the fourth largest air force in the world. This figure included extensive helicopter lift facilities.

North Vietnam's Chief of Staff, General Van Tien Dung, writing after the war, explained that the military build-up was backed by extensive logistic support. A strategic 8 metre-wide highway begun in 1973 was speeded up. With two lanes it could carry heavy trucks and armour. To fuel these vehicles a pipeline was built running from Quang Tri to the Central Highlands and Loc Ninh. NVA forces in the south rose from 140,000 in 1973 to 185,000 in March 1974. There were between 500 and 700 tanks and 24 regiments of AA

Right: A Communist anti-aircraft unit in Laois, which had already downed 116 US aircraft, August 1972. These AA units were supplied by the Soviet Union.

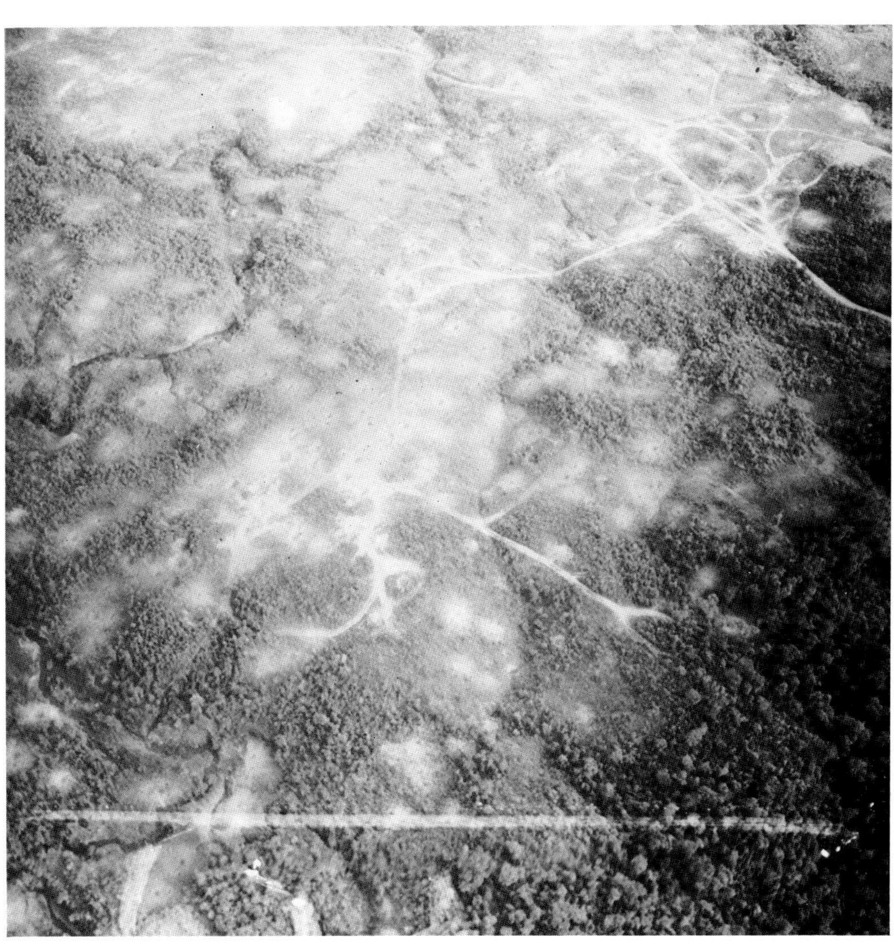

troops.

The ARVN had also received arms and equipment. The United States had used military and even chartered civil aircraft to bring armour, artillery, ammunition and communications equipment. However, each country was dependent on the willingness of its patron nation to keep up the flow of spare parts and ammunition. In 1973 Congress had voted \$2·270 billion, but a year later this was down to \$1·010 and in 1975 it would be down to \$700 million. Kissinger pleaded, and the US Ambassador to South Vietnam, Graham Martin, put it more clearly: cutting aid would 'seriously tempt the north to gamble on an all-out military offensive'.

General Dung could write:

The enemy became passive and utterly weak ...The reduction of US aid made it impossible for the puppet troops to carry out their combat plans and build up their forces . . . Nguyen Van Thieu was then forced to fight a poor man's war.

Lack of spares had reduced the number of close support missions that could be flown by 40 per cent and the number of aircraft combat-ready, out

Left: US Navy and the South Vietnamese Navy co-operate in a counter-infiltration patrol along the South Vietnamese coastline. This operation was known as Market Time and was to prevent VC supplies moving south.

of 1,277, was down to 921. The ARVN had been trained by the US Army to be lavish with fire-power, but now they were being forced to husband their ammunition. Dung wrote:

Enemy fire-power had decreased by nearly 60 per cent because of bomb and ammunition shortages. Its mobility was also reduced by half due to lack of aircraft, vehicles and fuel.

In fact in some ARVN units ammunition was down to 85 rifle rounds per man per month and four rounds of artillery ammunition per day.

These cut backs came at a time when the dollar was suffering a fall in value and the price of oil had risen. Fuel for not only military vehicles, but for outboard motors, trucks and agricultural pumps was becoming expensive. Inflation moved upward in South Vietnam. There were more than a million unemployed and with the country under threat few investors were prepared to put money into the south.

Desertion, which had been running at 168,997 gross in 1971, was at 239,448 in 1975. The soldier's pay had been undermined by inflation and his loyalties were stronger for his family group, which he had to support. There was also the knowledge that the Saigon administration was unlikely to catch him.

Corruption included soldiers who paid men to stand in for them and others who paid their officers to move them to safer postings – they were known as 'flower soldiers'. Corruption led to the fall of Phuoc Long province in Military Region III. It was the first South Vietnamese province to fall completely since 1954 and John C. Donnell, an American in Saigon, noted: 'Corruption in the Army was believed by many to be so gross that outpost defenders were having to pay other units for artillery support and air supply'.

At the Politburo meeting in Hanoi between December 1974 and January 1975 the political and military leaders of North Vietnam noted that this defeat had produced no reaction from the United States. Dung wrote:

It was obvious that the United States was in this position: having withdrawn from Vietnam, the

United States could hardly return. All the conferes analyzed the enemy's weakness which in itself heralded a new opportunity for us ...US troops have withdrawn from the south, and our armed forces are present there.

The decision was taken to launch large scale attacks in 1975 to make gains for further operations in 1976. If the situation was favourable the operations in 1975 could be extended to capture the whole of the south.

The first attacks were in the Highlands – it was here that the French had fought their last actions at the close of the first Indo-Chinese war. This time, instead of ambushes from the treeline of the roads, the tactics were no longer hit and run. The assault on the south was classic Soviet-style steam rolling. In the attack on Ban Me Thuot, capital of Darlac province, the NVA employed three divisions against the ARVN regiment and territorial

Below: A French-designed river craft used by South Vietnamese units for fire support, minesweeping and patrol missions.

Above: Communist tanks in Vietnam. The North received T-54 and T-55 tanks for their attacks in 1975.

force battalions. In practical terms this meant a ratio of 5·5:1 in infantry, 2·1:1 heavy artillery, 1·2:1 in tanks and APCs. It took only 24 hours for this force to crush the town on 11 March.

As the north looked at the opportunities to seize the whole of the Highlands before the onset of the 1975 rainy season, the US House of Representatives voted to reject the $300 million supplementary military appropriation that President Ford attempted to push through Congress. Thieu, at a meeting at Nha Trang with Major-General Phan Van Phu, commanding Military Region II, now realised that South Vietnam was on its own. Thieu ordered Phu to pull back from Kontum and Pleiku to release men for a counter-attack on Ban Me Thuot.

Withdrawals are the most difficult operation in war, and Phu after passing the job on to a Ranger officer flew back to Nha Trang with his staff. The evacuation operation became a rout. No one wanted to fight as a rearguard and refugees who joined the withdrawal clogged the roads. While some ARVN units fought among themselves, equipment worth an estimated $253·5 million was left undamaged for the NVA to capture.

A collapse as rapid as this had not been anticipated by the NVA, but they were quick to exploit it. By 18 March they had taken Pleiku and Kontum. Hanoi sent three fresh NVA divisions across the DMZ to join with forces in Quang Tri. In order to cover Saigon, Thieu had taken units from the strategic reserve – the 1st Airborne from their locations in the north. The commander of Military Region I, General Truong, complained, and it was hard to blame him when Quang Tri province fell. The refugees who streamed south rekindled fears in the population of Hue of a repetition of the horrors of the Tet offensive.

A former Special Forces officer watching the TV film of refugees commented that this was behaviour uncharacteristic of the Vietnamese. Normally, he said, they would sit out the fighting. They dug bunkers, and would even dig one for their water buffaloes.

The ARVN troops around Hue and the former US base at Danang were in the grips of a fear for the lives of their families. In counter-insurgency operations it was normally excellent for morale for soldiers to return to a base where their dependents were living – now, with a massive conventional attack threatening, there were fears for these potential military and political victims.

Thieu had intended to adopt a strategy called 'Light at the Top: Heavy at the Bottom'. In essence this meant accepting the fall of the Highlands and parts of Military Regions I and II. He hoped by pulling forces back he would have enough strength to hold a line running from Nha Trang on the coast through the Highland resort of Dalat and south-westwards to Chon Thanh to Tay Ninh near the Cambodian border. In addition he aimed to hold enclaves along the coast which would cover the cities of Hue and Danang, and Tain Ky and Chu Lai with Quang Ngai. This would not only secure major bases and population areas, but prevent movement southwards along Highway 1.

The refugee disaster became a reality when most of the 150,000 inhabitants of Quang Tri came stumbling into Hue. Out of the chaos Vice-Admiral Chung Tan Cang, who had until recently held a desk job, emerged as a temporary saviour. He moved every available vessel northwards to evacuate civilians and soldiers from Military Regions I and II.

Hanoi now realised that their original timetable for the defeat of the south could be speeded up. On 30 March Danang fell to the NVA. With its capture three ARVN divisions had melted away and their arms and equipment had been captured. The north pushed more troops southward and this time it looked as if the men who went south would return alive. US estimates were that the north sent 178,000 troops south between September 1974 and April 1975; in April the figure was 58,000.

In early April, as the NVA II Corps moved south through the coastal towns, the NVA III Corps deployed along the ARVN defence line which now ran from Phan Rang on the coast westwards to Tay Ninh on the Cambodian border. However, as Saigon attempted to stabilise this line they were already under attack by NVA and VC forces within their enclave.

While Hanoi pushed its military preparations forward it also continued a political offensive holding up false olive branches. The grim Madame Nguyen Thi Binh, who represented the Provisional Revolutionary Government (a new name for the Viet Cong – and thus a front for Hanoi) announced in Algeria: 'We understand General Duong Van Minh is ready to negotiate for peace and we are ready to talk to him'. Since Minh, known as 'Big' Minh, was the obvious rival to

Far right, above: Some of the lucky ones who got away before the fall of South Vietnam. Refugees are transported on a mechanised landing craft, April 1975.

Far right, below: The invasion of Cambodia and South Vietnam by North Vietnam produced massive refugee problems in South-East Asia. This photograph was taken near Kao-i-dang camp on the Thailand-Cambodia border in June 1979.

Above: An F-5E Tiger fighter-bomber drops three bombs on VC positions. The US left South Vietnam with the fourth largest air force in the world but lack of spares and maintenance problems reduced its efficiency.

Thieu this was intended to undermine morale in Saigon.

General Dung arrived in Military Region III on 3 April and met COSVN chairman Pham Hung at Loc Ninh. Here Dung, Hung and his deputy General Tran Van Tra worked on plans for the final assault on Saigon. A three-front attack was planned, the main weight to fall on Xuan Loc. This village was on the junction of Highway 1 with the road to the coastal town of Vung Tau and the road westwards to the Bien Hoa airbase outside Saigon. While the tactics were under discussion the NVA III Corps continued their attacks. On 6 April the NVA 10th Division overran the refugee centre of Cam Ranh Bay; now the only areas of Military Region II still in government hands were the Phan Rang airbase and Phan Thiet City.

In less than a month 150,000 ARVN troops and militia in the northern portion of the country had been destroyed, dispersed or abandoned. Some 16,000 troops had been lifted off the beaches of Military Region I, but the only unit intact was a Marine brigade. In Military Region II only two regiments and the airborne brigade were battle-effective out of two divisions. In the same period $1 billion worth of equipment had been destroyed or abandoned and nearly half of the 400 aircraft flying in the area had been lost, some including F-5 fighters being captured intact. After the war was over, a North Vietnamese pilot was to com-

Below: The former USS *Brattleboro* was handed over to the South Vietnamese Navy and became the *Ngoc Hoi* PCE-12, another example of the US legacy to South Vietnamese forces.

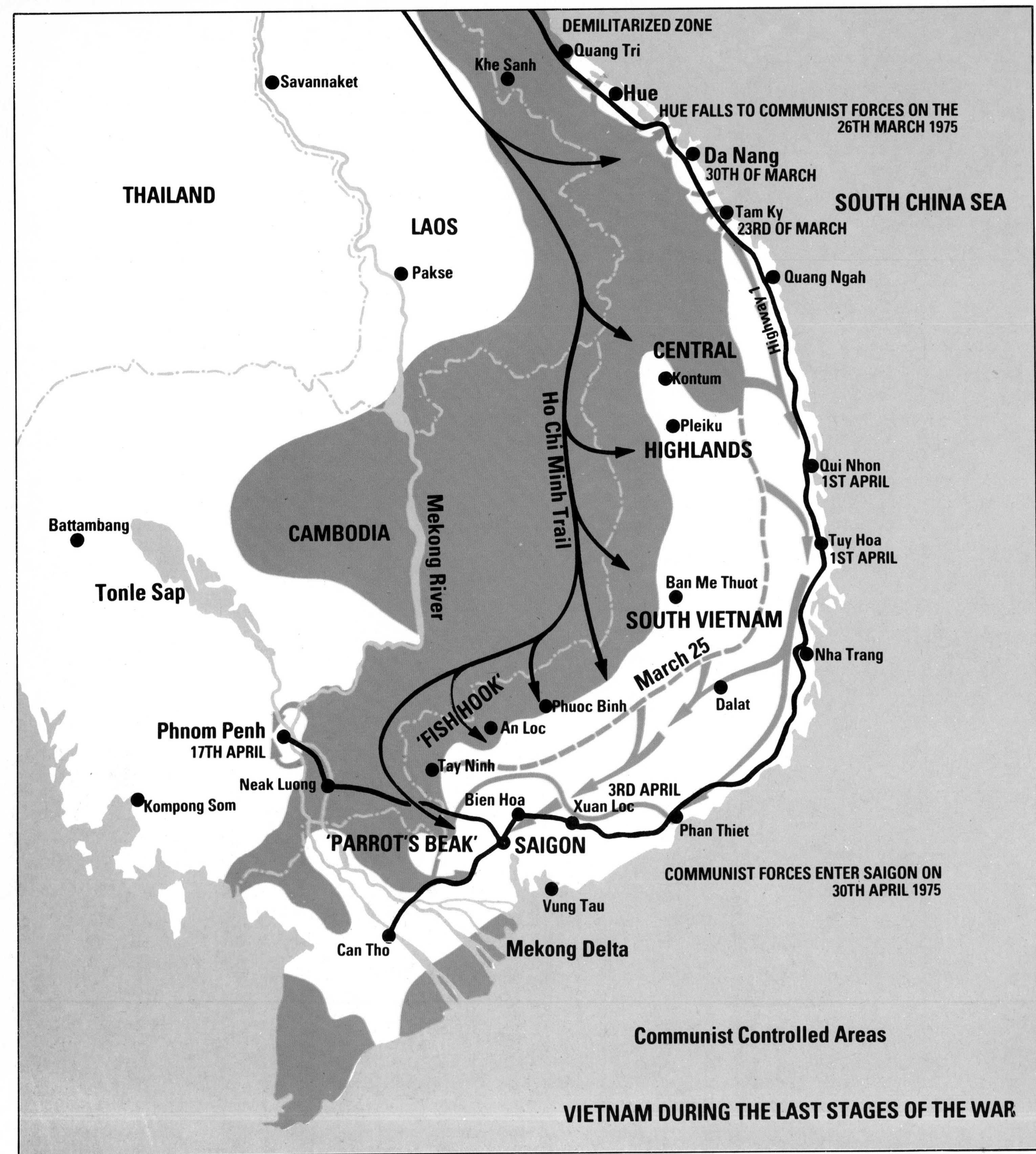

VIETNAM DURING THE LAST STAGES OF THE WAR

ment that he liked flying these aircraft since they were better designed than the Soviet fighters he had trained on and flown in the war.

The defence of Saigon now hung on six infantry divisions, an airborne and an armoured brigade and four newly-created ranger groups. In all they added up to 90,000 men. The NVA now had 300,000 men either in the south or barrelling down the excellent roads that crossed the country. By early April, there were 18 NVA divisions in action.

As the NVA I Corps moved southwards through North Vietnam, the II Corps pushed along the coastal roads of the south; III Corps was aligned along the ARVN defence line running from Phan Rang on the coast to Tay Ninh. NVA units were in action within the ARVN southern enclave; and the NVA IV Corps was moving against Xuan Loc while the NVA 232 Tactical 'Wing' aimed to cut Highway 4 out of Saigon. Incredibly by mid-April the ARVN were still holding, assisted by intelligence supplied by US analysts. At Xuan Loc the ARVN 18th Division and the 3rd Armored Brigade were putting up unexpected resistance. Around Saigon the 5th Division had the élite Airborne Brigade fighting alongside, while the 21st Division defended the delta city of Can Tho. The makeshift ARVN defence at Phan Rang, commanded by General Nghi, added additional problems for the NVA. It was difficult to move troops from Military Region II while this position was still intact.

Dung was under pressure from Hanoi. The rainy season was fast approaching and 19 May was Ho Chi Minh's birthday – a good day to capture Saigon. Dung decided therefore to by-pass Xuan Loc and to give added incentive to his troops designated the final phase of operations in the south the 'Ho Chi Minh Campaign'. However, shortly after dawn on the 21st the defences at Xuan Loc collapsed and the last four surviving battalions of the ARVN 18th Division with their commander General Dao were evacuated by helicopter. In an act of heroic bravery 600 ARVN troops under Colonel Le Xuan Hien volunteered to remain to cover this withdrawal. They died when they were swamped by 40,000 NVA troops.

On the same day Thieu summoned the former Prime Minister Khiem and the Vice-President Huong to tell them that he was resigning. He saw his continued presence as unhelpful in the attempt to find a political solution. All he desired was a constitutional hand-over that would avoid the danger of chaos.

In a two-hour broadcast to the nation Thieu explained why he was going and blamed the United States whose resolve, he said, had been destroyed by Watergate. Tran Van Huong was sworn in; he was 71, nearly blind and arthritic. For the Provisional Revolutionary Government Thieu's departure changed nothing, they wanted surrender and did not take up the offer of talks about a cease-fire put forward by Huong.

Between the 21st and the 24th the NVA had made advances that made offers of cease-fire irrelevant. Phan Thiet in Military Region II had fallen; with the fall of Xuan Loc, the NVA were pushing towards Bien Hoa and southwards to Vung Tau, where they would be able to cover some of the sea approaches to Saigon. Saigon had only the remains of the 18th Division, two Marine brigades, around Bien Hoa, and an airborne brigade and two infantry regiments north of Vung Tau. Against these battered forces the NVA were about to commit five divisions.

The NVA plan which had been finalised at the

Below: ARVN gunners plot targets for their guns during the operations in Laos. The NVA invasion of the South overwhelmed ARVN positions, which had been starved of ammunition and equipment.

HQ at Loc Ninh was drawn up by Dung's deputy, Genery Le Ngoc Hien. In the words of Frank Snepp, whose excellent book *Decent Interval* covers the last days of the war in Vietnam, the attack would resemble the peeling of an onion. The NVA would first remove the outer defences of Saigon and then, after the ARVN units had been destroyed, would push armour into the city with five main targets: the Presidential Palace, the General Staff HQ outside Tan Son Nhut, the HQ of the Saigon City Military Command, the General Police Directorate and Tan Son Nhut airfield. The first attacks would be on 27 April, and the second phase on the 29th. The NVA operations in Tay Ninh and the delta would continue since they helped to tie up ARVN forces.

As the NVA forces grouped around Xuan Loc the South Vietnamese Air Force put in attacks with a range of weapons. A CBU-55 was fitted into a C-130 transport and the aircraft took off from Tan Son Nhut. Over Xuan Loc the pallet was off-loaded and exploded almost on top of the NVA 341st Division HQ. In the explosion from the fuel over 250 NVA soldiers died, or suffocated in the vacuum that followed.

This attack was followed by 'Daisy Cutters' – the 15,000 lb bombs which had been intended to blast down primary jungle for helicopter pads. To these were added pallets of 500-lb bombs. Frank Snepp also mentions in *Decent Interval* an attack made against a convoy of mobile SA-2 anti-aircraft missiles. They were hit by radar homing Wild Weasel missiles and the attack aircraft were American.

NVA artillery fire increased and Bien Hoa airfield became unusable. The F-5A fighters were pulled back to Saigon and the A-37s flew to Can Tho.

Far right: The evacuation of Saigon produced many examples of waste. This UH-1 Huey helicopter was pushed into the sea to make way for other helicopters landing refugees on the USS *Blue Ridge* on 29 April 1975.

Below: A Vietnamese UH-1 Huey helicopter ditches in the sea near the USS *Blue Ridge*, after having delivered military personnel and families aboard the ship during the evacuation of Saigon.

On 28 April Duong Van Minh accepted the premiership of South Vietnam; it was a curiously symbolic move since Minh had been one of the moving forces behind the overthrow of Diem in 1963. The NVA launched their attacks from the east, pushing on Nhon Trach and then with that phase under way the NVA 232nd Tactical 'Wing' pushed past a town on Highway 4 only 12 miles south-west of Saigon. To the north-west the NVA I Corps cut the Tay Ninh-Saigon highway and trapped the ARVN 25th Division at Cu Chi and another NVA unit cut the road to Vung Rau. The NVA launched their first air attacks using captured A-37s, hitting aircraft on Tan Son Nhut.

Rockets were hitting Saigon regularly, random explosions that killed rich and poor and were not directed at military targets. After midnight on 29 April NVA 130-mm guns began shelling Tan Son Nhut. They destroyed a US Air Force C-130 and the US Embassy staff realised that the final phases of their evacuation plans would have to be done by helicopter.

The NVA armour that entered the city on the 30th met little organised resistance. Some Europeans remained behind to see the outcome of the last battle. The West German journalist Peter Scholl-Latour found himself as one of the last clients of a Saigon bar girl. With other journalists they talked of the future:

When the Viet Cong take over I'll go and plant rice

for them – what's wrong with that? I come from a peasant family anyway.

As police control collapsed, the beggars and cripples and shoe shine boys around the Continental Hotel became more aggressive. Only the local bookseller favoured by Scholl-Latour remained calm, and the West German noticed that at the top of his display was Graham Greene's *The Quiet American*.

The US evacuation of Saigon, which some felt had been dangerously delayed through optimism about the possible political solution, was rushed through the night and day of 29 and 30 April. In his memoirs the NVA commander General Dung pays tribute to 'the largest evacuation operation by helicopter in US history'. With 70 helicopters and 865 Marines, 630 sorties were flown to evacuate 1,373 Americans, 5,595 South Vietnamese and 85 'third country nationals'. Incredibly, of these, 2,100 (including 978 Americans) were lifted out of the Embassy compound.

The humanitarian aspects of the operation were criticised by some members of Congress. Why had the South Vietnamese been evacuated? President Ford's press spokesman, quoting Ford, announced that the actions had been done on moral not legalistic grounds, and said that the President 'did it because the people would have been killed'. However, one of the lasting images of the evacuation, code named 'Operation Frequent Wind', was of some South Vietnamese being held at bay by US Marines with their M16s trained on them, and of an unknown white evacuee leaning out of a helicopter to punch a Vietnamese who was trying to force his way aboard.

For the citizens of Saigon there was the trauma of the NVA military and political presence. As the T-54s rolled into the city the NVA soldiers and tank crews saw wealth and a style of life that they had never imagined. In their olive-green uniforms they began to wander about the streets. Parades followed and monuments erected by the South Vietnamese government were destroyed. At Tan Son Nhut an inscription which read 'The Noble Sacrifice of the Allied Soldiers will never be forgotten' was covered with a layer of white paint. Over it, the new masters of Saigon, now Ho Chi

Far left: Refugees on board a US merchant ship being evacuated from Saigon.

Top left: A South Vietnamese helicopter pilot and his family are safely aboard the USS *Hancock*.

Below: Soviet backed Vietnamese forces and Kampucheans in Phnom Penh celebrate the overthrow of Pol Pot's regime.

Far right: Vietnamese refugees being transported to the *Transcolorado* on 5 April 1975. Many refugees were not able to take any of their belongings with them.

Below: Refugees are escorted to the processing station on board the USS *Hancock*, which remained offshore to receive refugees during the evacuation of Saigon.

Minh city, painted a quotation from Ho: 'Nothing is more Precious than Independence and Freedom'. At 10.30 on 5 May the ugly 'Monument to the Unknown Soldier' was destroyed among a flutter of revolutionary banners.

The Italian-born journalist Tiziano Terzani, who watched the takeover, quoted a Vietnamese:

On the first day the people were glad to save their necks, on the second they try to get back their Hondas, on the third they organize themselves to go on living by their little business deals.

In the United States *Time* magazine produced a cover for their 12 May issue which had a dominant shade of red. With his face framed by the sickle shape of Vietnam, a quizzical Ho Chi Minh smiled out. Saigon was marked by a star and the name Ho Chi Minh City.

Inside, the correspondence pages had a one-line letter from a reader in Memphis: 'Let's hear it for "Might makes right!"' However, the most revealing comments were short interviews with American men and women actively involved with the war. They ranged from General William Westmoreland to a student paralysed for life by a bullet fired by a National Guardsman at Kent State University. Jane Fonda commented on the end in Vietnam:

What happened is what happened to us 200 years ago: a revolution for independence, playing itself out in Viet Nam. To say Saigon has 'fallen' is to say that the 13 colonies 'fell' two centuries ago.

Daniel Ellsberg, the former Rand Corporation consultant who made public the Pentagon Papers, the secret US political study, said that the war was coming gloriously to a conclusion:

It was the will of the American people, expressed to Congress, that ended this war now. That's the best possible celebration of the Bicentennial of the American Revolution that I can imagine.

General Westmoreland said:

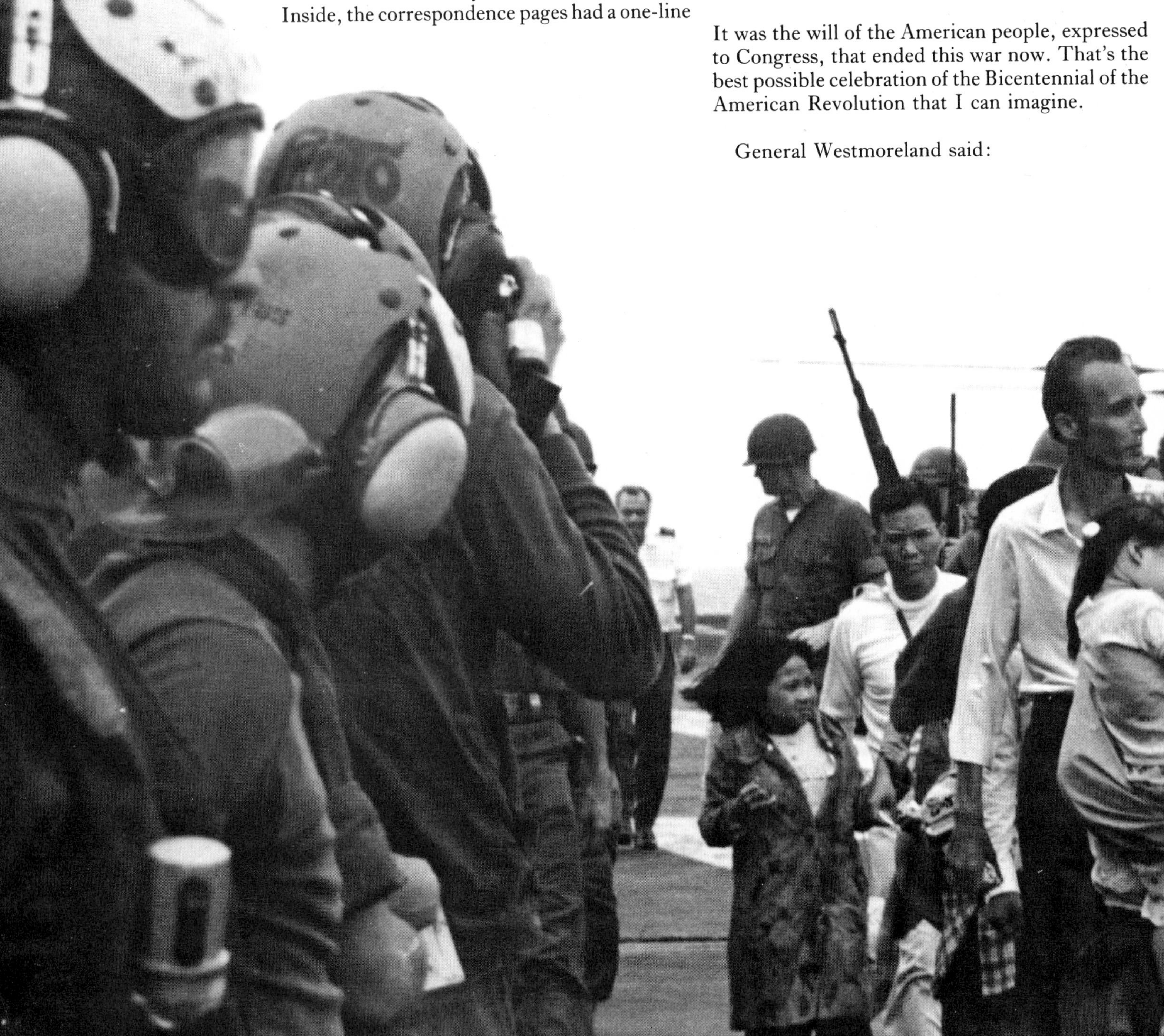

It was a sad day in the glorious history of our country. But elements in this country have been working for this end. We failed. We let an ally down. But it was inevitable after Congress pulled the rug out under the President with the War Powers Act. Hanoi was home free at that moment, for our only trump was gone.

However, the most reasoned and personal was the comment by Commander Richard Stratton. He had spent six years and two months as a prisoner of war in North Vietnam. His striped uniformed figure bowing to North Vietnamese in front of TV and press cameras was one of the traumatic images of 1967. In Stratton's view:

American disengagement from Viet Nam was inevitable, but the manner in which we did it was embarrassing. I certainly thought we owed it to the Vietnamese to show a little more class than that. We led them down the primrose path and left them hanging on the end of the limb. Then we sawed it off. So why should we be surprised when we see them fail? As for me, I did everything I could. I can face myself in the mirror. I don't know how many others can say the same thing.

13. AFTERMATH

IN AUGUST 1976 JOURNALIST Peter Scholl-Latour returned to Ho Chi Minh city. The first stop was a re-education centre for prostitutes. In an old training school for Catholic nuns he saw 600 girls who the authorities planned to reform by dint of hard work: reading lessons, mat weaving and basket making. The girls who were at the centre were simple, rather plain youngsters and Scholl-Latour noted that the 'up-market' women, the *poules de luxe* had escaped. Either that or they had found new patrons among the men from the north. Other visits were to a centre for reformed drug addicts and an orphanage; among the children were Eurasians and half-caste black and Asian girls and boys.

The trip also took the TV crew to rural areas where some of the population of Saigon had been re-located, and to zones of development where young men and women from bourgeois backgrounds were purging their anti-social origins by three years' hard work in the country.

By chance the West German TV crew visited 'Vietnam's very own Gulag Archipelago'. The Plain of Reeds, bordered by the Mekong delta and the Cambodian border, was a lake in winter and a slimey mass of decaying vegetation in summer. It had been a free-fire zone in the war. An attempt to interview two former ARVN officers did not work because the men were clearly too frightened to say anything, so the West Germans could not establish the truth of reports that thousands were being held in the area.

In order to film a shot of men at work on the reclamation work near the village of Phuoc Tay, the TV crew climbed on to the roof of their vehicle. The men who were going to do the work were clearly guards, not labourers. With the advantage of the height the crew saw a crowd of men working in the distance in the thick slime. They wore the tattered remains of army uniforms and were so covered in mud that they looked 'more like part of the countryside than human beings'. Told that these men were local peasants who had volunteered to work in the area, the TV crew were able to go closer to film them. They were all men between 20 and 40, and continued their work with crude shovels and two wheelbarrows as well as the traditional balancing pole and baskets, ignoring the West Germans. As the crew suspected, their interpreter admitted that these were former ARVN soldiers — largely officers.

We stood and watched the 'marsh soldiers' of the new Socialist Vietnam, slaving and toiling and suffering before our very eyes. We were quite speechless.

Scholl-Latour saw the camp where these men were housed:

It had all the classic features of a concentration camp; barbed-wire fencing, floodlights, watch-towers with machine-gun posts. One or two ragged figures were shuffling about, others were lying motionless on the ground, probably half-dead with malaria.

Tiziano Terzani revisited Ho Chi Minh city in 1981. In 1975, he recalled, the ambitious post-war plan projected an annual growth of 14 per cent; the reality now is a growth rate of 2 per cent with a population growth of 3 per cent. The slave labour in the Plain of Reeds seen by Scholl-Latour has proved a disaster as the soil was not rich enough to produce the quota of rice ordered by Hanoi. A model agricultural settlement at Le Minh Xuan which was once shown to visitors is now off-limits. During the war the north was supported by Moscow and the south by Washington. However, the Americans now send nothing and the Soviet Union has cut back on aid, yet the population has expanded by six million. The USSR is estimated to be sending $3 million a day to Vietnam. Corruption has become part of the way of life in Ho Chi Minh city. It is used to get housing permits, travel documents and permission to see a doctor. For the boat people who buy spaces on overcrowded vessels in order to leave the country, payments have to be made in gold. The salary of government servants is such that they cannot live reasonably and so, as one puts it, 'The State pretends to pay us so we pretend to work'. Former Thieu government servants are banned from posts.

Books published before 1975 are now held under lock and key in the libraries, and the book stores in Ho Chi Minh city stock mainly Vietnamese titles, though Terzani saw Russian technical manuals and a French language biography of Leonid Brezhnev.

Part of the problem for the new Vietnam is that spare parts for the equipment originally supplied by the United States cannot be acquired. Even Soviet-supplied economic aid suffers from spares problems. Scholl-Latour commented after a visit to Hanoi:

Foreign experts from East and West despaired at the technical and economic ignorance of a people whose fighting skills had compelled the admiration of the world. The Vietnamese had opted for the Moscow brand of Socialism and adopted Soviet methods of running industry and agriculture. Now they were suffering.

Within Vietnam, long after the war ended, there are reports that talk of bandits and terrorists, but which seem to point to signs of armed resistance still troubling the government in the remoter regions. The Communist press carried a report in 1983 of a deception scheme that trapped a leader of

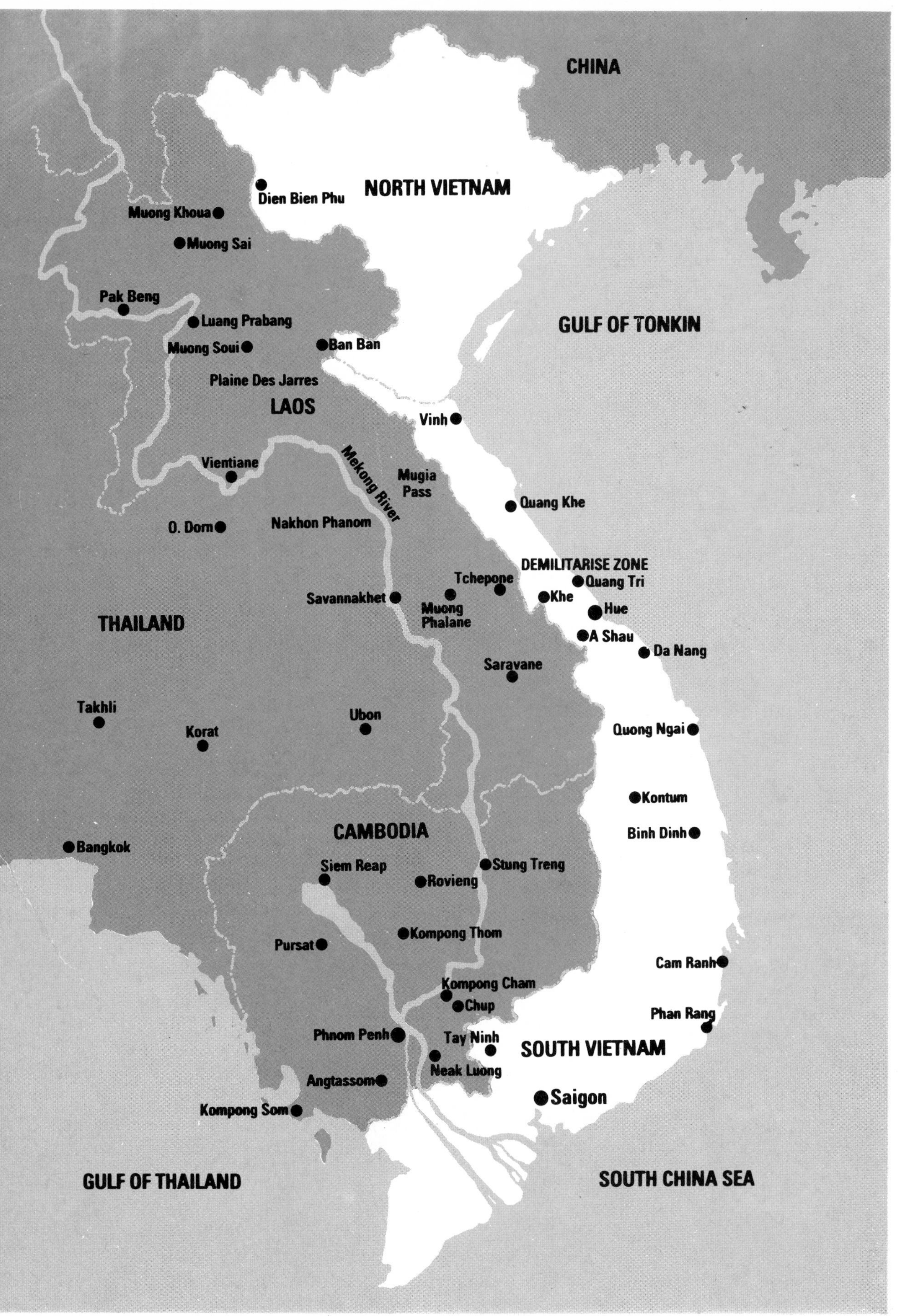

a group operating in the highlands.

Tragically war, and the effect of war, seems now to be almost endemic in an area that has been a home for people who were once noted for their industry and generosity. Its involvement in the Vietnam conflict has also left a bitter legacy in the United States; a legacy that still divides a generation.

39681

14. CAMBODIA AND LAOS

Previous page: A USAF CH-3E of the 20th Helicopter Squadron on a troop-carrying mission over the jungle of South-East Asia. Helicopters such as this were used to insert special forces teams into the North and also across the border.

Below: Cambodian sailors parade during an independence celebration in Phnom Penh. The strong French influence in the area can be seen in the officers' and ratings' uniforms, closely modelled on those of the French Navy.

TO THE WEST OF VIETNAM, running from North Vietnam's border with China to the southern delta and South Vietnam are the two countries of Laos and Cambodia. They were the dominoes that the United States predicted would fall if the south became communist.

Cambodia and Laos had been part of the French colonial empire. During the First Indo-China war they provided troops for operations under French command, but in turn the territory of northern Laos became a target for Vietminh attacks. Following the fall of the border positions with China much of the French military effort in the north was directed against the Vietminh incursions into Laos. In July 1953 Laos accepted increased independence from France, though agreed to remain as part of an Associated States of Indochina; Cambodia refused. Between August and October that year the French negotiated with King Norodom Sihanouk of Cambodia and he received almost complete independence and control of his military, political and economic affairs. France, however, retained control of some forces in eastern Cambodia for operational purposes.

At the Geneva Conference of April-July 1954 Cambodia, which had declared its independence on 9 November 1953, and Laos which had been independent since the later 1940s, though linked through treaty to France, were both recognised as free and neutral states. A small French presence was retained in Cambodia and Laos as military advisors and training teams. By 29 December 1954 additional agreements with France finally severed any vestige of that country's former colonial rule.

Laos, however, was too close to her warlike neighbour North Vietnam to enjoy a lasting peace. The Pathet Lao forces in the country were backed by the USSR and China while the USA supported the Royalist Forces. A three cornered struggle developed between the right wing forces of General Phoumi Nosavan, neutralist troops under Premier Prince Souvanna Phouma and the communist Pathet Lao under Souvanna's half brother Prince Souphanouvong. The main area for the fighting was the Plane of Jars, or *Plaine des Jarres,* an area so named because of the prehistoric stone storage jars found there.

In July 1959 the Pathet Lao launched attacks against Royalist army positions in a series of concerted actions throughout the country. The United Nations agreed to investigate the Laotian claim that these attacks had been made with the assistance of North Vietnam.

In the late 1950s the parachute battalion commanded by a captain Kong Le was one of the more successful units on the government side. However, on 5 August 1960 Kong Le seized Vientiane the capital, and accused the USA of colonialism and demanded that a truly neutral government be set

up under Souvanna Phouma. Prior to this Souvanna had been pressured into resignation by the USA, replaced by Phoui Sananikone – who in turn had been deposed by a right wing army faction led by Phoumi Nosavan in December 1959.

Souvanna attempted to be genuinely neutral, accepting aid from both east and west, but was opposed by Phoumi Nosavan and Boum Oum who were supported by the USA and Thailand. Boum Oum commanded the 25,000 strong Royal Army and as these forces advanced on the capital the USSR used Il-14 transports to move arms and equipment from Hanoi to support Kong Le in Vientiane. Long range artillery duels followed, causing severe damage to the political capital of Laos and killing or wounding 1,600 people, mostly civilians. Kong Le withdrew to the Plane of Jars where he linked up with the Pathet Lao and Phoumi Nosavan secured Vientiane.

Soviet assistance to the Pathet Laos-Neutralist forces included trucks and AA guns and in turn the USA provided a modest increase to the Royalist air force with six North American AT-6 Texan (Harvard) trainers, modified for ground attack operations. The Royalists were later to lose these aircraft in a spectacular accident when a loaded machine-gun 'cooked off' and fired when the AT-6s were parked on the ground. The aircraft were lined up nose to tail, and in a series of sympathetic explosions were all destroyed.

However, before their demise they supported the Royalist push through the Plane of Jars. US Special Forces were tasked with improving the training of the Royalist troops, and CIA sponsored operations by the 'civilian' company of Air America, kept a supply of arms and equipment flowing to these forces.

In a piece of political pragmatism President

Below: American supplies arrive in Laos during the early days of the Laotian war. Here Laotian forces can be seen in the foreground. The uniform of the man on the left is clearly that of a French paratroop officer. The aircraft in the background is not readily identifiable as a Government controlled aircraft and would probably be one of those operated by the CIA under the name Air America.

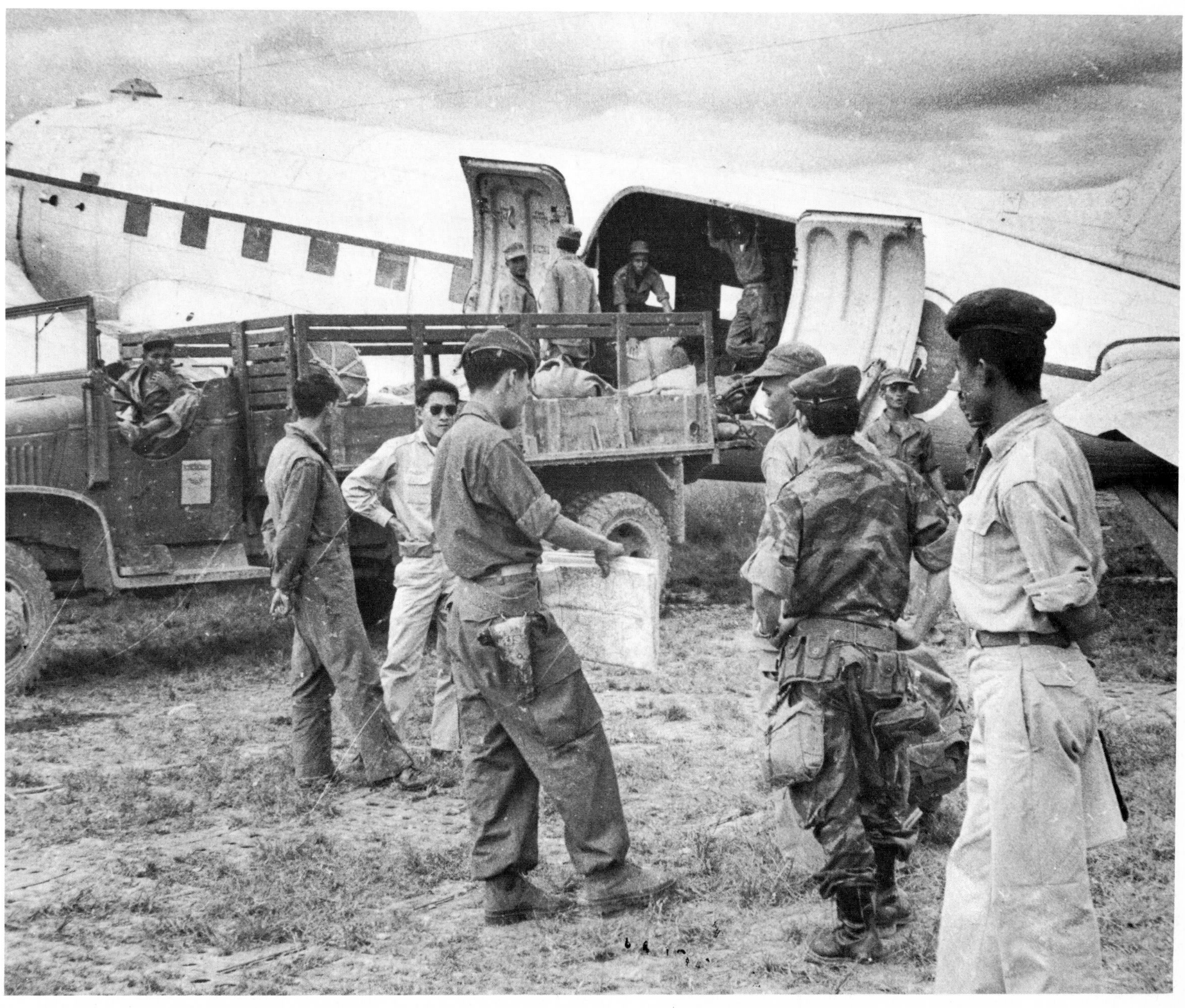

Kennedy and Nikita Krushchev decided that they would make Laos genuinely neutral. But the Chinese and the North Vietnamese each wanted a border that was respectively secure, or allowed movement along the Ho Chi Minh trail. Plans were made for a re-convening of the Geneva Conference in May 1961, and at that point Phoumi Nosavan reacted against this big power planning over his head: he refused to form a coalition government and moved troops up to the sensitive Muang Luong-Nam Tan area near China.

Tough North Vietnamese troops crossed the border and on 6 May 1962 sent the 5,000 Royalist troops reeling back in panic. Phoumi Nosavan was obliged to accept the presence of Pathet Lao and Rightist leaders in a government that was headed by Souvanna Phouma and which took power in the late summer of 1962.

These agreements did not bring an end to the fighting in Laos. The NVA were keen to keep the Ho Chi Minh trail secure, and therefore employed the Pathet Lao in aggressive defence. The United States in turn kept a force of Meo tribesmen under Major-General Vang Pao to harass the Pathet Lao and to gather intelligence.

The war began to fall into a pattern. The NVA maintained around 100,000 troops in Laos, some keeping the Ho Chi Minh trail operating, some assisting the Pathet Lao, and some controlling its operations. The Royalist Neutralist government received assistance through the CIA and special forces who funded, equipped and trained the 30,000 men of Vang Pao. In the dry season it was the turn of the NVA and Pathet Lao to emerge from their bases and push westward into the Plane of Jars in the north, the 'panhandle' in the centre and the Bolovens Plateau in the south. As foot and vehicle mobility decreased with the onset of the monsoon the Royalist, neutralist and Meo guerilla forces backed by US air power, both for troop lift, re-supply and attack, would roll back the enemy.

Peter Scholl-Latour recalled a visit to the Plane of Jars in the autumn of 1966. Meeting a US Special Forces team he was told that they were 'relief workers', and noted that there were also three American women, whose work was to teach, run the hospital and organise the food distribution. The cynical pilot, an ex-French Air Force

Below: An old tactic is employed by Pathet Lao guerillas. Here, the guerillas use panji stakes to create a mantrap. The stakes are sharpened bamboo and will penetrate through the sole of a boot and into a man's foot. A further refinement is to cover them with excrement which will cause infection.

sergeant, who flew Scholl-Latour to the Plane of Jars remarked:

The Meo have never had it so good. Since they started fighting for the Americans they've had everything they could possibly want. Every Meo tribesman is issued with a pair of rifles to keep under his palliasse, and they can go out and fight to their heart's content.

The West German journalist noted that the Meo no longer carried the traditional flintlock muskets, each man had an M16.

He also noted that another tradition had persisted. In the middle of war the Meo still cultivated opium poppies. When he remarked about this to his American host the reply was simply 'The Meo have to live somehow and you can't grow rice at this height'. The rumour that was current at that time, wrote Scholl-Latour, was that the CIA was running the biggest and most efficient drug ring in the world.

The fighting was conducted largely by the Meo, a more traditionally war-like group, and the Kha mountain tribes who were recruited by the North Vietnamese. The Kha had long been exploited by Laotians in the Mekong valley and this was a chance to revenge themselves. They were promised a new Socialist Laos for their efforts.

By 1973 a cease-fire, declared on 22 February, had left the Communists in control of vast areas of the country – including the land that gave access to both Cambodia and South Vietnam. The US involvement, as would happen in Cambodia, had been either removed or greatly scaled down.

In 1975 increased left-wing violence showed that the coalition under Prince Souvanna Phouma was virtually powerless. By the end of the year it had been dissolved and a People's Democratic Republic of Laos proclaimed.

The Socialist Laos that eventually became a reality in 1975 was not headed by the 'Red Prince' Souphanouvong who had lived out the campaigns in the caves of Sam Neua and Vieng Xai, but by an anonymous half-Vietnamese *apparatchik* named Kaystone Phomvihane whose aim was to make Laos a North Vietnamese satellite.

Scholl-Latour had remarked that the bulk of the population in Laos were an easy going peaceful race who had absorbed the teachings of Buddha to make them a tolerant and rather detached nation. They continued to celebrate religious feasts and watch the traffic of prostitutes between the huge US Air Force base at Udorn in Thailand and their capital of Vientiane where the girls worked the clubs and bars favoured by the Air America pilots. The West German observed another tolerant and more charming nation to the south. The Cambodians are an attractive and cultured people and their country has one of the great wonders of the world; the Temples of Angkor Wat. The photographer Larry Burrows took time off from the Vietnam war to photograph the temples for Time Life and produced some beautiful and mysterious studies of carved rock and the encroachment of the jungle. Scholl-Latour had other memories.

In 1965 under a full moon he watched the temple dancers act scenes from the Ramayana. It was a cross roads of Indian and Chinese culture. But besides the temples and their history, he was to recall the country's capital, Phnom Penh, as the most beautiful city in Asia:

Here nothing much had changed since the days of French colonial rule. The dark-skinned Khmer girls, with their softly curling hair, had an earthy sensuality and a carefree abandon that made them very different from the more subdued Vietnamese women.

Above: Cambodian troops in American-built armoured vehicles. This Chaffey light tank is working outside Route 1 near Phnom Penh. It was supplied to the Cambodians by the French and just visible on the turret is the battle honour name painted on, a common practice in the French Army.

Top: SP-4 Don Perez, Rear Scout to Co H, 75th Rangers keeps watch during a patrol north-east of Xhan Loc in 1970. He is armed with a captured North Vietnamese AKM. This weapon would be similar to those used by men during cross-border operations.

Above: US Navy SEALS await a mission in April 1970.

Right: A 12.7 mm heavy machine gun used by men of the Khmer Rouge, dug in outside the temple of Angkor Wat. The temple was practically undamaged during the fighting but is difficult for foreigners to visit.

To complete this picture of an Asian paradise was added a fertile land that gave a rice yield high enough to support the whole population.

The national leader, Prince Norodom Sihanouk, could trace his ancestry back to the sculptured monarchs on the walls of Angkor Wat. Though he was addressed as 'monseigneur' by the French during colonial days, he was more of a god king to the rural population. He had two publicly stated ambitions, to be an enlightened leader and to keep his country free from the military unrest that was on his northern and eastern borders.

However, the growth of the Ho Chi Minh trail and the presence of large numbers of Viet Cong and NVA along his border placed him in an impossible position. He could not help but know about the traffic that went through the harbour of Sihanoukville and along what was bitterly called the 'Sihanouk' trail into Vietnam. This was an additional supply line for the VC and NVA, and was moreover much more efficient than the Ho Chi Minh trail. Ships were faster than trucks and porters, and the final journey to the battle front in South Vietnam was far shorter through Cambodia.

Whilst Sihanouk had struggled for freedom from the French he had crossed into Thailand on 14 June 1953, going into voluntary exile to be free to press for complete independence from the French Union. Later, in November 1963, he refused US assistance and at the end of the year withdrew his embassy from Washington. He had already dropped out of SEATO in 1956. But these gestures towards neutrality would only be effective if they were backed by a strong army and air force, for example the world's two most famous neutrals Sweden and Switzerland maintain quite awesome defensive forces. Sihanouk, however, fearful of *coup d'état* not only kept his army small, but, to the frustration of the French advisors, employed it on non-military tasks like road construction and static guards.

Within Cambodia itself the opposition until the early 1960s had come from the so-called Khmers Viet Minh, a Communist group that campaigned for a Communist Federation of Indochina. Sihanouk was forced to crack down on them as they were reinforced by a new generation of trained Communist teams who were also nationalists. They stirred up a rebellion in Battambang province and linked up with the Viet Cong in the jungles of Ratanakiri. They also gave themselves a new name – the Khmer Rouge.

The Cambodian police who were sent to put down the rebellion did so with ghastly brutality. Horrified by this some of the younger ministers in the Cambodian government defected to the Khmer Rouge, among them a man called Kieu Samphan. He had been a member of Sihanouk's left-wing interim government and was later, under a new name, to become the first head of state in a new Communist Cambodia.

During 1966, as the war in South Vietnam became more intense, the United States Army began a series of top secret cross border raids. The Studies and Observation Group (SOG) had been organised as far back as 1964 to make cross border raids into denied areas of Laos, Cambodia and even North Vietnam. Among its activities were sabotage, ambush, prisoner snatching for interrogation, and intelligence gathering. Employing men from local ethnic groups and arming them with 'sterile' weapons (or weapons that could not be traced directly back to the USA) they were a shadowy and little known organisation. And in 1966 the commander of SOG (or to give it its full title MACVSOG), Colonel John K. Singlaub, got permission to escalate actions into Cambodia. It was during this time that networks were set up to allow US pilots to escape and evade capture if they were shot down over hostile territory.

The reconnaissance operations in Cambodia and Laos, which went under the code name OPS 35, were called Daniel Boone in Cambodia and Prairie Fire in Laos.

The NVA transport along the Ho Chi Minh trail was observed and possible targets located and attacked with aircraft on call by radio. In the confusion following an air attack there was also the opportunity to seize a prisoner. However, some Nung tribesmen, with their sterile weapons and clothing would be mistaken for VC and there were incidents when the US personnel present would step off the track while their Nungs engaged the enemy in conversation.

The NVA activity and the USAF operations along the border and in Laos were known to Sihanouk, but he still attempted to remain neutral. In March 1970, despite warnings from his advisors, he set off on an extended foreign tour to attempt to persuade Moscow and Peking to pressure Hanoi to remove her forces from Cambodia. He had correctly judged that the sanctuaries in Cambodia were now too much of a provocation to the USA and South Vietnam and wanted them to be reduced.

He left Cambodia assuming that the 35,000 strong army under General Lon Nol would remain loyal. Lon Nol urged Sihanouk to return, but the king remained abroad, and the very middle class intelligentsia that he had created by improving schooling and university opportunities pushed the army into seizing power. Lon Nol, once the loyal commander, became the new national leader.

The coup was supported and assisted by US intelligence operators who urged the Cambodians that they needed to drive the Viet Cong and NVA out of their country. But as Lon Nol was beginning to receive the publicity treatment reserved for a new Asian ally, he was partially crippled by a stroke, and he became merely a pawn in the military and political wrangles of South-East Asia.

Sihanouk settled in Peking and the North Vietnamese felt free now to advance into the eastern provinces of the Mekong. They also declared support for the Khmer Rouge, and advanced into Cambodia as far as the temples of Angkor Wat.

Realising that they had kicked open a hornets' nest by backing Lon Nol and then by invading Cambodia, the US attempted to shore up the Cambodian government. In April 1970 they agreed to a Cambodian request for \$7·5 million of arms and equipment. Saigon helped too by sending thousands of captured AK47s which were better than some of the World War II vintage arms from the US.

On 1 May Cambodians who had been trained by US Special Forces attempted to open up the now Communist controlled river route between

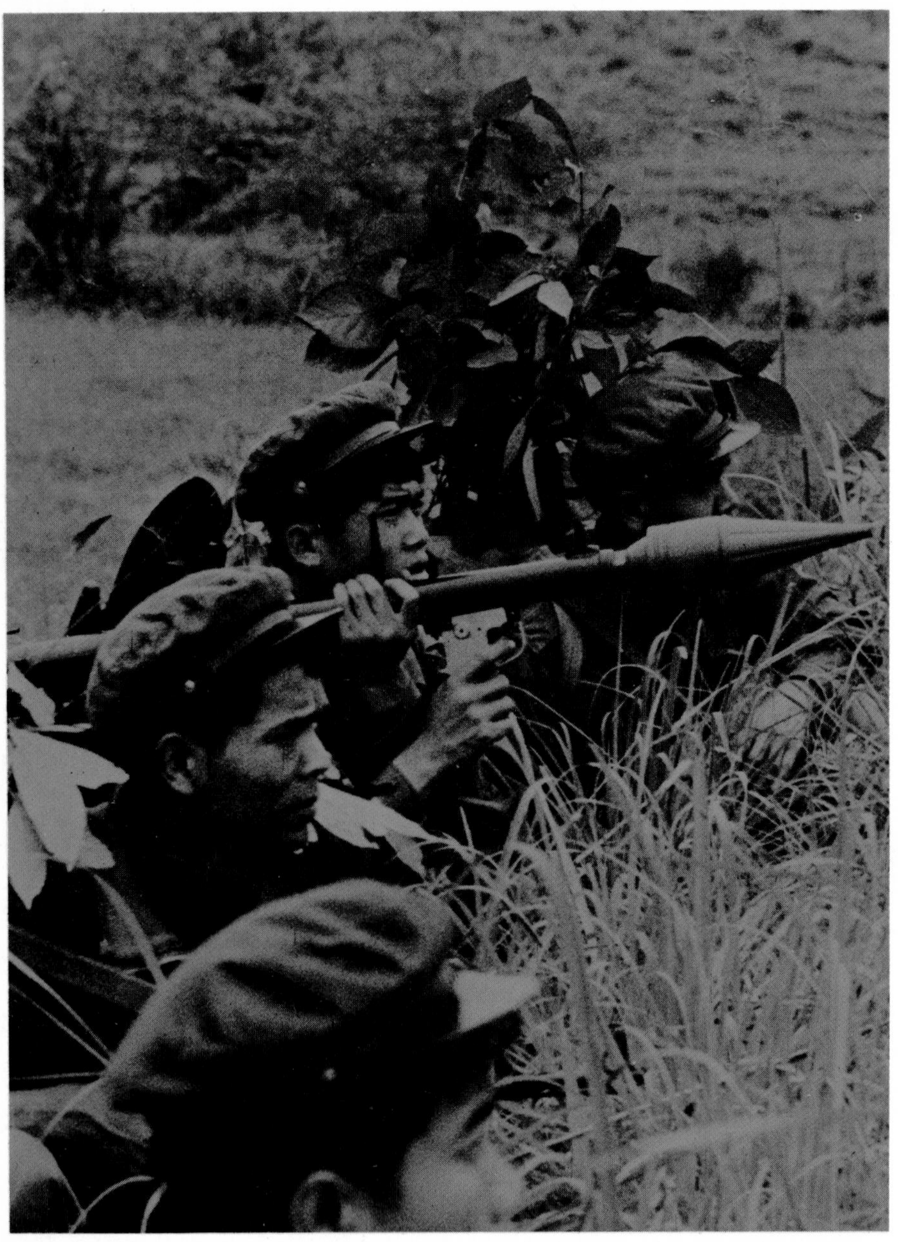

Above: Communist forces in Laos wait in ambush with a B-40 anti-tank rocket. This was one of the most widely used weapons in South-East Asia and proved to be light and very effective.

Phnom Penh and South Vietnam. They failed, but a week later a stronger force with US assistance broke through, and a South Vietnamese armoured column also opened up a road link.

However, within Cambodia the war was following a traditional Maoist pattern with Lon Nol being driven out of the countryside and holding only the cities. Phnom Pen became an ugly city with barbed wire and sand bags, and refuse piling up in the streets. While this battle was under way, the South Vietnamese continued to make forays into Cambodia to reduce the effectiveness of the Ho Chi Minh trail and to take some of the pressure off the Lon Nol forces. In 1971 the South Vietnamese and Cambodians began to suffer defeats at the hands of new well trained NVA forces and the NVA began to reduce the cities around Phnom Penh, until finally by 1975 there was a siege perimeter around the capital itself.

The charge of the war which had begun under NVA control moved to the Khmer Rouge and with this came a new and dreadful barbarism. The Khmer Rouge produced what one commentator has called 'Stone Age Communism'. Death was the only punishment suitable for opponents of the party. But death came not always by firing squad, but more commonly from clubbing with pieces of timber, or asphyxiation with a plastic bag. These methods saved bullets and were often employed by the very young men and women, almost chil-

dren, that the Khmer Rouge favoured for their party executioners.

In Phnom Penh Lon Nol had passed much of his power to his corrupt brother Lon Non. Lon Nol had the astrologers he had valued earlier jailed because their predictions did not match up to his aspirations.

With the inevitability of a Greek tragedy the final days in Cambodia drew to a close. Some of the foreign embassies in Phnom Penh decided to remain, while others evacuated the city. When the Khmer Rouge arrived all the foreigners who were left were ordered to go. They crossed over a bridge into Thailand and the photographs of their departure also gave the outside world a glimpse of the young men who were to grow more notorious as news of their activities inside the country leaked out.

Scowling at the camera the Khmer Rouge were armed with a mix of Warsaw Pact and US

Below: An AC-119G of the 17th Special Operations Squadron over Tan Son Nhut airforce base in October 1969. Aircraft such as this would have been used to cover movements down the Ho Chi Minh trail from North Vietnam to the South via Laos and Cambodia.

Above: With a B-40 rocket launcher to the front, a patrol of Khmer Rouge soldiers moves through the deserted streets of Phnom Penh, following its capture in 1975.

weapons, dressed in the simple black uniforms common in the Far East, and with the curious caps and the black and white *karma* sweat band cum neck cloth.

The fall of Phnom Penh, which was preceded by rocket and artillery fire and a tightening of the seige lines, came on 17 April 1975, only two weeks before the fall of Saigon.

In an area that had been torn by war for years, it seemed that the fall of three national capitals – Vientiane, Phnom Penh and Saigon – would bring a sort of grim peace. Not only was peace to be almost impossible to find, but worse was to come.

In a ruthless application of raw Marxist theory Pol Pot, the new leader of Kampuchea (as Cambodia had been renamed) ordered the population of Phnom Penh out of the city. They were to purge themselves by work in the fields, and moreover money was to be banned. The insane fundamentalism was to lead to starvation among both the rural population – now flooded with town dwellers – and predictably among the citizens of Phnom Penh who had no agricultural experience. Many were also to be killed as others had died before from clubbing and being buried alive. From a nation that had been reasonably wealthy and secure, war and the insane policies of Pol Pot had turned Kampuchea into a disaster area. Also the Khmer Rouge leadership were very reluctant to receive any form of international disaster aid, since this reflected badly on their new socialism and so because of this many more died.

There were attempts within Kampuchea to overthrow the regime, notably in September 1976 and early 1977, and the rural resistance from the Khmer Serai Kha (Free Khmer Movement) began to grow. An insurrection in the eastern provinces of Kampuchea was blamed on the Vietnamese.

Already there were signs that the two new Socialist States were not to be happy neighbours. The first clashes came in 1974 and there was further fighting over the islands of Phu Quoc and Tho Chu almost immediately after the fall of Saigon.

On 30 April 1977, exactly two years after the fall of Saigon, the Kampucheans crossed the border to a depth of 6 miles catching Vietnamese units off their guard on what was a national holiday. They withdrew, but choosing another national holiday attacked on 24 September 1977 and this time pushed 93 miles into Vietnam. The raid had also been timed during a visit to Peking by Pol Pot which would lull the Vietnamese into lowering their guard. A third raid followed, this time with armoured vehicles and support from Chinese crewed AA-guns. These weapons shot down some Vietnamese aircraft during the operation.

With their patience exhausted the Vietnamese went over to the offensive. They attacked in October 1977 and again in June 1978. The offensives were commanded by General Tran Van Tra who had operated from the Parrot's Beak during the Second Indo-Chinese war. In the second attack in 1978 he pushed to within 10 miles of Kompang Cham and used armour, artillery and aircraft – including much equipment captured with the fall of South Vietnam. There were reports that with large numbers of helicopters the Vietnamese

forces were able to use tactices which reflected US concepts of air-mobility.

Late that year the Vietnamese went back into Cambodia and this time they stayed. On 3 December a new group in opposition to Pol Pot was announced. The Kampuchea National United Front for National Salvation (KNUFNS) was dedicated to the removal of Pol Pot and establishment of links with Hanoi and Moscow. It was headed by Heng Samrin, a former officer and commissar in the Khmer Rouge, and a political officer named Chea Sim. On Christmas Day 1978 KNUFNS forces and Vietnamese troops crossed the border in strength and with 12 Vietnamese Divisions of battle experienced troops, armour, air power as well as artillery the Kampucheans had little chance.

By 15 January 1979 they had reached the border with Thailand and there was some fear that they would not stop. They did, but a flood of new refugees crossed over. Initially there had been reports that the Vietnamese were correct and careful soldiers, but later refugees reported the use of area weapons that made little distinction between civilians and combatants.

Kampuchea remains unstable, in Laos the Vietnamese control is almost total, while in former South Vietnam there are still reports of unrest. Albert Camus in his philosophical study on revolution *L'Homme révolté* (The Rebel) has summed up a tragic truth:

While man is struggling to free himself he retains his hopes and ideals. Once he has achieved the goal of destroying his oppressor, he in turn becomes a new oppressor.

Sadly, this is the story of Indo-China.

Below: Khmer Serai troops cross paddy fields during operations against the Khmer Rouge. The contrast is marked. The Khmer Serai with their mixture of Soviet and Western equipment and one man in the middle with his portable cassette player, appear a raggle-taggle army in contrast to the grim men patrolling the streets of the capital of Kampuchea.

Index

All page references in italic denote illustrations

Picture Credits

The publishers would like to thank the following, who supplied photographs:

Bell/Helicopter Textron: p 143 centre.
Camera Press: pp 158, 159, 167, 171, 180, 181, 182, 185.
Defense PR Canberra ACT: pp 64–65.
ECPA: pp 8, 9, 10–11, 12–13, 14–15, 16–17.
Keystone: pp 183, 186, 188–189.
McDonnell Douglas: p 140 top.
MARS: pp 42 centre, 84 top.
Network: p 163 bottom.
Popperfoto: pp 48–49.
United Press: p 71.
United States Air Force: pp 42 top, 43, 46–47, 50–51, 61, 63, 88, 89, 92 bottom, 96–97, 100–101, 102, 114 bottom, 116, 122–123, 126–127 bottom, 128–129, 130–131, 132–133, 134–135, 137, 138–139, 141 top, 147, 152, 164 top, 178–179, 187.
United States Army: pp 18–19, 20, 21, 23, 24 top, 25, 39, 44–45, 49 top, 53, 54–55, 56, 57, 60, 66–67, 68 top, 70, 74, 79, 80–81, 84 bottom, 85, 86–87, 98, 100 inset, 104, 105, 107, 109, 112–113, 114 top, 120, 121, 124, 125, 126–127, 148–149, 153, 156–157, 184 top.
United States Marines: pp 24 bottom, 30–31, 34 centre, 35, 36–37, 38, 40, 48 top, 52, 58–59, 62, 76–77, 78, 90–91, 92–93, 94–95, 103, 106, 110–111, 115, 118–119, 122 inset, 126 inset, 127 inset, 142, 145, 146, 150–151, 154.
United States Navy: pp 26–27, 28–29, 32–33, 34 top, 51 inset, 68–69, 72–73, 82–83, 133 inset, 136, 140–141, 143 top, 144, 164–165, 168–169, 170, 172–173, 174–175, 184 centre.
USIS: pp 6–7.